AMERICAN PATRIOT

The Transcript of the Tom Brady Deflategate Appeal Hearing

BOSTON, U.S.A

American Patriot:*The Transcript of the Tom Brady Deflategate Appeal Hearing*

ISBN-13: 978-1516842100

ISBN-10: 1516842103

Table of Contents

Prefatory Matters

APPEALS HEARING

New York, New York

Tuesday, June 23, 2015

9:28 a.m.

* * *

COMMISSIONER GOODELL: Good morning and welcome. As you can see, we have a court reporter here, so there will be a formal record of all of the proceedings this morning. And we just ask you all to speak up and try to avoid speaking across from one another so we have the correct record.

We all know why we are here this morning. This is in response to an appeal filed by Tom Brady. I'm particularly interested in hearing anything Tom has to say and I look forward to hearing directly from him. You also heard and got a letter from Gregg Levy on how we will proceed this morning so that hopefully all of those issues have been addressed and we will follow those procedures as best we can.

I will obviously oversee this, but as you all know, I am not an attorney. I am somebody that will focus on the testimony and I will ask Gregg Levy to administer the proceedings this morning. Obviously we will confer from time to time, and so I will ask Gregg to take the lead on that front. I will interject, obviously, as I feel necessary.

So Gregg, do you have anything you want to add?

MR. LEVY: The only thing I want to add is that counsel, whoever is speaking, identify themselves so the record is clear for the court reporter.

COMMISSIONER GOODELL: Do we have any objections that need to be made?

MR. KESSLER: I think we are ready to go unless you want us to do appearances.

MR. LEVY: I don't think that's necessary. If you intend to give an opening?

MR. KESSLER: Yes.

MR. LEVY: Let's get started.

MR. KESSLER: Yes. Good morning, Commissioner.

COMMISSIONER GOODELL: Good morning, Jeffrey.

Opening Statement by Mr. Kessler

MR. KESSLER: On behalf of Tom Brady and the NFLPA, we are happy to have an opportunity to present to you what we believe are very important, convincing and to some degree new grounds for overturning the discipline that has been imposed. We have heard your public statements that you have an open mind and that you are interested in receiving the evidence and that's what we intend to do today.

I am compelled to say at the opening that as you know, we had moved for you to recuse yourself. We understand you have rejected that. We are proceeding on that basis without waiving our objection regarding that.

What I'm now going to turn to first is the main evidence that's going to be presented to you today, and I know you've indicated that's what you are particularly anxious to hear and what that evidence is going to consist of. But to give you context for this, I'm compelled to note one point at the outset.

I understand from communications that you have issued in this case that you have basically, you and Mr. Vincent together, whatever the combination was, have relied upon the conclusions, the factual conclusions of the Wells report and you mentioned in your decision you did not independently look at the notes and the investigators.

You didn't have any witnesses for yourselves. You are essentially relying on Wells' conclusions. I'm compelled to note at the beginning that the conclusion of the Wells report with respect to Mr. Brady is that he was generally aware of something.

It is our position that there is no policy, no precedent, no notice that has ever been given to any player in the NFL that they could be subject to any type of discipline, whether it's conduct detrimental discipline or whether it is under the policy that has been invoked here for being generally aware of something.

It would be the equivalent if a player knew or was generally aware that another player was taking steroids, okay, and had nothing to do with it, but had some general awareness of that. The only person who was punished under the Steroid Policy is the person who was taking the steroids. You don't get punished for being generally aware that somebody else is liable.

If the League wants to change that, of course, you could promulgate new policies or something else, but we really believe that, (A), there is no such policy. It's not in the CBA. It's not in the Personal Conduct Policy. It's not in the -- it's not in the policy cited here. It's not in any precedent of conduct detrimental and no player has ever been punished for such a thing.

The reason I'm making this point is the reason we are about to tell you why we thing the Wells report is wrong, we think the Wells report doesn't answer or doesn't provide the basis for any discipline of the player.

This is wholly apart from what you did on the team, because on the team, the Wells report made very different findings, that it was more probable than not that something occurred and that's what they said and the team was responsible. But for the player, it was very, very different and I assume while Mr. Wells testifies, I assume that was a deliberate decision he made.

Had he been able to conclude that it was more probable than not that Mr. Brady participated in any kind of inappropriate activities, that's what he would have said in his findings. He did not say that. So before I get into the facts, I just felt compelled to make that context point, which we think is very important.

Now let me talk about the evidence we are going to present to you today. You are going to first hear from Tom Brady who you said you want to hear from. Tom will answer every question about this matter that I will ask him, that the NFL's counsel will ask him and if you have any questions or Mr. Levy has any questions, he's prepared to answer anything relevant to this case, as, by the way, he was with Mr. Wells.

And I note that Mr. Wells made it very clear both in his report and public statements that he was completely willing to answer any question that Ted Wells posed to him -- there has never been a refusal by Tom -- or anyone on Mr. Wells' team asked of him about that.

What Tom will tell you under oath is that he never asked anyone to deflate footballs below any kind of limit of the League. He never authorized anyone to do that and he's not aware or does he have any knowledge that anyone did that. He will tell you that truthfully, honestly. You will get a chance to look him in the eye and see what you think about that.

But we believe you are going to conclude when you hear this evidence that he is not somebody who was responsible for anything that did or did not happen at the Patriots' facility regarding the footballs.

And, in fact, he will testify and explain that his concern about footballs has to do with the touch and feel of the football. You will remember in 2006, there was a movement by all the quarterbacks to prepare their footballs. None of that had to do with ball pressure, and he will explain that.

And, in fact, it will be clear in the evidence it had to do with the same way a baseball player works in his glove to a right feel to soften the leather to make it feel right for that quarterback. He's never been particularly concerned about pressure at all except in one game, and there are -- things happen that create appearances that are not correct, which was the Jets game in 2014.

And what happened in the Jets game, you will hear is that he didn't even know there was an issue of pressure. What happened, the balls felt really big and fat and round to him like he had never felt them before, okay.

And, yes, he complained at that time to Mr. Jastremski, "What's wrong with the ball? There's something wrong with the balls," and ultimately found out the next day from Mr. Jastremski -- and this is important -- that while Mr. Jastremski had tried to have the balls set, it turns out at 13, which is well within the League limit, they were registered at 16, which is an astounding amount of pressure.

No one knows how they got to 16. That's what he noticed. That's the only time he's ever even thought about this issue of pressure. And that when it came to the championship game, he had no idea what was going on with the pressures of the balls. He felt nothing unusual.

He didn't feel a difference in the first half to the second half on the balls because he didn't know what had gone on was the balls had more air put into them at the halftime, as you know. None of that affects him. He didn't know of it. He wasn't generally aware of it.

We think you are going to find him to be credible on this issue. And we urge you to ask him any questions that you have about that.

We also are going to then submit the Declaration of Robert Kraft and Mr. Kraft would have been here to testify. You probably know he's in Israel. So he was not able to be here to testify.

But Mr. Kraft wanted to put in evidence here to indicate that his discussions with Tom about this and what he believes about Tom's credibility in terms of his relationships over a very long period of time and what happened here, so we hope you will give weight and consideration to somebody who we know you trust his judgment very much and we know that no one knows Tom Brady, at least in the NFL better than Robert Kraft, although I am sure there are, obviously in his personal life, that know Tom Brady better than Mr. Kraft does.

We are also going to put in a declaration from a forensic person who dealt with the issue of e-mail and texts. And you know from your decision that there was an aspect of the discipline. We don't know how much -- and I will talk about them in a second -- that was exacerbated in the minds of Mr. Vincent in his letter for a failure to cooperate in providing these e-mails and texts.

First of all, you are going to hear from Tom that the only reason he didn't provide that is because his lawyers told him it wasn't proper or necessary and he just did what his lawyers and agents told him. He would have been happy to produce them.

Number two, there were no incriminating texts being withheld or e-mails, and there never have been any incriminating texts or e-mails. And now he has gone through and produces exactly what Ted Wells had asked for at the time that existed at the time and exists today.

Whatever is there has been there and what does it show? It shows exactly what's in the Wells report. There was nothing being withheld. I mean, can you look at it and say, gee, why didn't he just produce it? He was following the advice of his lawyers and agents at the time. And part of the issue is that when Mr. Wells was asked to provide authority for why he was entitled to look at these e-mails and things, no authority involving players was ever cited.

And no one ever told his lawyer, agent or Mr. Brady that if he didn't provide it, that somehow that was going to be a lack of cooperation with a penalty. Now, we can ask why that wasn't done. It was there. But he certainly was never told that, that there was that type of obligation imposed upon him in that way. That's going to be provided by declaration from the forensic people who looked at that.

Then we are going to have Mr. Ted Snyder testify who was the Dean of the Yale School of Management, who is one of the leading experts in statistical analysis in the world. He previously was the Dean of the Chicago Business School. He is one of the most respected academic people in this country, and particularly his statistics expertise is second to none. He worked with a team of people to study the testing in the Wells report and what that shows.

And what he is going to explain and this is not, by the way, the fault of Mr. Wells, it's not the fault of Exponent, okay, there was simply so many unknowns about how the testing was done -- and I am going to explain that in a second -- that nobody is able to give an opinion as to whether these balls were tampered with or not.

And the reason is as follows, and I will do this in my very nonscientific way. We now all know that there's something called the Ideal Gas Law. And what that means is all balls deflate when they go from hot weather to cold weather, to make it very simple. That's one of the factors. So the Colts' balls went to lower pressure. The Patriots' balls went to lower pressure. That just happens. So the mere fact that a ball is tested at lower pressure doesn't tell you anything. It doesn't tell you whether or not there's been any tampering. What you have to come up with is, can you figure out whether the evidence shows that natural causes don't explain this in a way that a researcher, a tester would agree, which is something called statistically significant and it makes a difference?

What it turns out is there are so many unknowns which are in the Wells report. The Wells report will say we don't know the exact time that the balls were tested. We don't know the exact order in which the balls were tested.

We don't know exactly if Gauge A was done, the so-called logo gauge or the non-logo gauge.

We don't know the temperature in the room at the time the ball was tested, a whole variety of factors, which would directly affect this result. So we know there are unknowns. So what did the Snyder team do? They said, okay, we are just going to test the different scenarios.

What happens if you vary this which is an unknown? What happens if you vary this which is an unknown? And what they found is the result change in such a way, in other words, the unknowns matter that the only conclusion you could come to is that you can't tell. You can't come to a statistically significant result that is reliable here.

Now, why did this happen? And again, this is something, sometimes you learn about this. It is my belief that the League has never thought about the Ideal Gas Law, frankly, before this thing. I dare say that there's not a referee in the NFL who knew anything about it.

I don't think there is anyone in Game Operations who knew anything about it. The original pressure rule goes back to 1920. I don't know when the Ideal Gas Law was first articulated, whether it was known or not because of that. No procedures are in place.

So think of drug testing. When we do drug testing, we have A samples and B samples. We have procedures for handling. We have chain of custody. We know exactly what should be tested. You can tell that somebody tests positive or tests negative. With respect to this issue of balls, there are no procedures to figure out if a lower pressure means it was tampered with or not and the result is none of this was recorded.

So no one wrote down what is the temperature in the room? That matters. No one wrote down, says, oh, were the Colts' balls, you know, inflated? Were the Colts' balls tested after the Patriots' balls were inflated or before? Because it matters on time. Time is a huge impact.

Why? Very simply, when you come back into the warm room, guess what happens? The balls heat back up. So you have to know every minute that you are in the room affects the balls heating back up, so the pressure is going back up. So these are the most essential things. So there were no procedures. So because of that, you can't tell.

And our view is, if this is something that needs to be approved and fixed, it should be, but you can't punish a player for that. You can't just assume, well, we didn't collect any of the proper information for this, so we are just going to assume that, (A), the player was generally aware, and (B), that something happened. In our view, this just isn't a basis for doing this.

Based on that testimony, we are also going to call Mr. Vincent who we understand we now could call about game day to talk about the procedures so you could see why this is missing and what maybe should have been done versus what was done.

And, again, I'm not ascribing blame to anyone. I don't think anyone knew about the Ideal Gas Law and knew this had to be accounted for. It's just the facts were the facts. We are going to have Mr. Vincent who will testify about that.

We are also going have Mr. Wells testify, because I think he will candidly admit -- because I think Ted Wells is an honest person -- what he knew and what he didn't know and what he was able to look at and what he wasn't able to look at and the limitations of what he could find here with respect to that. And so we will spend some time with Mr. Wells.

Given my four-hour limitation and the need to reserve time for cross-examination, I don't know what the NFL is going to do with witnesses, whether they are going to call Exponent, which they said they might, any of those witnesses, those are all the witnesses I think we are going to be able to call and still have enough time in order to have cross-examination time at all.

So that's going to be the evidence you are going to hear from our side. And we think when you hear all of this, you are going to look at this if, as you said, with an open mind, and say, this is really not a basis to suspend Mr. Brady who, in every other way, obviously, has been one of the most exemplary citizens in the history of the NFL. This is not somebody who has ever violated any NFL Policy.

This is not somebody who has ever done anything except do his best for his team and for this League in every way imaginable. And we don't believe this would be an appropriate basis for this discipline.

Finally, briefly, I know Mr. Levy has said we should put our legal arguments in briefs. I'm not going to spend time on them much at all, but I do want to note them here, I feel on this record before it closes, I have to note what our legal arguments are going to be. The first one I already mentioned is generally aware is not a proper standard for players. There is no precedent for it. There is no notice for it.

And we believe that without notice, which is a very, very important principle here, one of the reasons it's such an important principle is because we know from Judge Doty's decision in Peterson, that at least after of now unless the Eighth Circuit overturns it, it is the established law that players have to have notice as to what the policies are that apply to them and what they are going to be held responsible for.

There is no way that there is any argument that Mr. Brady knew that there was some general awareness standard, before you get to anything else. But the notice argument has three layers. The first one is, "Even if the NFL policies applied to him that are at issue, there was no notice because of generally aware."

But let's assume generally aware was the standard. I will get by that. The second thing was the policy that was invoked, which is the integrity of the game policy as you know, is directed, and this is in evidence -- is directed only at owners, head coaches, general managers, the club. It's never given to the player. And, in fact, it's clear on its face who its given to.

You probably know, Commissioner, every year, the players are given certain policies. For example, they are given the Personal Conduct Policy. They are given team rules, okay. They even sign acknowledgements as to which policies they get. One policy they've never been given is this integrity of the game policy which talks about the balls.

That's where -- that's exactly what Mr. Wells cited. He said my authority under this policy, it clearly applied to the club. It clearly applied to club personnel, you know, people who work at the club like GMs and coaches and equipment room men, locker room people.

We don't dispute any of that. But it was not a player policy. And therefore, neither Mr. Brady nor anyone else had any knowledge of this. Now how do I know this is correct? I know this is correct because not only is there no mention of this, but what you will also find out is that in the past, you have never looked at players for this issue.

And I will give you an example. There was an incident last year involving the Minnesota Vikings, which I don't know if you are aware of or not, where the Minnesota Vikings heated the footballs during the game. And the League conducted an investigation and instructed the club -- first of all, they gave them a warning only. That was the only penalty that was imposed. And they said you can't do this. In fact, there is a specific rule about you can't -- you can't heat the footballs during the games.

Now, I would even have to agree as a player advocate that the player on that team, the quarterback probably was generally aware that the ball felt warmer in freezing cold, okay. There wasn't even an investigation of that quarterback, let alone any thought of discipline. And why? Because the integrity of the game policy didn't apply to players.

We had another incident a few years ago involving the New York Jets. So in the New York Jets Case, it involved -- this is NFL Exhibit 73 -- it involved Mr. Cortez Robinson, who is a club employee of the Jets. Ironically, it's a Jets game against the Patriots. This was on November 24, 2009.

And in that game, it was found that he had attempted to use unapproved equipment to prep the kick balls, the K-balls prior to the kickoff. And, in fact, he was disciplined by the Vice President of Football Operations, Mr. Ron Hill, okay. And he said because your attempt to use this could be viewed as an attempt to gain a competitive advantage.

So what happened? He was suspended for the rest of the season, the equipment person was. The player, the kicker, wasn't even investigated. Why? Because this policy doesn't apply to the player. And, in fact, it's interesting because Mr. Hill was the Vice President of Football Operations.

He's the right person to interpret this policy. The Competitive Game Policy says if you know of any violations, please tell, you know, the Vice President of Football Operations. Today that's Mr. Vincent in terms of that, I believe. They are not people who discipline players ordinarily.

You know, we know under the Conduct Detrimental Policy other people discipline players' personal conduct. It's not the Vice President of Game-Day Operations, because these have never been directed at players. There is no history. And I can say to you without equivocation there has never been a player in the history of the NFL who has been suspended for anything having to do with equipment.

There is another player policy -- there is one player policy -- there's a player policy involving uniforms and things, which I will talk about, not that there is no policy. So Commissioner, this you may recognize. This is called League Policies For Players (indicating). This is what the players are given.

And it's interesting. It said "for players." What is not in here is the competitive integrity rule that Mr. Wells used in his report or anything about that. So we looked through those League Policies For Players and said is there anything that could arguably be applicable to this?

And the only thing that we have been able to find that could possibly apply to this is that there is something called, on page 15 of this policy, "Foreign Substances on Body Uniform." Has to do with, like, receivers putting Stickum on their gloves, things like that.

And then it says "Other Uniform Equipment Violations," okay. And it doesn't mention balls at all, but I'm trying to be creative. Was there anything that could possibly apply to this? And what it specifically says under this thing is the first offense will be a fine. That's what it says.

This is Mr. Brady's -- we don't believe it did anything, but this would be a first offense even if it came under this policy, which we don't believe this policy applies either, because there is nothing here about the balls. And it's clear Mr. Wells didn't use this policy; he used the other one. But even this policy would have it.

And by the way, the fine is $5,512 for the first offense. That's it. That's the only notice that a player has ever had about anything regarding equipment in the players' policy in terms of that.

So we believe both under the established rule of notice and what's called fair and consistent treatment, I know that you may remember from bounty and from Ray Rice, in the cases, and I know you are not a lawyer, but generally, it's been held by all of those arbitrators that fair and consistent treatment is the rule.

And, in fact, I think you have acknowledged this at various times yourself that there is a need for consistency and notice and fairness. I don't think you have yourself ever disputed notice, fairness and consistency.

We don't think it could come under notice. We don't think it could come under fairness. We don't think it could come under consistency in terms of these different issues.

So, finally, I would just note on the last issue of delegation, I understand you've already ruled, I guess, that Mr. Vincent's role was proper, so I am not going to reargue that. I understand -- if that's not correct, you can advise me -- but I understand from your two decisions you have already ruled on that.

I note there's another delegation issue we believe arises so I want to mention that, because it is clear to us now after reading the letter yesterday that there was no independent fact-finding by either Mr. Vincent or you in imposing the initial discipline. We think that also, unfortunately, raises another improper delegation issue.

We don't think under the CBA paragraph 15 of the player contract or Article 46 or, frankly, even under the NFL Constitution that delegating the fact-finding to someone outside the League and just having the League or Mr. Vincent, either you or Mr. Vincent decide the penalty based on someone else's facts was appropriate under, at least, the legal system as we understand it there.

So I'm not going to say any more about it. But I do want to note it and we will address that further in our post-hearing briefs. Thank you for bearing with me in doing this. I probably used more time than I wanted to given my limitations, but thank you very much.

Opening Statement by Mr. Nash

MR. NASH: I will try to be just as brief and maybe even briefer. This is a procedure under the Collective Bargaining Agreement, Commissioner, as you know. It's a matter that obviously is very serious. And starting with the delegation point that Jeffrey just said, this also is a fact-finding proceeding today.

You are here to hear evidence, as you just said. And so following this hearing, it will be up to you to make a judgment under the CBA regarding two issues. The first is whether Mr. Brady conducted conduct detrimental or engaged in conduct detrimental; and the second, assuming you make that conclusion, what is the appropriate discipline?

Now, as to the first point, I'm not sure what Mr. Kessler was saying about fact-finding. But I will say that under the CBA, there is no question that you can rely on the independent investigator in making the judgment, your judgment as to whether Mr. Brady engaged in conduct detrimental.

In fact, this is something that you and your predecessors have always done. It would not be reasonable to suggest that you would be the person to interview every witness or to look at every document every time an issue of potential conduct detrimental arose.

This case involves an investigation that I think was as thorough as any that has ever been done. It was done by an investigator, Mr. Wells and his colleagues, who is a person of unquestioned integrity. He interviewed over 66 witnesses. He reviewed documents.

And importantly, he gave Mr. Brady and his counsel as well as the Patriots and their counsel every opportunity to provide evidence, including some of the arguments that you heard today, and in fact considered these. Everything I think that you just heard Mr. Kessler describe about the evidence that you are going to hear today are things that were considered in the report and they are addressed in the report.

So we are not going to put on any evidence, any particular evidence beyond the report today, except we may have some witnesses in rebuttal and we will see what they have to say. But I will say just generally that all of these points that were made have been made and have been considered in the report.

One other point that I think is important, and there has been a lot that has been said about the Wells report, but as I think you are aware and Mr. Wells is here to tell you, this was truly an independent investigation. He was not given a task to find any particular conclusion, nor would he have agreed to do the investigation under those circumstances.

His investigation, as he will tell you, was conducted to find the truth, to find the facts and that's exactly what he did. And he did it in a thorough manner and under the Collective Bargaining Agreement, you are entitled clearly to rely on that report as you are entitled and should rely on whatever it is that they want to present here today.

Most importantly, it will be up to you to listen to Mr. Brady and consider what he has to say. And then it's your judgment. Under the Collective Bargaining Agreement, it's your judgment. And as far as the argument about standard of proof or burden of proof, this is not a criminal trial. It is not a civil trial.

This is, as I said, a proceeding under the Collective Bargaining Agreement regarding a very important subject, conduct detrimental, the integrity of the game. I don't think there can be any reasonable dispute that the underlying issues here involving the integrity of the game. The conduct of the Patriots in this matter, as I think everyone is aware, called into question the integrity of the game.

And under the CBA, you are obviously authorized and it is your responsibility to address that. Whether it's more probable than not, it's your judgment to make, listening to Mr. Brady, considering all of the evidence that is in the Wells report whether you, in your discretion, believe that he engaged in conduct detrimental and it's your judgment alone under the Collective Bargaining Agreement.

As far as the arguments whether Mr. Brady was under notice, I think Mr. Kessler is conflating what was done in the Wells report with your ultimate judgment on conduct detrimental. And most importantly, I think there's a lot of evidence that you didn't hear about in what Mr. Kessler had to say.

I don't have any doubt that you will hear Mr. Brady come in and tell you, I think, probably what he told Mr. Wells, the things that Mr. Kessler said. But in considering his testimony, I think you have to consider it in the context of the other evidence that's in the report.

And I would suggest that the other evidence of Mr. Brady's involvement and the violation that occurred here, the conduct detrimental that occurred here is substantial. The evidence in the Wells report is not as was said in the notice of appeal, purely speculative or just circumstantial.

As the report itself says, the conclusions are based on substantial evidence. That includes the basic evidence that there is no -- I think there is no dispute that at the halftime of the AFC Championship Game, the footballs of the Patriots were deflated and they were deflated more than the Colts' footballs. I don't think there is any dispute about that.

There is going to be evidence, it sounds like today, from experts about what was the cause of that? But I would submit, Commissioner, that those arguments and those very points are all documented in the report considered by Mr. Wells and the two experts who he retained.

And on that point, I should say and he will tell you that Mr. Wells wanted to find any explanation other than conduct detrimental or a violation of the rules for what happened at the game. That's why he retained an expert. The expert was tasked to look into all of this.

In addition, Mr. Wells retained a second expert to also check the work of the first expert. Now, I'm not going to go through all the details of the Ideal Gas Law, but what I can say and the experts are all here that from Exponent, Mr. Marlow from Princeton, who is an expert in physics, what

they will tell you is that they've considered all of these points, the timing point that Mr. Kessler raised, the change in temperature, and their basic conclusion that, for the Patriots' balls, those factors could not explain the level of deflation in the balls, and that the more reasonable conclusion was human intervention.

The human intervention part is something that wasn't addressed at all just now by Mr. Kessler. But there, again, the report contains substantial evidence that the deflation of the footballs was caused by human intervention. It's documented in the report.

Mr. McNally broke protocol. He disappeared from the locker room. Walt Anderson and the others interviewed in the report all were unequivocal that it was something that had never been done before by Mr. McNally and shouldn't have been done.

There is also in dispute at first he didn't say so, but ultimately Mr. McNally had to agree that he went into the bathroom with the footballs, clearly a breach of protocol. So there was substantial evidence of human intervention.

And then on top of all of that are the texts that are documented in the report of between Mr. McNally and Mr. Jastremski. And by the way, I think I heard some discussion that Mr. Brady was either not aware of the inflation rules that applied to footballs or his only concern was the surface or the grip.

I think there's evidence in the report and I think he would even say here today that he certainly was aware that there was a minimum inflation level. He knows what the rules are. This idea that he didn't have notice that somebody purposely deflated a football after the officials checked it was somehow not a violation of the rules, clearly he knew about that.

He's on public record as saying that he prefers the footballs to be inflated at the lower end. And he's made other statements to that effect. So there is no question that he was aware of that.

And I don't think you can reasonably accept the argument that you just heard that, because there is not a specific rule or document that would tell a player that if you are involved in an effort to cause footballs to be deflated below the rules that somehow you are not subject to discipline. On that point, there is no question that Mr. Brady was fully on notice of your authority to address conduct detrimental and the integrity of the game. It's in his player contract. It's in his CBA. He knows very well. It's in paragraph 15 of his player contract that he is subject to suspension for conduct detrimental.

Mr. Kessler talked about other cases including the Rice case. But as Judge Jones said in the Rice case, your authority to address this, these kinds of situations is broad. It's the agreement between the League and the Players Association.

And the Players Association and Mr. Brady himself, all players are under notice that if they engage in conduct detrimental, that you reasonably conclude is conduct detrimental, that they are subject to a suspension.

Again, this is not a minor, I would submit the report does not show some minor rules violation, some minor -- this is not and we will address all this in our brief, but the Vikings' case that was talked about, that was a ball boy who warmed up the ball and was not aware of the rule.

That doesn't, I think, provide any defense here for Mr. Brady and it certainly doesn't provide any basis to ignore all of the other evidence in the report.

On the argument about the failure to cooperate, as you know, during the investigation, Mr. Brady was asked to provide what the report describes as, "critical evidence." There is no dispute. I don't think Jeffrey just disputed that he did not do that. I think the argument I heard is that he didn't do it because his lawyer told him not to do it. I don't think that would be a basis to excuse a failure to cooperate.

I don't think you will hear any argument that -- reasonable argument that Mr. Brady didn't know failing to cooperate in an investigation like this could subject him to discipline. And I think it's a critical point when you consider all of the evidence in the report itself, because let's be clear what evidence we are talking about.

As the report documents, and I didn't hear whether Mr. Brady is going to testify about this, but as you know, following the AFC Championship Game, really for the first time, Mr. Brady all of the sudden had all these contacts by phone, by text and in person with Mr. Jastremski, the person he relied on to ensure that the balls that he used in the game were to his liking.

He was interviewed about this. It's all documented in the report. There are numerous calls. And the explanations that he provided and the witnesses provided, I would submit, you should consider as they are documented in the report.

And I don't think you are going to hear any evidence today to come to any conclusion other than it would be simply implausible, implausible to accept the idea that Mr. Brady didn't have any knowledge about either Mr. Jastremski's activities or Mr. McNally's activities.

It would not be plausible and I think, again, putting aside arguments about more probable than not, the bullet question I think in this proceeding is for you to make in terms of your judgment as to whether you believe after listening to Mr. Brady he engaged in conduct detrimental. He would submit that the evidence in the report on this point is substantial.

I would also submit that the refusal to provide the information that Mr. Wells asked for that bore directly on this point not only is absolutely a failure to cooperate, but it is reasonable to draw the inference that the failure to do so, his failure to provide that information suggests that there were -- there was probative evidence in the texts.

Now, as far as this last-minute, the Declaration from Mr. Maryman, I think we addressed this in the letter and I don't spend a lot of time on it, I'm actually quite puzzled by the declaration. I don't see how it can help Mr. Brady's arguments here.

First of all, there's a discussion about the e-mails. What the report documents is that the information that was most critical to Mr. Wells and the investigators are the texts. I think the players, like Mr. Brady, communicated by text far more than they do by e-mail.

We were not provided with the context of any texts during the relevant period. In fact, and we will hear from Mr. Brady, I suppose today about this, in fact, if you look at this expert declaration that was just submitted, there is a large gap in terms of Mr. Brady's phone. There are no text records for the relevant period.

I think the assumption could be they were somehow either destroyed. But even if that's not known, there is certainly no explanation as to why if Mr. Brady had cooperated when he was asked, if he had cooperated in a timely manner, that would have been available.

And interestingly, according to the declaration, and we can give you more in our brief about this, it appears that the phone was -- the new phone became available on March 6th, the date of his interview with Mr. Wells.

All of this, all of this, Commissioner, while not a direct statement from Mr. Kessler, and not a direct text telling somebody please deflate a football below a certain amount, all of this is highly probative and as the report says, substantial evidence, substantial evidence of his knowledge of a very serious matter, of a very serious matter.

You, as the Commissioner of the NFL, who is responsible for protecting the integrity of the game, can consider not just what you just heard from Mr. Kessler, not just a denial from Mr. Brady, but you can weigh that in the context of all of this evidence. And I would submit at the end of the proceeding, it's going to be your judgment.

It's your judgment, Commissioner. You know that as to what the appropriate finding should be. What I can say with quite certainty, it is, you are plainly authorized under the CBA to make that judgment. To the extent that you decide to affirm the discipline, the evidence in the Wells report is substantial and provides a more-than-adequate basis to affirm the discipline.

And, finally, it is certainly fair and consistent. The fact that -- the argument that because no player before has engaged in something like this in this context, we are talking about the AFC Championship Game.

Again, we are not talking about a ball boy heating up the ball who doesn't know the rules in Minnesota. When you read the Wells report, we are talking about much, much more. And in this context, in order for him to convince you that the discipline is not either fair or consistent, I would suggest that it's his burden. He would have to show you that there was some similar incident.

And by "similar," it has to be the same overall facts. And on that point, one other thing about the Wells report that I think needs to be emphasized, you can parse various parts as Mr. Kessler did; he didn't address a lot of the evidence in the report, but you can parse things.

But the Wells report makes clear that the conclusions are based on substantial evidence and they are based on the totality of the evidence. It's not just based on the scientific report. It's not just based on one text or one phone call. It's based on all of the evidence.

Commissioner, I would submit that's the judgment, that's the way you should approach the judgment, is you listen to the evidence. I would submit that when you listen to the evidence today and when you weigh that against all of the evidence that we are going to put into the record including the Wells report, it is certainly within your discretion to conclude that Tom Brady engaged in conduct detrimental, serious conduct detrimental, and that the discipline imposed was fair and appropriate.

A Response by Mr. Kessler

MR. KESSLER: I would like to use five minutes of my very valuable time just to respond to a few points that Mr. Nash raised. The first one is, he emphasized at the end, he kept using the word "the player engaged," "the player engaged in conduct detrimental." No player has engaged in similar conduct.

I'm sorry, but Mr. Nash is wrong. Mr. Wells did not make any finding and there is no finding that Mr. Brady engaged in anything other than being generally aware of somebody else's conduct. He has no response to that. He can point to nothing. He can brief this afterwards. And I'm saying right now he will find no precedent for generally aware. So the whole premises of his argument of "engaged" is just not what the Wells report found.

Number 2, on the e-mails, he seems to not understand the Maryman Declaration. So let me just explain it a little bit. I didn't think I had to. It says, so, for the phone texts, the phone doesn't exist. It didn't exist at the time. In other words, Mr. Brady's practice, you will hear, because of living the life he lives as a celebrity, for better or worse, he gets free telephones.

And based on that, he gets rid of his phones constantly because he's afraid of in this world of social media what would happen if somebody got his private information with himself and his wife and other things and what that would become. So that has been his practice for years and years.

So what did we provide? We provided all the phone logs that show the text messages. I didn't even know this, but your phone bills, you can actually get the records, show all the text messages. And what does that show? It shows all the text messages from the relevant time match up to all the texts to Mr. Jastremski, okay. There are none to Mr. McNally, which is consistent with Mr. Brady's testimony that he didn't really know Mr. McNally in any material way at all.

So there are no texts to Mr. McNally's number. The Jastremski texts match up and the Schoenfeld texts match up. So everything that was a text there was basically in the Wells report. So for Mr. Nash to come and say you should assume that there are bad texts and Mr. Brady's going to testify there were no such texts and the phone records show there were no such texts, there is no way you can draw that adverse inference about him. And it's not right for Mr. Nash to suggest it.

With respect to the issue of cooperation, as Mr. Nash knows, and as I believe you know, the only -- assuming there was a lack of cooperation for the moment, and we believe why we think you should not find that in this case because there was no policy that said it, he wasn't told about it, assuming you say I think this was a lack of cooperation, here, we do have a history of very comparable behavior in Mr. Nash's word.

So Brett Favre in an incident you may remember involving sexting on his phone, he was found to have refused to cooperate in the investigation and he was fined $50,000.

When that came up in bounty, you will remember Mr. Hargrove was fined -- was suspended; I'm sorry -- for refusing to cooperate in the investigation. Commissioner Tagliabue said the following with respect to that: He reversed Mr. Hargrove's suspension and he said, "Although not entirely comparable to the present matter," talking about the Favre situation for Mr. Hargrove, "This illustrates NFL's practice of fining, not suspending, players for serious cooperation violations of this type."

That's the history. It's been a fine. So if Mr. Nash had said I still think it's cooperation, it should be a fine, that would be one thing. But there is no history in the light of bounty, I don't see any way under fair and consistent a suspension would be imposed just on this cooperation issue.

And finally, on the issue Mr. Nash said, well, it's not a big deal that it's not in any policy or notice. Mr. Brady should just know that this, he would be punished for this. Well, that's not what the cases say.

So in Peterson, Judge Doty said the new policy couldn't be imposed instead of the old policy because the player had no notice of it even though the player surely knew from the old policy that domestic violence was prohibited, but it had to do with what the punishment can be and that's what Judge Doty held. And right now that's binding law on the NFL League.

It says, Commissioner Tagliabue in bounty, specifically said that in the case of bounty, the League's history was to hold the clubs responsible, not the players, and therefore, he found that as a reason to overturn the discipline there. And he said because that was the history.

That's the exact history here. That's why the conduct detrimental doesn't apply. This is the competitive integrity policy which is directed at holding the clubs responsible for this. Now, that can change. It can promulgate a new policy, but it matters. It's simply not correct legally that it doesn't matter.

And I know Mr. Levy will give you legal advice on this based on the caselaw. But I just believe when you get that advice and look at the evidence, you are going to conclude that notice, fairness and consistency matters. So thank you very much for that extra time.

MR. LEVY: Why don't you call your first witness.

MR. KESSLER: I will. I will now call Tom Brady to the stand, please.

Testimony of Tom Brady

Direct Examination by Mr. Kessler

Q. Good morning, Mr. Brady. Could you please just state your name for the record so we have that.

A. Thomas Edward Patrick Brady, Jr.

Q. Thank you. And what college did you attend?

A. University of Michigan.

Q. And what year were you drafted into the NFL?

A. 2000.

Q. And by which team?

A. New England Patriots.

Q. Okay. And how many seasons have you played in the NFL?

A. 15.

Q. And have they all been with the Patriots?

A. Yes.

Q. And how many Super Bowls have you led the Patriots to during your career?

A. Four.

Q. Now, how many did you go to?

A. Six.

Q. I know you are focused on how many did you win?

A. Four.

Q. Okay. Has anybody won anymore?

A. Same, Montana.

MR. KESSLER: That's all I am going to do on Mr. Brady's background, which I think is well-known to the Commissioner regarding this.

COMMISSIONER GOODELL: Sure.

Q. Mr. Brady, I'm going to direct all of your testimony now to the issue of game balls and the incidents that are in the Wells report and all of that information.

So let me first ask you, sir, and if you would just explain to the Commissioner more than me, who selects the footballs you use in the NFL games?

A. I do.

Q. Okay. And could you explain to the Commissioner how do you decide what balls you would like to use, what factors, what process do you go through? If you could explain that to him.

A. Well, we have a, I would say in a very general situation, I have played a lot of games and we have different practices, I think, depending on -- depending on the game. I think every quarterback likes the balls a certain way. And it really has to do with feel. It really has to do with comfort of gripping the ball. And I think we go through pretty, you know, extensive, rigorous process to take what may be a brand new football and try to break it in as quickly as possible so it can be available to be one of the game balls that you use on game day.

So what typically happens is over the course of the week, in our situation, John would break the balls in.

COMMISSIONER GOODELL: John who?

THE WITNESS: Jastremski.

A. He would break in the last three or four years, I don't know however long it's been, he has been the one that I've dealt with that has been responsible for prepping them so that I can go in before the game and choose what I like and what we are going to play with on that particular day.

And it's a very feel-oriented process. It's not, you know, I grab the ball. I feel with my hands. If I approve it, you know, I flip it to John, you know, to sort through however many he may make up for the game. There could be 30 balls. There could be 40 balls. I could select 12. I may select 24 depending if we think we are going to use additional balls. So I think it's really a process for me to -- I don't even really think about. Is it important to me? Absolutely. I think the ball is important to every quarterback, which is why we are a part of that 2006 that we could break them in.

But for me, it's always been about how does the ball feel in my hand? Can I properly grip it and, you know, is this, what I feel is going to be the best to go out there and perform on the field with? So that's basically it.

Q. Mr. Brady, did the issue of inflation level ever come up as a factor when you are choosing your balls or deciding upon the balls; is that something you think about at that time?

A. Never.

Q. Okay. Do you discuss the inflation level of the balls with Mr. Jastremski during the process when you are selecting the balls?

A. Never.

Q. Okay. Now, once you approve the footballs for the game, when is the next time you come into contact with the balls?

A. On the field.

Q. During your whole career now, I want to be very clear about this, I am asking during your whole career, have you ever asked anyone from the Patriots to alter the footballs in any way after you've approved them?

A. No.

Q. Okay. Now, have you ever specifically, so again, very specific question, have you ever told anyone on the Patriots after you've given to them that they should change the inflation level of the footballs after you approved them or do anything about the inflation level after you approved them?

A. No.

Q. Now, what would be your reaction if Mr. Jastremski or anyone else in the Patriots was doing something to the footballs after you've approved it? How would you feel about that?

A. I would disapprove of that.

Q. Why? Why would it matter to you?

A. Because I go through, like I said, this extensive process to pick out the balls for the game, and that's the ball ultimately that I want on the field that I play with. So once I pick the ball out, then I don't want anything other than that ball to be the one that I am on the field playing with.

Q. Now I am going to ask you now, I am going to turn to the October 2014 Jets game.

MR. KESSLER: And to give you, Commissioner, context, this is the game about which this various e-mail traffic and discussing the Jets' ball that's in the Wells report. That's the one we are focusing on right now.

Q. Now, what do you recall was your reaction to the footballs when you felt them in the October 16, 2014, game against the Jets? Was there anything different? What happened?

A. Before the game or after the game?

Q. Well, first, yeah, let's go before the game. Was there anything different?

A. Well, we chose a different process. So I would say we have a pretty standard process for how we break the ball in or how John breaks the balls in. It's a very rigorous process. It's probably, you spend a significant amount of time on each ball.

COMMISSIONER GOODELL: What does he do, Tom? Do you mind?

MR. KESSLER: Sure.

THE WITNESS: Well, I don't know all the specifics. I know there's sandpaper. I know there's dirt. I know there's a leather conditioner that we use that I got from my old college coach that we use on the ball quite a bit.

And we take leather receiving gloves that the receivers use and we try to get the tack from the leather on the receiver gloves and really rub that into the -- (indicating) -- each of these balls have nubs on them. Sometimes if the ball is too nubby, I like to sand down the nubs. I don't like it when there's no nub because then there's no traction on the ball.

So you want your hand to be able to grip the ball, but you don't want it so flat that you can't. So they try to, basically, moisten the ball with the leather conditioner. And it's -- it's -- that has been a very helpful way to break in a new ball quickly, not that there is any way to break in quickly.

I think even before John, John Jastremski took over that process, which like I said, it's a very extensive process, so I'm not sure how the other equipment managers do it, but a lot of players would just basically use the ball in practice until it broke in enough that they could -- that they would want to use it in the game.

Sometimes that may take two weeks, three weeks, four weeks, it takes a long time to break in a football if you are just playing catch with it. At some times in my career, I have seen ball boys manually throwing the ball back and forth to one another, I mean, literally hundreds of times to try to break the ball in. So to use that conditioner, it's been a significant way to kind of speed up the process.

COMMISSIONER GOODELL: You said there were different processes?

THE WITNESS: Yeah.

COMMISSIONER GOODELL: And you said you did something different at the Jets game?

THE WITNESS: Yeah.

COMMISSIONER GOODELL: What was the difference, I guess just so I understand, and how many different processes did you have? I understand there are multiple steps that you just described.

THE WITNESS: There was really, we basically prepared them one way up until that particular game. We played in a game late, not in 2014, but in 2013. It may have been the last game of the year. We played the Buffalo Bills and there was a torrential downpour and we used a lot of the Lexol leather conditioner on the ball. And John, not knowing that, what he does always before the game with the Lexol, and it turns out that when the Lexol is exposed to the -- to the wet weather, the ball gets very oily and it makes it nearly impossible to grip.

So when we went into that particular Jet game, there was going to be inclement weather and I -- we came to I think a mutual decision. And he said, believe me, we are going to use a lot of these old footballs that are from training camp which, I don't know, four or five weeks, six weeks ago that we would never typically use in a game because they don't have any Lexol on them.

But they are already broken in so that when the water hits the ball, the water will absorb into the ball and it will create, you know, enough tackiness with just the water that you will be able to grip it when you throw it.

So I was a little hesitant, but I went with it. You know, I felt the balls before the game. I said all right, you know, let's go for it. And then I got on the field and hated it.

Q. Tell the Commissioner --

COMMISSIONER GOODELL: In the Jets game?

THE WITNESS: In the Jets game.

Q. Tell the Commissioner what did you feel different in the football during the Jets game?

A. Well, the ball was very hard, so it didn't feel like the ball was the way I approved them before the game. And for one reason or another, I don't know what happened to the balls.

COMMISSIONER GOODELL: But they were the same balls, to your knowledge?

THE WITNESS: I have no idea. To my knowledge, yes, they should have been.

Q. And did you react to that with anybody on the team?

A. Yes. Can I just say one other thing?

Q. Sure.

A. So when you use -- just to be clear, when I say "soft" and "hard," a lot of times the only thing I have ever felt a football when I say that is the softness of the leather. So when I say I'm trying to break in the ball, I'm breaking in the -- I'm making the laces softer, I'm making the leather softer, like you refer to it like a baseball mitt.

So when we use those balls in the Jet game, they were balls that were really old balls so the leather was soft. Does that make sense? The leather was soft. The ball wasn't soft. The leather felt like I could grip it.

Q. Now I would like you to turn to, so you felt the ball, but you didn't like it. Who did you express your feelings to during the game?

A. To John. It was over the course of the first half that, you know, I was just, I was very pissed off. I was very pissed off at -- partly because I felt like I got talked into using these balls that we had done, like I said, a different protocol, and I felt like it didn't work out very well.

Q. Mr. Brady, during the course of a game, is it fair to say you are somebody who gets fired up and intense during a game?

A. Yes.

Q. Is that a fair statement?

A. Yeah.

Q. Okay. Did some of that intensity get directed at Mr. Jastremski during this game?

A. I mean, yes, I think it did. It did. I was pissed off. So it's kind of a good attitude for me to have all the time on the football field, you know. And I know that he got the brunt of it because I didn't like -- for the first time in my career, I didn't like the way the football felt.

Q. Now, the next day after the Jets game, did Mr. Jastremski then tell you anything he learned about the balls?

A. I don't know if it was the next day or days after that game.

Q. Sometime after the Jets game, what did Mr. Jastremski tell you he learned about the ball?

A. That the balls were, you know, inflated to, you know, much higher than what they were agreed upon before the game.

Q. Do you recall what number he used?

A. 16.

Q. 16 psi? Okay.

And how did you react to that? First of all, before he mentioned that, at that time, did you have any prior knowledge as to what the exact psi levels were set for in this NFL rule from 1920?

A. Zero.

Q. No knowledge at all until then?

A. Zero.

Q. Okay. So after he told you it was something called 16, what did you say to him? How did you react to that?

A. Well, obviously, I felt like somebody did something to the balls. I thought possibly the referees added balls -- added air to the balls, just because maybe they squeezed them, felt that these balls feel soft and just, you know, squeezed air into the ball.

So I told our -- I asked our equipment manager, Dave Schoenfeld. I said Dave, what does it say in the rule book as to how the balls should be inflated? And he brought me a piece of paper that was highlighted and it said the balls should be between 12 and a half and 13 and a half. And then I told Dave –

COMMISSIONER GOODELL: That was in the days following the Jets game?

THE WITNESS: Yes, I don't know, two days, three days, four days.

COMMISSIONER GOODELL: Whatever it was?

THE WITNESS: Yes.

I said make sure when the referees get the balls, give them this sheet of paper that highlighted, because really I don't want that to ever happen again. I don't want to go out there on the field and play with a ball that's –

Q. The sheet of paper was, the rules say between 12 and a half and 13 and a half?

A. Yes.

Q. And so you were telling him make sure the officials don't make it more than that? Don't make it 16, right?

A. Yes.

Q. Other than that comment, have you ever, after that time, told Mr. Jastremski or anybody else in the Patriots anything else about the pressure of footballs? Was there any comments at all that you make to them –

A. No.

Q. -- until this happened?

A. No.

COMMISSIONER GOODELL: Tom, why would you go to Dave -- is it Schoenfeld -- the equipment manager?

THE WITNESS: Yeah.

COMMISSIONER GOODELL: Why did you go to him and not Jastremski?

THE WITNESS: Because he's his boss.

COMMISSIONER GOODELL: Jastremski was the one who went through the process with you in the past?

THE WITNESS: Right.

COMMISSIONER GOODELL: And prepared them for you, and you didn't ask him about the pressure?

THE WITNESS: I may have had Dave -- no, I didn't. I didn't ask John about it. I don't think I did. I mean, it could have been the two of them there together at the same time. I'm sure John eventually found out.

Q. Tom, at the time of this, did you even know who on the Patriots would be with the officials when the balls were being looked at to show them the rule to tell them that? In other words, did you even know it was Jastremski or somebody else?

A. No, I never thought about it.

COMMISSIONER GOODELL: Just so I'm clear, this is a Jets game in New York?

THE WITNESS: No.

COMMISSIONER GOODELL: It's not? It was in New England?

THE WITNESS: Yeah.

Q. Now, let me show you next something from the Wells report, because Mr. Nash in his opening mentioned that there were these e-mails from other people or texts from other people that are not you. But it's talking about you, so I want to give you some chance to give context to what this seems to refer to, even though you obviously don't know what the e-mails say or mean other than that you are looking at them now.

Take a look at in the Wells report, which is NFLPA Exhibit 7. I'm sure it has an NFL number as well. And take a look at page 86 of the Wells report.

COMMISSIONER GOODELL: Is this it?

MR. LEVY: Yes.

MR. KESSLER: Do you have it, Commissioner?

COMMISSIONER GOODELL: Yes.

Q. So the Jets game we are talking about was October 16th. You will see these are a pair of e-mails from Mr. Jastremski to Panda that are October 17th. You will see that's the day after the Jets game, just to give context to everyone.

By the way, I will represent to you because it says in Mr. Wells' report that Panda is Mr. Jastremski's fiancé, so that we know who he's communicating with is his fiancé, the day after the Jets game, okay?

And you will see what he writes is, "Ugh...Tom was right."

Do you see that? And then it goes, "I just measured some of the balls. They are supposed to be 13. They were, like, 16, felt like bricks."

Do you see that?

A. Yeah.

Q. Now, at this time, when he says, "Tom was right," what had you discussed with Mr. Jastremski during the game? Did you say anything about the pressure at that time or the psi during the game?

A. No.

Q. What did you tell him?

A. I don't -- that the balls sucked, yeah.

Q. I think you said they felt hard or fat or something like that?

A. I didn't like them.

Q. Does this reference to you in any way indicate that you had a conversation with him during the Jets game about pressure or psi or anything like that?

A. No.

Q. Thank you. Now, when you told Mr. Schoenfeld to show the referees the rule, did you ever tell him you wanted him or anyone else to make a psi level below 12.5 that you now learned was the limits?

A. No.

Q. Okay. Did you ever tell anyone in the Jets organization -- I'm sorry, the Patriots organization -- that they should do -- they should try to get the balls to be less than 12.5?

A. No.

Q. Now, let me now mention, because it came up in the Wells report, the 2006 rule change that you were involved in. Were you one of the quarterbacks to lobby for the rule change in 2006 regarding preparation of footballs?

A. Yes.

Q. Who were some of the other quarterbacks who were involved in that?

A. I know Peyton was, Trent Green, Drew Brees; who else?

Q. Were most of the quarterbacks in the League involved at that time?

A. All of them. And everyone ultimately that we sent a petition to, you know, said, hell yeah, let's do it. Let's agree with it.

Q. And let me just refer, we have NFLPA Exhibit 203 is a copy of the petition. Is this the petition that you and other quarterbacks signed asking for the ability to prepare your footballs as a rule change?

A. Yes.

Q. Okay. Now, in this petition, was there any discussion of the pressure of the balls or inflating balls or anything about that subject at all?

A. No.

Q. During the time in 2006, did you have discussions with anybody about inflating footballs or the psi's of footballs or even what those requirements were?

A. No.

Q. Did you ever learn the 12.5 to 13.5 standard during that 2006 process?

A. No.

Q. Okay. Now, was this rule ultimately presented to the NFL Competition Committee?

A. Yes.

Q. And did the Competition Committee adopt this rule change to let the quarterbacks prepare their balls?

A. Yes.

COMMISSIONER GOODELL: Mr. Kessler, who did this come from?

MR. KESSLER: The petition?

COMMISSIONER GOODELL: Yes.

MR. KESSLER: The quarterbacks and the League all signed it.

COMMISSIONER GOODELL: I know. I signed it. But who did it come from?

THE WITNESS: Peyton.

COMMISSIONER GOODELL: Peyton?

THE WITNESS: Manning.

MR. KESSLER: And then this was presented to the Competition Committee and that's what happened.

Q. Now, in the Wells report, Mr. Wells said, and this is one of the points that Mr. Nash said or Mr. Wells reached his conclusions, and he wrote, "It is reasonable to infer" -- that's the words he used -- "that you were likely to have become familiar with the NFL rules regarding the 12.5 minimum inflation level in 2006 when you were lobbying for this rule."

Regardless of what Mr. Wells said was reasonable to infer, did you, in fact, become aware of the rule at that time?

A. No.

Q. Was there any discussion of that rule at that time?

A. No.

Q. Now, let me now turn to the AFC Championship Game against the Colts.

MR. KESSLER: Commissioner, do you think we should have a break? Should I continue? Okay, we will continue.

COMMISSIONER GOODELL: Do you want a break?

THE WITNESS: No.

Q. Looking at that game, do you recall approximately what time the game was going to start that night, roughly?

A. 7:30, 8:00.

Q. Would it refresh your recollection if I said it was around 7:00, 6:50, 7:00?

A. It was a night game.

Q. That sounds about right? Okay.

How many hours before, approximately, would you have made your final approval of the balls on that day for the AFC Championship Game?

A. I think between three and four hours.

Q. Okay. Now, when you selected the footballs, who was assisting you in the selection process at that time?

A. John.

Q. Anybody else besides Mr. Jastremski or was it just the two of you?

A. Just the two of us.

Q. Okay. Now, at the time that you made that selection, did you give Mr. Jastremski -- did you say anything to him about the pressure level of the balls on that day?

A. No.

Q. Did you in any way suggest to him to do something to the balls to make them less than 12.5?

A. No.

Q. Did you even suggest to him anything about the pressure whether it was to make it at any level?

A. No.

Q. What were you talking to Mr. Jastremski about when you were selecting the balls, if you remember; what kinds of factors were you talking about?

A. Just the way the ball felt. And this was a different -- can I talk about just, again, was a different process than what we had normally gone through.

COMMISSIONER GOODELL: The AFC Championship Game?

THE WITNESS: The AFC Championship Game.

A. So knowing that I didn't want to go back and use two-month balls in this AFC Championship Game like we did for the original Jets game, I think on Friday we found out the weather was going to be inclement.

And we decided to break in brand-new footballs with, like, 36 hours to go before the game because I didn't want any Lexol on the balls. And I didn't want to do the same thing that happened in the Jets game.

So we kind of referred back to an old process that the previous equipment manager who was responsible for the preparation of the game balls did, which was like I said, that really extensive manual throwing, gloving process that makes up for a lot of the Lexol.

What you gain from the Lexol, kind of the weeks of breaking the ball in, that kind of, you can get through those. So I asked John to make up 24 brand new balls without putting any Lexol on them.

COMMISSIONER GOODELL: Have you ever done that procedure before?

THE WITNESS: No. It had been many years.

COMMISSIONER GOODELL: When you played in inclement weather, did you ever decide to do that?

THE WITNESS: No.

COMMISSIONER GOODELL: This is the first time in the AFC Championship Game you said, I want to break in 24 new footballs in a different process than you have ever done before?

THE WITNESS: Well, that's the way -- before John took over, the guy John Hillebrand, that's how he broke the balls in. We didn't use much Lexol with John Hillebrand. That's not what he wanted to do. When John Jastremski took over, we used a lot more Lexol.

COMMISSIONER GOODELL: Was the Jets game in inclement weather?

THE WITNESS: I don't think it ended up -- no. It was supposed to be, but it didn't end up being. It may have -- it may have rained; I don't remember.

Q. Which game are we talking about?

A. The Jets game.

Q. The original?

COMMISSIONER GOODELL: Back in October.

A. So what happened was I don't want any -- we definitely need to use new balls, but I don't want any Lexol on the balls. So you basically have to go through this rigorous ball preparation with, like, 36 hours to go.

COMMISSIONER GOODELL: But over the three years that John was there —

THE WITNESS: Yeah.

COMMISSIONER GOODELL: -- you never did that before? You never did a 24, 48-hour process to take new balls and break them in?

THE WITNESS: No.

COMMISSIONER GOODELL: But you decided to do it because you felt —

THE WITNESS: Right. But we also had a lot of backups to that, too. I said, look, in case I don't like this when you are done, make sure we have, like, that night, I think I had, like, probably 50 balls to choose from.

COMMISSIONER GOODELL: Okay. Q. Now, Mr. Brady —

THE WITNESS: And, sorry, when I felt them that night, I liked them so we went with them.

COMMISSIONER GOODELL: "That night" was what?

THE WITNESS: The night of the game.

COMMISSIONER GOODELL: Okay.

Q. Mr. Jastremski never was with you prior to this year when you went to the Super Bowl, right?

A. No.

Q. Okay. Mr. Hillebrand had been with you and he was preparing the balls when you got to the Super Bowl sometimes; is that correct?

A. Yes.

Q. During the game, now, when did you next get the balls after you gave them to John on game day? You picked your balls and you gave it to John. Do you know where he took them or what happened after then?

A. No. Normally I just leave because I do it in the equipment room.

Q. So that was, you gave the balls to him. When did you next see any of the balls?

A. On the field.

Q. On the field?

COMMISSIONER GOODELL: Just so I am clear, for warmup or game?

THE WITNESS: Game.

Q. Now during the game you got the balls. Did they feel okay to you?

A. Yes.

Q. In other words, you didn't notice anything unusual about the balls or your balls felt okay?

A. I didn't think about it. They felt fine; I didn't.

Q. You had a process like you had in the Jets game?

A. That was the only time I reacted to not having a ball.

Q. They felt like they normally feel after you select them?

A. Yes.

Q. After halftime, did the balls feel any different to you than they did in the first half of the game?

A. No.

Q. Now, did you know during the game that the referees had put more air into the balls to get them to 13 psi at the halftime? Were you aware of that during the game?

A. No.

Q. So could you even tell the difference between whatever the inflation was in the first half versus the second half in terms of your feel? Did you have any sense of that during the game?

A. No.

Q. Now, just to ask, do you recall how you played in the second half of that game?

A. We played good. We played really well.

Q. Is it correct that at least your statistics of passing a touchdown were better in the second half after the ball was raised to 13 by the referees? You didn't know it, than they were in the first half?

A. Yeah.

Q. Was that correct?

A. What did I do? I don't --

Q. Okay. You don't focus on your own statistics; what do you focus on in the game?

A. Whether we win or lose.

Q. Yes, okay.

A. We did good in the second half. We played really well.

Q. That's sufficient. Now what I want to do is focus on the events after the game is over. When did you first become aware after the game now that someone was making allegations that the Patriots had done something to deflate the balls during the game? How did you learn about that?

A. On the radio show the following morning.

Q. The following morning?

A. Yeah.

Q. Okay. And what was your reaction when you heard about that?

A. I couldn't believe it. I think I said it's ridiculous.

COMMISSIONER GOODELL: Just so I am clear, you were being interviewed or you just heard it on the radio?

THE WITNESS: I was being interviewed by the host on the show.

Q. Now, after this radio interview, you heard this allegation; did you speak to anyone in the Patriots about this allegation?

A. I spoke to John.

Q. Okay. And did you ask Mr. Jastremski if he knew anything about the efforts to deflate the footballs or anything like that?

A. Yes.

Q. What did he tell you?

A. That he has no idea what happened and that he couldn't explain it.

Q. And you know Mr. Jastremski a long time, I mean, for these three years?

A. Well, I have known him for 12 years since he has been working on the team because he was actually kind of the quarterback ball boy at one point during training camp, so.

Q. You generally found that in your dealings with him, he has been honest and upfront with you over the years?

A. Absolutely.

Q. Do you believe that?

A. Absolutely.

Q. So when he told you he didn't know anything about it, did you believe him?

A. Absolutely.

Q. Okay. Now, there are records that Mr. Wells has noted that in the weeks after the game, now, so you now have two weeks to Super Bowl, you had various text messages and phone conversations with Mr. Jastremski?

A. Yes.

Q. Now, first of all, what was most of those phone conversations about? Why were you talking to Mr. Jastremski in those two weeks?

A. Because we were obviously going to the Super Bowl, still had the season to play and I knew there was another extensive process of breaking in all the brand new Super Bowl footballs.

So we had numerous conversations on the processes that we would go through to break them in because the ones we had gone through the AFC Championship where we didn't use the Lexol, we were going to play in a dome.

The last time we played in Arizona, it rained after the game. So I didn't necessarily want to chance it with putting a bunch of Lexol. So we were just determined when he was going to get the balls whether we were going to use them at practice or not. I think most of the conversations centered around breaking in those balls.

Q. The Commissioner may already know this. I didn't know this. Do you have to prepare more footballs for a Super Bowl than for other games in the NFL season?

A. Yeah.

Q. Why is that? Could you explain to the Commissioner. Maybe you know all this. What's different about the Super Bowl?

A. Well, you know, we break in, I think almost -- I think you use the ball for one play and then they take it out of the game. So I think there's almost 100 balls that we broke in.

Q. How many balls do you have to select for a Super Bowl as opposed to a normal game?

A. I think around 100 as opposed to 12.

Q. That's, like, almost ten times as many balls?

A. Yeah.

Q. So in your experience in past Super Bowls, is that an expensive process for someone like Mr. Jastremski to go through in that two-week period of time?

A. Absolutely.

Q. And he had ever done that before for a Super Bowl?

A. No.

Q. And you were aware of that?

A. Yes.

Q. Now, take a look again. I want to refer you to some of the e-mails or texts, the things that Mr. Wells cites. So look at page 104 of the Wells report, which is NFLPA Exhibit 7.

Now, you will notice this is a text from you to Mr. Jastremski at 9:51 in the morning of the 19th, which is the, I believe the day after the AFC Championship Game, so after the radio interview and remember you said you had a phone conversation with him?

A. Yes.

Q. So was this text after that phone conversation you had with him?

A. Yes.

Q. Okay. Now, what did you mean or why were you sending a text to Mr. Jastremski saying, "You are good, Jonny boy?"

And then he writes back to you, "Still nervous. So far, so good, though. I will be all right."

What do you understand that to be referring to, if you could explain that to the Commissioner?

A. I wrote, "You good, Jonny boy," like, you doing okay? Because he was obviously nervous the fact that these allegations were coming out that they would fall back on him. And I was just, I guess, expressing my concern for him.

Q. Now, you then wrote to him, "You didn't do anything wrong, bud." Why did you say that? Was that based on your conversation with him?

A. Yeah, I said, "You didn't do anything wrong, bud." That's how I, you know.

Q. And then he writes back, "I know. I will be all good."

A. Yeah.

Q. Did that set of texts refer in any way to your knowing that he had done anything to deflate footballs or anything like that at all?

A. No.

Q. Now let me refer you next, the Wells report notes that, "There came a time that you invited Mr. Jastremski in this two-week period to the Super Bowl to come to the quarterback room."

I think it was on that day. Do you recall inviting him to the quarterback room?

A. Yes.

Q. Well, first of all, just to explain to the Commissioner, describe the quarterback room. Is it kind of some secret sanctuary like the Bat Cave that only the most special people get invited in? What kind of people are in the quarterback room every day?

A. All the quarterbacks, coaches.

Q. Can any one of your backup quarterbacks invite whoever they want into the quarterback room?

A. Absolutely.

Q. Okay.

COMMISSIONER GOODELL: Had John ever been in it?

THE WITNESS: Up to that point, I have no idea.

COMMISSIONER GOODELL: But not with you or you don't remember?

THE WITNESS: I don't remember.

Q. Now, normally, when you are preparing for a game, do you prepare in the quarterback room or do you prepare at your home, usually?

A. Home.

Q. Okay. On this particular day, were you preparing in the quarterback room at that time?

A. Yes.

Q. Okay. And so, why did you call Mr. Jastremski to the quarterback room? Was there some significance to that?

A. Because I was doing all my Seahawks preparation and I was just thinking about the Super Bowls and asked him to come to the quarterback room as opposed to me going to try to find him somewhere.

Q. Okay. Now, during that time in the quarterback room, what was the purpose of asking him? What did you want to talk about?

A. The Super Bowl.

Q. Okay. So did you call him there because you wanted to discuss something about the allegations that were being made at that time?

A. No.

Q. Is it possible that something came up about is he feeling okay because you heard that?

A. Sure, absolutely.

Q. But anything beyond that, do you remember any conversations about the allegations?

A. I don't remember.

Q. Okay. Now, by the way, there has been some discussion from the Wells report about Mr. McNally and whether you knew him or not, okay. Prior to all these allegations, did you know the name Jim McNally?

A. No.

Q. Now, did you know who it was, even, who met with referees in their locker room when they are testing the balls? Did you even know which person physically on the Patriots was the person who went in there and did that?

A. No.

Q. Okay. Now, in the New England stadium on game day, are there lots of people who come in just for game day as kind of part-time people working in various ways?

A. Yes.

Q. Okay. And do you get to sort of know over the years their faces, whether or not you know their names?

A. Yes.

Q. So is it possible that you actually knew -- I will even ask it differently. Have you subsequently learned who Mr. McNally is among those people?

A. Yes.

Q. And is he somebody you actually sort of knew as a face, somebody to go, like, wave to but you didn't know who he was, his name?

A. Yes.

Q. Okay. Now, other than that, do you have any relationship with Mr. McNally at all?

A. No.

Q. Now, there is discussion in the Wells report about Mr. McNally getting some autographed jerseys or footwear or other things that you would autograph; are you familiar with that?

A. Yes.

Q. Describe for the Commissioner what your practice is when you get asked to sign jerseys or shoes or other things by people who are, you know, at the stadium or around the locker room or any of those environments; what is your normal practice?

A. I get asked I would say on a daily basis to sign any number of things. I think I told Mr. Wells I don't think I have ever turned anyone down. So if someone asked, I signed whatever they would ask.

Sometimes they would put it in my locker and walk away and there would be things there and I would just sign them. But if somebody asked for an autograph, I would give it to them.

Q. Have you signed autographs for merchandise of people who you don't know what they are? Someone comes over and says, "Could you give me this for somebody else?" Would you sign that even if you don't know the person?

A. Absolutely.

Q. Have you ever handed signed merchandise to people in the locker room at the stadium when you didn't really know what their name was?

A. Yes.

Q. You just said here, they asked, someone did it and you gave it to them?

A. Yes.

Q. So there's a statement here in the Wells report, and I don't know who the source is because you can't tell from the report, that someone says that you handed a signed Jersey or shoes or something to Mr. McNally at one point, okay.

If you did that, did you know somebody named Mr. McNally when you did it?

A. No.

Q. Now, let me turn now very briefly to the subject of electronic communications. Now, did there come a time after February 28th, so now we are well past the Super Bowl when you learned from your lawyers or your agents that there had been some request made for e-mails and texts that you might have?

A. Yes.

Q. Okay. Now, we know that those were -- nothing was turned over or the request was not responded to. How did you make the decision about that? What were you relying upon? How did you decide that?

A. Well, I was relying on their advice as my lawyers and what they basically said, There's been a request, but we don't think it's proper for you to turn your phone over, so you don't need to do that.

Q. If they had told you that you should turn over anything, would you have done so?

A. Absolutely.

Q. Okay. At the time that the request was made, okay, you know what e-mails you did and what texts you did. Were there any e-mails or texts that you were worried about which showed you knew about deflating or anything like that? Was there anything you were trying to hide or conceal in your mind?

A. Absolutely not.

Q. Okay. Were there any such texts where you wrote to somebody talking about deflating footballs or other things in connection with the AFC Championship Game?

A. No.

Q. Were there any e-mails like that?

A. No.

Q. Now, you were interviewed by Mr. Wells and his team, correct?

A. Yes.

Q. And did they spend a number of hours with you?

A. Yes.

Q. During that time, did they ever tell you that if you didn't turn over some texts or e-mails or respond to that that you were going to be disciplined in any way, you know, that you were going to be violating some, you know, specific policy about that or anything like that? Did they ever tell you that?

A. No.

Q. If you had been informed by them and they said look, this is your duty to cooperate, would you then have produced them no matter what your agents and your counsel said?

A. Yes.

Q. Okay. Have you ever had anything to hide on this issue, Mr. Brady?

A. No.

Q. Now, Mr. Brady, let me ask you about your patterns of phones, okay, because not everybody has this pattern, okay. First of all, do you have access to basically cell phones for free?

A. Yes.

Q. So it is essentially costless to you to get another cell phone?

A. Yes.

Q. Okay. Now, have you had a practice, and tell me when it began, how long ago, of destroying or, I guess, asking somebody to destroy or get rid of your cell phones periodically?

A. I think for as long as I have had a cell phone.

Q. Okay. Since you have been in the NFL?

A. I don't remember all the way back, but yeah, I've had a cell phone since being in the NFL.

Q. So whenever you first started having, I don't know when cell phones started, but whenever you started having cell phones in the NFL, that has been your practice, correct?

A. Yes.

Q. Okay. And did you do anything unusual here in terms of getting rid of your phone? And I will explain what I mean. In other words, did you hear about the Wells investigation or the request for this and then say, oh, let's get rid of my cell phone or anything like that?

A. No.

Q. Did you do anything unusual except your normal practice, when you are done with a cell phone, to get rid of it and have it destroyed?

A. That's what I do.

COMMISSIONER GOODELL: Just, Jeff, can I ask a question? How often do you normally dispose of your phone? When you say "get rid of," does it run out of time?

THE WITNESS: Well, if it -- a new version may come out of a particular phone, if I break the phone, I've stepped on the screen a few times, it just fell out of my bag at my locker, I'm not seeing it, I stepped on it, I think three or four times, sometimes the touch panel breaks.

COMMISSIONER GOODELL: But it's not a very regular practice, irrespective of you breaking it, to just get rid of it or when a new version comes out? I'm trying to understand that, or is it every month you change it just for security reasons?

THE WITNESS: No, I don't do that.

COMMISSIONER GOODELL: Does your number change when that happens?

THE WITNESS: No. The number would stay the same.

COMMISSIONER GOODELL: Okay.

Q. And, in fact –

THE WITNESS: The only time I changed it was after the report came out and there was -- a lot of people started guessing what my phone number was and then I changed my number.

MR. KESSLER: And, Commissioner, the phone log we produced, just for your information, covers that whole period for which we don't have the cell because the number was the same number. And we got all the phone records from the company and that has been submitted.

COMMISSIONER GOODELL: Do you have multiple phones?

THE WITNESS: No.

Q. Mr. Brady, when Mr. Wells interviewed you, did you answer every question that he or his colleagues asked you?

A. Yes.

Q. Did you refuse to answer any question that he or his colleagues asked you?

A. No.

Q. By the way, did he ever ask you if there were any texts or phone messages that you had that would have discussed deflating footballs or anything like that?

A. Did he ask me?

Q. Yes, did he ask you that?

A. Yes.

Q. And what did you tell him?

A. No.

Q. That there were none?

A. Right.

Q. Let me now turn to a few more of the –

A. Can I just say something as I think about the process –

Q. Yes, please.

A. -- of getting rid of the phone?

Q. Anything you would like to tell about the Commissioner.

A. I think whenever I'm done with the phone, I don't want anybody ever to see the content of the phone, photos. Obviously there is a log with the smart phones of all my e-mail communications. So in those folders, there is player contracts. There's, you know, endorsement deals. There's -- along with photos of my family and so forth that I just don't want anyone to ever come in contact with those.

A lot of people's private information that, had that phone -- if it shows up somewhere, then, you know, all the contacts in my phone, you know, wouldn't want that to happen. So I have always told the guy who swaps them out for me, make sure you get rid of the phone.

And what I mean is destroy the phone so that no one can ever, you know, reset it or do something where I feel like the information is available to anybody.

Q. Mr. Brady, we've already gone through a few of the texts and the e-mails that are in the Wells report that either you sent or that mentioned you. What I'm going to do now is, there are a very few of these that actually mention you or are alleged to mention you.

I am going to ask you about each of them. And I know these are not your e-mails, but Mr. Nash has said that we should look at these e-mails.

MR. KESSLER: And so what I want to tell the Commissioner, I'm covering every one that Mr. Wells claims relates to Mr. Brady in some way, either mentioning him or with him.

Q. So we've done a few already. I'm going to go through a few more now. Take a look at the Wells report. And this is on page 77 on the Wells report. It goes from 77 to 79 in terms of that. So at the bottom, these are not e-mails that you sent or texts you sent.

This is between Mr. Jastremski and someone called Bird. I will represent to you Mr. Wells has reported that Mr. McNally's nickname is Bird. So this is a set of text messages between Mr. McNally and Mr. Jastremski. And you will see the date is 10/17, okay, which is the morning after that Jets game that we previously discussed with you.

So this is what was written. Bird writes to Jastremski, "Tom's sucks. I am going to make that next ball a fucking balloon."

Do you see that?

And then Jastremski writes, "Talked to him last night. He actually brought you up and said you must have a lot of stress trying to get them done."

John Jastremski to Bird, "I told him it was. He was right, though."

Then John says, "I checked some of the balls this morning. The refs fucked us. A few of them were at almost 16."

Do you see that?

A. Yes.

Q. Now, just in context, this was after you had gotten somewhat agitated with Mr. Jastremski about how the ball felt during the game, right?

A. Yes.

Q. Now, when it says here that, "Talked to him last night. He actually brought you up," did you ever bring up Mr. McNally at that time?

A. No.

Q. Did you even know that, by name or not, did you even know who it was who went to the referees' room when balls were blown up or not? Did you know anything about that, or tested?

A. No.

Q. Do you remember saying anything to Mr. Jastremski about somebody having a lot of stress about getting something done?

A. No.

Q. Now, in the Jets game, if you look at the last one, you see the reference to 16. That's the one they thought was -- that they tested and they found was at 16, right; is that correct?

A. What do you want to know?

Q. Do you remember that you were told it was 16?

A. Yes, in the Jets game.

Q. Right. So my question is, in the Jets game, did anybody make any efforts to deflate or reduce footballs or were the footballs turned out to be 16? What happened at the Jets game?

A. The balls were overinflated.

Q. Okay. And are you aware of any efforts at the Jets game by anyone to try to deflate or take air out of balls at the Jets game?

A. No.

Q. Now, I would like you to look at, on page 86 of the Wells report, we already covered this one; I'm sorry. This is the one that says, "Tom was right and it's supposed to be 13." We already covered that one, sorry.

Let's now go to page 105 of the Wells report. This is now the last one of all the ones that allegedly refer to you. And it says here, this is John to you, this is 1/19/2015. So this is after the AFC Championship Game, okay.

And John wrote to you, "For your information" -- "FYI, Dave will be picking your brain later about it. He's not accusing me or anyone. Trying to get to the bottom of it. He knows it's unrealistic you did it yourself."

John then says, "Just a heads-up."

And you write, "No worries, bud. We are all good."

What's your understanding of what they say referring to here in these texts with you and Mr. Jastremski?

A. That John was telling me that Dave would be picking my brain about it and that he wasn't accusing him and he was trying to get to the bottom of it and he knows it's unrealistic that I did it.

So that was just the heads-up. And I wrote back, "No worries bud, we are all good," because I obviously didn't think we had anything to do with it.

Q. Now, when he wrote, "It's unrealistic you did it yourself," did you have any knowledge that Mr. Jastremski or Mr. McNally or anybody had done anything to the balls?

A. No.

Q. Did you understand him to be saying here that, well, I did it, but you could have done it? Did you view it as a confession by Mr. Jastremski? Is that your understanding of the text?

A. No.

Q. What did you understand he was saying here when he said, "It's unrealistic you did it yourself"?

A. That he knows, he knows, "It's unrealistic that you did it yourself, but he's still going to ask you about it."

Q. Did it in any way indicate that Mr. Jastremski did it or Mr. McNally or anyone else in your mind at the time if you remember when you read it? Did you think that?

A. No.

Q. Okay. As you are sitting here today, I am going to ask you to be very clear. Did you ever give anyone any directions or instructions or authorization, anything, for the AFC Championship Game that they should alter, change, lower the pressure of footballs?

A. Absolutely not.

Q. Okay. You never authorized it?

A. No.

Q. Okay. Do you know somebody did it despite your authorization?

A. I don't know what you mean.

Q. In other words, are you aware that, even know you didn't authorize it, they did it anyway?

A. No.

Q. Are you aware of that?

A. No.

Q. Do you know that?

A. Absolutely not. I wasn't there.

Q. Okay. As you are sitting here right now, do you still believe Mr. Jastremski that when he told you he didn't know anything about it and he didn't do anything?

A. Yes.

Q. Has anyone in the Patriots organization, anyone else ever told you that they did anything to deflate the footballs on that day after they were tested by the referees?

A. Absolutely not.

Q. One last question, Mr. Brady. There's a policy at issue in this case that I will show you.

MR. KESSLER: What exhibit is that, John?

MR. AMOONA: I believe it's 115.

MR. KESSLER: 115. While we are doing that, I'm just going to note for the Commissioner that Exhibit 95 is the Competition Committee report in 2006, which discusses the change and the reason for it.

And you will find it has nothing to do with ball inflation or psi or anything like that. It's a full Competition Committee report that's in the record. I assume, Dan, we agree all exhibits are in evidence?

MR. NASH: Yes. Let me -- we will check. We will get back to you on that, but I think that's right.

MR. KESSLER: That is our normal practice. But I'm assuming all exhibits offered by both parties would be in evidence.

Q. 115, if you could look at Exhibit 115. This is a very thick exhibit. I think we will be able to deal with this quickly. But look first at the cover of it so you can see what the cover of it is.

Do you recall ever being given a copy of this policy? I think the title is "Policy Manual For Member Clubs."

A. No.

Q. Okay. Now, if you turn to the section on "Competitive Integrity." I think that is, it's like, if you look in the index, you will see that is -- I don't have a copy in front of me.

MR. KESSLER: What is it, John, for the record?

MR. AMOONA: A2.

Q. Do you recall ever getting a copy of this Competitive Integrity Policy?

A. No.

Q. You will see at the top it's directed -- who does it say it's directed to? Do you see at the very top? Who is listed?

Here, I got it now. If you look at it, you will see at the very top, it says, "The following updated memorandum was sent on February 11, 2014, to chief executives, club presidents, general managers and head coaches from

Commissioner Goodell regarding the Policy on Integrity in Game and Enforcement and Competitive Rules."

Do you see that?

A. Yes.

Q. To your knowledge, was it ever sent to you as a player?

A. Not that I can remember.

MR. KESSLER: I have no further questions. But if the Commissioner has any additional questions or Mr. Levy, even before the NFL or at any time, we are certainly willing to answer anything the Commissioner would like to know.

COMMISSIONER GOODELL: Should we take a break? Are you okay? You want to take a break?

THE WITNESS: Sure.

COMMISSIONER GOODELL: Why don't we take a quick break, ten minutes.

(Recess taken 11:23 a.m. to 11:38 a.m.)

MR. LEVY: Any questions for the witness from this side of the room?

MR. REISNER: I think we will be asking some questions.

Cross-Examination by Mr. Reisner

Q. Good morning, Mr. Brady.

A. Good morning.

Q. Mr. Brady, did you hear Mr. Kessler say in his opening statement with respect to text messages that you have produced exactly what Ted Wells asked for? Did you hear that?

A. Yes.

Q. And you know that one of the things that the Paul, Weiss investigative team asked for was copies of all text messages that you sent or received that referred to ball deflation and ball inflation and other topics identified as relevant, right?

A. Not sure what you are asking.

Q. You knew that one of the things that the Paul, Weiss investigative team asked for was any text messages that referred to ball inflation and ball deflation, right?

A. I'm not sure I was aware of exactly what was asked for other than what –

Q. Did you know that one of the requests was for all text messages that related to ball inflation and ball deflation?

A. I don't remember.

Q. And do you know whether any search was done of text messages referring to ball inflation or ball deflation?

A. Yes.

Q. Tell us what search was conducted for those text messages as far as you know.

A. Well, there was a forensics -- forensics team that Steve had, I guess, hired to examine some phones that I had.

Q. So there was a forensic team that was hired to examine the text messages on phones that were provided to that forensic team, correct?

A. Yes.

Q. And those were phones that you used, correct?

A. Yes.

Q. I want to direct your attention to what's in evidence as NFLPA Exhibit 6, which is the Supplemental Declaration of Brad Maryman. Do you have that document in front of you?

A. Yes.

Q. And is Brad Maryman the forensic expert that was engaged to review the telephones?

A. Yes.

Q. And you see there is a reference in paragraph 1 to, "Two mobile phone devices used by Mr. Thomas Brady, Jr.," correct?

A. Yes.

Q. And that refers to the mobile phone devices that you provided for his review, correct?

A. Yes.

Q. And directing your attention to paragraph 4 of the document, it refers to the first phone and says that, "It's dates of active use were from March 6, 2015 through April 8, 2015."

Do you see that?

A. Yes.

Q. And directing your attention to the next paragraph which refers to the second phone review, it says that, "The dates of active use were from March 23, 2014 or May 23, 2014 through November 5, 2014," correct?

A. Yes.

Q. And those were the only two phones that were provided to the forensic expert, correct?

A. Yes.

Q. And do you see that there is a gap from November 6, 2014 to March 5, 2015, in the phones provided to and received by and reviewed by the forensic consultant?

A. Yes.

Q. And did you use a cell phone to make calls and send and receive text messages during this gap period of November 6, 2014, to March 5, 2015?

A. Yes.

Q. And that gap period of November 6, 2014 to March 5, 2015, includes the day of the AFC Championship Game on January 18, 2015, correct?

A. Yes.

Q. And that gap period also includes the period immediately following the AFC Championship Game after questions were raised about possible deflation of footballs, correct?

A. Yes.

Q. And that gap period also includes a number of months leading up to the AFC Championship Game, correct?

A. Yes.

Q. It includes almost all of November, right?

A. Yes.

Q. All of December and January, all of February, all the way up to March 5, 2015, correct?

A. Yes.

Q. Do you know how many text messages you sent and received during that gap period?

A. I don't.

MR. REISNER: I'm going to ask that NFLPA Exhibit 1 be placed before Mr. Brady.

Q. These are phone records that have been produced by your counsel in connection with this proceeding. And I want to direct your attention specifically to the portion of this exhibit with the Bates Stamp Numbers NFLPA Brady 00067 through NFL Brady 00206.

And you will see that this document includes 99 pages of text phone records between November 6, 2014 and March 5, 2015 that list approximately 9,900 text messages that were sent or received during that period.

So my question is: Do you know why a phone that was active during this period was not provided to your forensic expert for review?

A. We didn't have it.

Q. Do you know where that phone is now?

A. No idea.

Q. Are you certain that you disposed of that phone?

A. I gave it to my assistant.

Q. Do you know when you provided it to your assistant?

A. I have no idea.

Q. And when you provided it to your assistant, did you provide it to your assistant for the purpose of it being disposed of?

A. Yes.

Q. Exhibit 96 submitted by the NFL refers -- it's a letter from your agent, Donald Yee, to Commissioner Goodell, dated June 18th.

MR. REISNER: Why don't we have that placed before Mr. Brady.

THE WITNESS: Thank you.

Q. And if you look at the first page of this letter down toward the bottom, the letter states, referring to you, "His custom and practice is also to destroy SIM cards when he gets a new phone and to destroy the actual device when he is done with the phone."

Do you see that?

A. Yes.

Q. And does that accurately reflect your practice?

A. Yes.

Q. And you say you don't recall precisely when you gave this phone to your assistant for destruction, correct?

A. Yes.

Q. But if you were following your practice, you would have done it around the time that you got a new phone, correct?

A. I'm not sure.

Q. Well, the letter that you just said accurately describes your practice says you destroy SIM cards when you get a new phone and "to destroy the actual device when he is done with the phone," right?

A. My assistant does that.

Q. Right. So if your actual practice was being followed, the phone would have been destroyed, the phone you were using would have been destroyed around the same time you started using another phone, correct?

A. Right.

Q. And directing your attention back to the Declaration of Mr. Maryman, NFLPA Exhibit 6.

A. Yeah.

Q. The date of active use of your new phone, according to paragraph 4 of his declaration, was March 6, 2015, correct?

A. Yes.

Q. Do you remember anything else that happened on March 6, 2015?

A. No.

Q. Was March 6, 2015 the date that you were interviewed by Mr. Wells and his team?

A. Possibly; I don't know. Was it?

Q. If I represent to you that March 6, 2015 was the date you were interviewed by Mr. Wells and his team, you have no reason to doubt that, correct?

A. Right, correct.

Q. And because your forensic expert didn't have access to the phone that was being used during what I'm calling this gap period, he couldn't review the text messages, the content of the text messages that were sent and received during this gap period, correct?

A. I think we tried to provide him with everything that we possibly could, you know, to that point. If the phone was already taken out of service, then it was –

Q. You couldn't provide him with a phone that had been destroyed, correct?

A. Or that I had given to my assistant, whether he destroyed it or not.

Q. That you gave to your assistant for the purposes of destruction, correct?

A. Possibly.

Q. Was that your purpose? Was that your plan when you provided the discarded phone to your assistant, that your assistant would destroy the phone?

A. That was kind of the normal routine.

Q. So that was your expectation when you provided that phone to your assistant that the phone would be, in fact, destroyed, correct?

A. Yes.

Q. And if you were following your ordinary practice, that would have been around the beginning of the date of active use of the new phone that you were using, correct?

A. Possibly.

Q. If you were following the practice described in Mr. Yee's letter, that's what would have occurred, correct?

A. Not sure.

Q. Okay. At the interview on March 6th by Mr. Wells and his team, were you asked questions about text messages that you sent and received?

A. Yes.

Q. And at that time, were you aware that there was an outstanding request from the Paul, Weiss investigative team for text messages?

A. The only thing that I knew about phone and electronic communications was an e-mail that Don had sent me at some point that said there was a request to turn over your phone. There's really no reason to do that and we are not going to provide them that. And that's the last I thought of providing my phone.

Q. Were you aware on or about February 28, 2015 that a request had been made to you for text messages?

A. I think the only thing that I remember was the e-mail from Don that said there's been a request made, along those lines, but we are not going to allow, you know, them to take your personal cell phone.

COMMISSIONER GOODELL: Was it around that time?

THE WITNESS: I don't know; I'm not sure. I don't remember when I got that message or –

Q. Do you recall at your interview on March 6th by Mr. Wells and his team being told that the Paul, Weiss team was seeking text messages?

A. I don't remember that.

Q. Do you remember being told during that interview that Mr. Wells didn't care whether he got the actual phone or not and that he would rely on your counsel to review the text messages and that would satisfy his request for the text messages? Do you recall hearing that discussion during the March 6th interview?

A. I don't remember that.

Q. Mr. Kessler said that certain materials had been provided by your counsel in connection with this proceeding, correct?

A. Yes.

Q. Do you know whether the materials produced by your lawyers in connection with this hearing include the content of any text messages?

A. I'm not sure.

Q. So if I represented to you that the materials produced by your counsel in this proceeding don't include the content of any text messages, you have no reason to doubt that, correct?

A. Correct.

Q. And are you aware if the phone records produced by your counsel show that, on February 7, 2015, you and John Jastremski exchanged three text messages?

A. I'm not sure; I don't remember.

Q. Let's look back at NFL Exhibit 96, the letter from Mr. Yee to Commissioner Goodell. And I'm directing your attention to page 3 of the letter in the middle of the page.

After Number 2, Jastremski, toward the end of that paragraph, it says, "The phone bills also show three text message exchanges on February 7, 2015 between 8:21 p.m. and 8:33 p.m. These occurred after the Super Bowl and were not mentioned or referenced in the Wells report."

Do you see that?

A. What page are you on?

Q. Page 3 of the letter.

A. Yeah.

Q. Number 2 is Jastremski?

MR. KESSLER: Two in the bottom half, Tom.

Q. Two in the bottom half.

A. Yes.

Q. It says toward the end of that paragraph, "The phone bills also show three text message exchanges on February 7, 2015 between 8:21 p.m. and 8:33 p.m.," referring to text messages between you and John Jastremski, correct?

A. Yes.

Q. And that period of February 7 is in that gap period that the forensic examiner didn't have a telephone for, right?

A. Right.

Q. So we don't know what the content of those text messages were, right?

MR. KESSLER: Are you going to ask him? You can ask him. He's right here.

Q. So you haven't been able to produce the content of those text messages, right?

A. No.

MR. KESSLER: Okay, I will have some questions on redirect. You don't want to know the content?

MR. LEVY: Jeffrey.

MR. KESSLER: Sorry.

Q. And directing your attention to that gap period again from November 6, 2014, through March 5th of 2015, do you know whether anyone has reviewed those messages to determine whether there were any messages referring to the deflation of footballs or other topics that are responsive to the Paul, Weiss requests?

A. If someone reviewed those?

Q. Do you know whether anyone has been able to review those messages to determine whether there are any messages referring to the deflation of footballs or other topics responsive to the Paul, Weiss requests?

A. No.

Q. Now, I want to ask you some questions about your knowledge of the NFL rule with respect to the inflation level of footballs.

A. Yes.

Q. You are presently aware that the NFL rules require that footballs be inflated to between 12.5 and 13.5 pounds, correct?

A. Yes.

Q. And when did you become aware of that?

A. After the Jets game.

Q. So during the period from when you entered the League in 2000 through the beginning of the 2014 season, you were unaware that the NFL rule was that balls should be inflated to between 12.5 and 13.5 pounds per square inch?

A. I think so.

Q. And in 2006, you were involved in efforts to change the rules regarding ball usage, correct?

A. Yes.

Q. Around the time that you were involved in efforts to change the rules around the ball usage, did you read the NFL rules regarding the ball?

A. No, at least I don't remember reading it.

Q. Now, you have said publically that you like footballs to be inflated at a level of 12.5 psi, correct?

A. I said that after the championship game.

Q. And so, how long have you known that 12.5 is your preferred level of inflation?

A. After the Jets game.

Q. And how did you come to learn that 12.5 is your preferred level of inflation? A. We basically just picked a number at that point, I guess, historically, we had always set the pressure at -- before John Jastremski took over, it had been historically set at, like, 12.7 or 12.8.

That's what I learned after the fact. And I think based on that Jets game, I said why don't we just set them at 12.5, bring this letter to the ref and I didn't think about it after that.

Q. You say you "just picked the number." Did you pick that number 12.5 for any particular reason?

A. Ball pressure has been so inconsequential, I haven't even thought about that. I think at the end of the day, the only time I thought about it was after the Jet game and then after this was brought up, after the championship game. It's never something that has been on my radar, registered. I never said "psi." I don't think I even know what that meant until after the championship game. It was never something that even crossed my mind.

Q. How did you come to pick 12.5 as the number?

A. We looked in the rule book.

Q. How did you come to pick 12.5 as the number for your preferred pressure level for the footballs?

A. I don't know how we exactly did it. I don't remember how we came to that other than the experience that I had in the Jet game when they were grossly overinflated and then they showed me the rule book or the copy of the page in the rule book. And I said, why don't we just set them here, 12.5, and not think about it ever again.

Q. Did you pick 12.5 because it was toward the lower end or the lower end of the permissible range?

A. I'm not sure why I picked it in particular, other than having to put some -- I think John said he did either 12.5 or 12.6. You know, we had to pick some number that we were ultimately going to set them to, so I said why don't we just set them all to 12.5 and that was it.

Q. Is it fair to say that you prefer the footballs inflated to a pressure level at the low end of the range?

A. Like I said, I never have thought about the ball, the air pressure in a football. The only time I have ever thought about the air pressure in a football was after the Jets game when they were at the level of 16.

So whenever I went to pick the game balls, I never once in 15 years ever asked what the ball pressure was set at until after the Jet game. So whether it's 12.5 or 12.6 or 12.7 or 12.8 or 12.9 or 13, all the way up to the Colts game, I still think it's inconsequential to what the actual feel of a grip of a football would be.

So the fact that there could be a ball that's set at 12.5 that I would disapprove of, there could be a ball that's 13 that I could approve of. It all is depending on how the ball feels in my hand on that particular day.

So I don't think my liking to a football could be a very psychological thing. I just want to know that there is consistency in what I'm playing with.

COMMISSIONER GOODELL: You mentioned before John –

THE WITNESS: Right.

COMMISSIONER GOODELL: -- he had set the equipment, the ball guy who prepared the balls?

THE WITNESS: Yeah.

COMMISSIONER GOODELL: Was it 12.7 or 12.8?

THE WITNESS: Yes. I think that's what they set them to; I don't know. That's what I learned three weeks ago at Mr. Wells' hearing.

COMMISSIONER GOODELL: And so you were not aware of that at the time?

THE WITNESS: No.

COMMISSIONER GOODELL: You became aware of that after the Jet game?

THE WITNESS: After the Jet game, yeah. I didn't know historically what we had set them at until before I think I met with Mr. Wells, and I think John had told Mr. Goldberg.

COMMISSIONER GOODELL: But after the Jet game, you said you wanted it down to 12.5?

THE WITNESS: Right, right.

COMMISSIONER GOODELL: So you made that determination after the Jet game, but before you met with Ted Wells?

THE WITNESS: Yes.

Q. So there came a time that you decided your preferred pressure level was 12.5, correct?

A. Yes, after the Jet game.

Q. And the reason that 12.5 was your preferred pressure level was because you like the balls inflated at the low end of the permissible range; is that fair?

A. I'm not sure what you are asking.

Q. You didn't just pick 12.5 randomly, correct?

A. No, we picked 12.5 because that was -- I don't know why we picked 12.5. We could have picked 12.6. I don't even remember it being a part of that conversation; I really don't. I don't remember exactly how we set it other than I had this experience at the Jet game where the balls were at 16.

I didn't like that. That's the first time I ever complained. So when I say 12 and a half and 13 and a half, I think I made the determination let's just set them at 12 and a half.

Q. Did there come a time that you were aware that Patriots personnel were asking to instruct the referees to set the balls at 12.5?

A. After the Jet game, yes. When I told Dave Schoenfeld and probably John, also, to bring that highlighted sheet of paper to say, just so they knew that -- like I said, I didn't know what the protocols were for the referees.

So I didn't want to -- I want the referee just to say, well, let's just inflate this to what I like them inflated to which, I don't know, the referee may say, well, I like them set at 13 or 13 and a half. I just wanted the referee to know that this is what it said in the rule book. This is Tom's preference going forward.

Q. And your preference was 12.5, correct?

A. After the Jet game.

Q. And that wasn't chosen randomly, but it was chosen because you preferred that inflation level, fair?

A. I never thought about the inflation level, Lorin. I never in the history of my career, I never thought about the inflation level of a ball.

Q. You had made public statements in 2009, 2010 observing that some quarterbacks like the balls heavily inflated and other quarterbacks like the ball less inflated, hadn't you?

A. I don't remember exactly what I said. But I think that speaks to how I feel about the ball. I know, for example, John Hillebrand, the guy who previously broke in the balls, when he would condition a ball, sometimes he would put them in the sauna because he felt that would get the moisten in the ball.

And when the ball would come to the sauna, the ball would probably be grossly overinflated. So however, you know, that experience of a really round football, until it came back to room temperature or whatever, ultimately I liked a ball that I could, you know, grip really loosely.

And just to, I think the irony of everything is I don't even squeeze a football. I think that's something that's really important to know is I grip the ball as loosely as possible. I don't even squeeze the ball and I think that's why it's impossible for me to probably tell the difference between what 12.5 and 12.7 or 12.9 and 13 because I'm just gripping it like a golf club.

I've tried to explain it. It's like a golf club. You don't squeeze the golf club. You handle it very gently. And that's the same way I hold a football.

Q. And a few years before the AFC Championship Game in January of 2015, you had made public statements to the fact that you like a deflated ball, correct?

A. I think that was in context to a joke about Rob Gostkowski spiking the football and how I felt sorry for the football. And that's all I remember.

Q. And you said you like a deflated ball, correct?

A. Yeah, but I didn't think it was in the context of what this hearing is all about, and certainly never below a permissible range.

Q. In any event, you knew that Patriots personnel were going to tell the refs to set the balls at 12.5, correct?

A. After the Jet game.

Q. At some point, you knew that was the instruction, correct?

A. Yes, after the Jet game.

Q. And did you know who on behalf of the Patriots was going to provide that instruction to the referees?

A. No.

Q. Did you know that the referees checked the air pressure of the ball in the officials' locker room?

A. I had no idea what the referees' processes were.

Q. Did you know that the Patriots had an officials' locker room attendant on game days?

A. No.

Q. And what was your understanding as to how the referees would be informed that the preference was for the balls to be inflated at 12.5?

A. I never, you know, really thought about it other than giving the, like I said, telling Dave to show this to the referee whenever they meet with the referees. I know the coaches meet with the referees before the games.

I know the referees come to the training room from time to time. So whenever Dave would come in contact with a referee or John, make sure they tell them that this is what we wanted.

COMMISSIONER GOODELL: Just so I'm clear, this whatever you wanted to show them was the rule?

THE WITNESS: Was that photocopy of the rule highlighted that the balls can be put between 12.5 and 13.5. So we put them at 12.5 and I didn't want them to just arbitrarily add significant air to them.

Q. And before the AFC Championship Game, you say you didn't know Jim McNally's name, but you knew who he was, correct?

A. I knew his face.

Q. And did you know what his responsibilities were?

A. He worked in the equipment room and that's a lot of the game-day employees that work, that come in for, you know, game days, there's a lot more people around the stadium when there's a game than obviously when there's a normal day of the week, practice.

Q. What was your understanding, if any, regarding his responsibilities to bring the balls to the ref before the game?

A. I wasn't sure.

Q. And did you see in the investigative report, the Paul, Weiss investigative report that Mr. Jastremski has stated that you knew Mr. McNally and his role as an officials' locker room attendant? Did you see that in the report?

A. Yes.

Q. And do you think that's inaccurate?

A. Yes.

Q. And did you read in the report that Mr. McNally has said that he had been personally told by you of your inflation level preference during the 2014 season? Did you see that in the report?

A. I saw it and I don't ever remember that.

Q. I know that Mr. Kessler asked you a number of questions about telephone conversations you had with John Jastremski after the AFC Championship Game. I want to ask you just a couple more questions about that.

And I think it would be helpful if you had a copy of the report in front of you when I ask you these questions. Do you have a copy of the report in front of you?

A. I don't think so.

Q. We have another one.

THE WITNESS: Thank you.

COMMISSIONER GOODELL: Are we done with all this other stuff?

MR. KESSLER: I think what we used you can move away.

Q. So I will ask you, Mr. Brady, to turn to page 101 of the report. At the bottom of the page, you will see there's a Roman Numeral VI that says,

"Communications following the AFC Championship Game" and there's a reference to January 19th, the day after the AFC Championship Game.

It says, "Jastremski and Brady spoke to each other on the telephone four times on January 19th for a total of 25 minutes and two seconds. They also exchanged a total of 12 messages."

Do you have any reason to think that that's not accurate?

A. No.

Q. And do you know whether in the six months prior to January 19, 2015, you had ever communicated with John Jastremski by text?

A. I'm not sure.

Q. And do you know whether in the six months prior to January 19, 2015, you had ever communicated with John Jastremski by telephone?

A. Yes.

Q. How many times?

A. I think once or twice.

COMMISSIONER GOODELL: Just so I am clear, once or twice in the six months prior to the Championship Game?

THE WITNESS: Yes.

Q. If you turn to page 102, there is a reference a text message sent by John Jastremski to you on January 19th at 7:25 in the morning. It says, "Call me when you get a second."

And the report says underneath that, "Brady called Jastremski less than one minute later and they spoke for 13 minutes and four seconds."

Do you see that?

A. Yes.

Q. And do you have any reason to believe that's inaccurate?

A. No.

Q. Do you recall what you discussed during that 13 minutes and four seconds with John Jastremski?

A. I don't remember exactly what we talked about.

Q. So let me ask you to turn to page 104 of the report. Under number 3, it says, "Approximately two and a half hours after they first spoke on the morning of January 19th, Brady followed up with Jastremski by text messages."

Do you see that?

A. Yes.

Q. And do you have any reason to question the timing of the text messages referred there, the text starting at 9:51 in the morning?

A. No.

Q. Let me ask you to turn the page, look at page 105. At the top of the page, Mr. Kessler already asked you about those January 19th text messages. And then the next box down lower is the text exchange where you asked John Jastremski to, "Come to the QB room."

Do you see that?

A. Yes.

Q. And when Mr. Jastremski came to the quarterback room, did you have a discussion with him?

A. Yes.

Q. And about how long did that discussion last?

A. I don't remember; probably pretty brief.

Q. To your knowledge, had Mr. Jastremski ever been in the quarterback room before?

A. I have no idea.

Q. Do you ever recall him being in the quarterback room before?

A. I don't remember. I'm not -- I don't know where he has been or where he's not been.

Q. If he says that's the first time he's ever been in the quarterback room, you have no basis to dispute that, do you?

THE WITNESS: No.

COMMISSIONER GOODELL: Can I ask, Tom, whether he had ever been in the quarterback room with you before?

THE WITNESS: I don't remember. There was a lot of renovations done to the stadium. I don't know if he was in the old quarterback room. But I would say the quarterback room is in, like, the hallway. I mean, you probably walk by this room 50 times a day. It's, like, right on Main Street.

Q. But if Mr. Jastremski says that is the first time he was ever in the quarterback room, you have no reason to doubt that, correct?

A. No.

Q. And do you recall what the two of you discussed in the quarterback room?

A. I don't remember. I was getting ready, like I said, I was watching a lot of film on the Seattle stuff. The computers weren't ready to bring home, so I decided to stay at the office. And I was thinking about the Super Bowl and figured I would text him to say, Come see me here rather than, like I said, me to go track him down at that time of the day.

Q. Incidentally, if that was Mr. Jastremski's first time in the quarterback room, about how many years had he been with the Patriots up to that point, if you know?

A. 12.

Q. Let me ask you to turn the page.

A. Can I say something else? There was a lot of renovation done to our stadium in the last year. So that particular quarterback room has been around for one year. We moved in at the start of last season. So, anyway –

Q. Directing your attention to page 106 of the report. Under the heading number 4 that says, "Jastremski speaks again with both McNally and Brady," there's a reference at the bottom of that page and it says, "At 5:21, Brady sent Jastremski the following text message."

And this is still on January 19, 2015 at 5:21, a text messages that says, from you to John Jastremski, "If you get a sec, give me a call."

Do you see that?

A. Yes.

Q. And if you turn the page to 107, it says, "Jastremski called Brady 11 seconds later. And over the course of three calls, they were on the telephone for 11 minutes and 58 seconds."

Do you see that?

A. Yes.

Q. And the third entry of those three block messages is, "Telephone call," again, on January 19th, at 5:30 between you and John Jastremski that lasted 11 minutes and one second.

Do you see that?

A. Yes.

Q. And do you recall what you and John Jastremski discussed during that 11-minutes-and-one-second telephone call?

A. I don't remember exactly what we discussed. But like I said, there was two things that were happening. One was the allegations which we were facing and the second was getting ready for the Super Bowl, which both of those have never happened before. So me talking to him about those things that were unprecedented, you know, he was the person that I would be communicating with.

Q. And you see down a little lower on page 107 there's a reference to, "Later that evening, McNally called Jastremski twice and they spoke for 13 minutes and 34 seconds."

And there are references to two different telephone conversations between McNally and Jastremski at 7:30 and then again at 10:26, the first call lasting eight minutes and 24 seconds, the next call lasting five minutes and 10 seconds.

Did Mr. Jastremski tell you during any of your telephone conversations that he was simultaneously in contact or close to simultaneously in contact with Mr. McNally?

A. No.

Q. Turn the page to page 108. This is the next day, January 20, 2015. The report says, "Jastremski and Brady spoke to each other twice by telephone on January 20, 2015 for a total of nine minutes and 55 seconds."

Do you see that?

A. Yes.

Q. And do you have any reason to doubt the timing described in the report there?

A. No.

Q. And there's a text in the middle of the page from John Jastremski to you at 7:24 in the morning. It says, "Call me when you get a second."

Do you see that?

A. Yes.

Q. And the report says underneath, "Brady called Jastremski within the hour and they spoke for six minutes and 21 seconds." And this is the morning of January 20th. Do you recall what you discussed with John Jastremski during that six-minute-and-21-second call?

A. I don't remember exactly what we talked about.

Q. And down lower on the page at 1:08, it says, "At 5:13 on January 20th, Brady again checked in with Jastremski by text messages."

And it refers to a text messages sent by you to John Jastremski at 5:13 on January 20th that says, "You doing good?"

Do you see that?

A. Yes.

Q. Do you have any reason to doubt the timing of that text message?

A. No.

Q. And if you turn the page to page 109, at the top of the page, it says, "Jastremski called Brady less than 15 minutes later and they spoke for three minutes and 34 seconds."

Do you recall what you discussed with John Jastremski during that referenced phone call?

A. I don't remember exactly what we talked about, but like I said, this was an unprecedented time for myself and for John going to the Super Bowl. I also told you that there were, I would say during the football season, I'm basically at the football stadium every day.

On this particular week, there was a couple days that we had off, so if I did need to communicate with John about the footballs, I would do it from home and I wouldn't be at the stadium. So it would be hard to do. But typically during the season, I'm at the stadium every day.

COMMISSIONER GOODELL: So you weren't in the office or at the stadium on the 19th or 20th?

THE WITNESS: I think the day after the game, we went in and then I think we had two days after that. So the Tuesday, Wednesday we were off. And I think we practiced Thursday, Friday, Saturday.

COMMISSIONER GOODELL: And you wouldn't have gone in?

THE WITNESS: I don't think I went in. I think I just stayed at home and worked those two days.

Q. And directing your attention to the bottom of page 109, there's a block referring to a text message at 7:27 in the morning on January 21st from you to John Jastremski.

It says, "Hey, bud, give me a call when you get a sec."

And the report states underneath that, "For the third straight morning, Jastremski and Brady spoke by phone, this time for 13 minutes and 47 seconds starting at 7:38 a.m. They spoke again for seven minutes and five seconds at 11:45:16 a.m."

Do you see that?

A. Yes.

Q. Do you have any reason to doubt the timing of the phone calls referenced in the report?

A. No.

Q. Do you recall the substance of either of those two telephone calls referenced in the report?

A. I don't remember exactly what we talked about, but like I said, there were two things happening simultaneously and I really wanted John focused other than what he needed to get accomplished with the footballs, so I was trying to make sure that he was good and that, you know, he felt responsible for, you know, the attacks.

And I was trying to make sure that he was composed so that he could do his job over the course of the next two weeks.

Q. Have you seen the text messages referenced in the report sent between Jim McNally and John Jastremski referring to inflating footballs, deflating footballs, "The only thing deflating Sunday is his passer rating"?

Have you seen those text messages?

A. In the report, yes.

Q. And have you seen the text message referenced in the report in which Jim McNally before the 2014/2015 season, he refers to himself as "the deflator" and says he "hasn't gone to ESPN yet"?

Have you seen that one?

A. Yes.

Q. And when you saw those text messages in the report, did they give you any concern?

A. I'm not really sure what the context of those text messages were between those two guys, so it's hard for me to speculate on what they talked about, the kind of language they use with one another. So obviously, those text messages didn't involve me.

I didn't know the spirit of their relationship, so I think it was kind of unfair for me to speculate that they did something wrong when they told me they didn't do anything wrong.

Q. So it didn't raise any concerns for you at all?

MR. KESSLER: Wait. After he read the report, you are asking?

MR. REISNER: No.

Q. The text messages referring to "inflation," "deflation," "needles," "cash," "the deflator," "haven't gone to ESPN yet," none of that concerned you?

MR. KESSLER: I have an objection. It's not established this witness ever saw those until he read the Wells report.

THE WITNESS: Correct.

MR. KESSLER: I want to know what he's asking him.

COMMISSIONER GOODELL: I think he asked him when he read the report, did he have a concern, I think is what I heard.

MR. REISNER: Yes.

Q. When you saw those text messages?

A. Yes.

COMMISSIONER GOODELL: In the Wells report?

MR. REISNER: In the Wells report.

A. Yes. Q. Did they raise any concerns for you?

A. About what? About that I was involved? Is that what I was concerned about?

Q. Any concerns at all. Did they raise concerns that something improper was happening?

A. I think that you can interpret however you want to interpret them. Me, personally, John said he didn't do it. I believe John. I never authorized anybody to do it.

I never talked about doing it, so I don't know what else I can say. I'm on the field playing. He said he didn't do it. I believed him. I can't speculate to something that I was never there for that I never saw that I never talked about.

COMMISSIONER GOODELL: So you asked him if he had done it?

THE WITNESS: Yes.

COMMISSIONER GOODELL: And he said no?

THE WITNESS: Yes, he said he didn't do it.

COMMISSIONER GOODELL: Did you ask him if he knew anybody else that had done it?

THE WITNESS: No, because I obviously didn't know that there was a -- that Mr. McNally -- I didn't know what his responsibilities were at the time. So John said, "We didn't do anything."

Q. Just to be clear, when you saw the text messages that I just described —

A. Yes.

Q. -- in the report, did they raise any concerns to you at all that something improper had happened?

A. I said it's not right for me to speculate on that. I don't feel like I was a part of those text messages. So, and I don't know what the relationship of those two were. Those were not text messages that I sent. I was not a part of those. I was not privy to those until after the report came out. I don't know what to --

Q. Had you seen those text messages during the interview -- withdrawn. Let me start again.

During your interview by the Paul, Weiss team on March 6th, you were shown copies of those text messages, correct?

A. Yes.

Q. And when you saw the copies of those text messages during your interview --

A. Yeah.

Q. -- did they raise any concerns, in your mind, that something improper was happening?

A. At the time, like I said, that was the first I saw them. So it wasn't in the context of the report as it's framed. Like I said, it's hard for me to speculate. Alls I can go by is what they told me, so.

MR. REISNER: Could we have one moment. Nothing further at this time.

MR. KESSLER: I just have a very few questions on redirect.

Redirect Examination by Mr. Kessler

Q. So you were shown a copy of the NFL 1639?

MR. KESSLER: Give this back to the witness.

Q. This was the letter from Mr. Yee in June that you asked about. And I'm going to direct your attention to page 3 that you were asked about. It's the second reference to Mr. Jastremski. This is talking about the text messages.

A. Yes. Q. And so, you will see that this says, "Result of search for text messages during relevant time period based on AT&T phone records."

Do you see that?

A. Yes.

Q. And the first one says, "McNally, there are no text messages between Brady and McNally." Does that recall with your recollection that you never texted Mr. McNally for anything?

A. Correct.

Q. In fact, you didn't know him?

A. Correct, well just by face.

Q. Right. And you didn't have any relationship with Mr. McNally; is that fair?

A. I mean, he worked in the equipment room. So you know, other than saying "hi" or, "Good to see you" or something like that.

Q. Did you ever discuss footballs or deflation or psi or anything like that with Mr. McNally?

A. No.

Q. Okay. Now, then it talks about Mr. Jastremski and that's what counsel asked you about. And it says, "All of the text messages identified in the Wells report between Brady and Jastremski show up on the phone records."

And then it says, "The bills reflect an additional text message from Jastremski to Brady at the same time as the others reflected in the Wells report."

And then it says that, "The phone bills also show three text messages exchanged on February 7, 2015 between 8:21 and 8:33."

You see that?

A. Yes.

Q. And those are the ones that counsel asked you to identify, correct?

A. Yes.

Q. So I'm now going to ask you the question that he didn't ask you. In that text message, do you recall whether there was any discussion of deflation or pressure or the Wells investigation or anything else that you recall in those text messages?

A. Absolutely not.

Q. Okay. For all the text messages you've ever sent Mr. Jastremski, okay, including all the ones that were identified on January 19th, January 20th, January 21st, did you ever discuss with him -- did he ever tell you that he deflated any footballs?

A. No.

Q. Did he ever tell you that anyone else ever deflated any footballs?

A. Absolutely not.

Q. Did you ever discuss with him any effort to conceal any deflation of footballs from investigators or anything else?

A. Absolutely not.

Q. What was your main focus from after the AFC Championship Game until the Super Bowl? What were you mostly focused on?

A. The Super Bowl.

Q. Okay. What did you want Mr. Jastremski to mostly be focused on?

A. The Super Bowl.

Q. Did you tell him that?

A. Absolutely.

Q. Were you concerned that he might get distracted by these other allegations being made?

A. Absolutely.

Q. Okay. And was that something you would have discussed with him, he needs to focus on the Super Bowl?

A. Absolutely.

Q. Now, do you recall that during this period of time, this two-week period of time, even Coach Belichick was distracted by this and had a news conference about ball deflation?

A. Yes.

Q. Okay. How long have you known Coach Belichick?

A. 16 years.

Q. Okay. When he is focused on the Super Bowl, does he usually get distracted by anything else other than Super Bowl game preparation?

A. No.

Q. Was it unusual for him to get up and have a press conference about something else other than Super Bowl?

A. Yes.

Q. Did Coach Belichick ever tell you that he knew anything else about ball deflation?

A. No.

Q. Anyone else in the Patriots organization ever tell you that?

A. No.

MR. KESSLER: I don't have any further questions.

MR. REISNER: I just have very briefly one or two.

Recross-Examination by Mr. Reisner

Q. During the telephone calls that you had with John Jastremski on January 19th and 20th and 21st that I asked you about, at that time, you knew that questions had been raised about the inflation levels of the footballs used during the AFC Championship Game, correct?

A. Yes.

Q. And during these telephone calls with Mr. Jastremski, did you discuss with him the fact that questions had been raised about the inflation levels of the footballs?

A. It's possible, yes.

Q. And did you discuss with him any concerns that he might have about questions being raised on that topic?

A. It's possible, yes.

Q. What do you recall about that, if anything?

A. Well, that they would be directed at him and that he was the person that prepared the footballs and like I said, the initial report was that none of the Colts' balls were deflated, but the Patriots, all the Patriots' balls were.

So I think trying to figure out what happened was certainly my concern and trying to figure out, you know, what could be -- possibly could have happened to those balls.

Q. And Mr. Kessler asked you about one of the e-mails that you exchanged during that time period -- pardon me -- one of the text messages that you exchanged during that time period. That's on page 105.

The e-mail that John Jastremski sent -- pardon me -- it's a text that John Jastremski sent to you on January 19th at 10:54 in the morning, the one that says, "FYI, Dave will be picking your brain later about it. He's not accusing me or anyone, just trying to get to the bottom of it. He knows it's unrealistic you did it yourself."

Around that time, were you aware that Dave Schoenfeld had been tasked with the responsibility to look into the ball deflation issues?

A. What do you mean?

Q. Were you aware that Dave Schoenfeld –

A. Yeah.

Q. -- had been tasked the responsibility by somebody at the Patriots to look into the ball deflation issues?

A. No.

Q. And during the text exchanges referenced there on January 19th, this was around the time that you were having telephone calls with John Jastremski as well, correct?

A. Yes.

Q. And you say that it is possible that you and John Jastremski were discussing the concerns that had been raised about ball deflation levels, right?

A. Yes.

MR. REISNER: Nothing further.

MR. KESSLER: Nothing from me. Perhaps the Commissioner has some questions?

COMMISSIONER GOODELL: I do have a couple. Can you go back to, I believe you said you changed the process prior to the Championship Game, the way you prepared the balls?

THE WITNESS: Yes.

COMMISSIONER GOODELL: On Friday afternoon, essentially –

THE WITNESS: Yes.

COMMISSIONER GOODELL: -- you made that change?

THE WITNESS: Yes.

COMMISSIONER GOODELL: Did you guys go into the -- did you ever walk through to observe the stadium on Saturday?

THE WITNESS: Yes.

COMMISSIONER GOODELL: You did?

THE WITNESS: Yes.

COMMISSIONER GOODELL: Yes?

THE WITNESS: Yes.

COMMISSIONER GOODELL: And did you guys communicate by phone on that change or was it at the office?

THE WITNESS: At the office.

COMMISSIONER GOODELL: It was all at the office or the stadium?

THE WITNESS: Yes.

COMMISSIONER GOODELL: And that process went basically Friday, Saturday and then Sunday you approved or didn't approve of the balls, essentially?

THE WITNESS: Yes.

COMMISSIONER GOODELL: Would the equipment managers do anything without your approval, essentially, that you are aware of with the footballs, just specifically the footballs?

THE WITNESS: I have –

COMMISSIONER GOODELL: I know it's a tough question, but I'm trying to understand would they -- you cared about the feel, they knew that from the process?

THE WITNESS: Yes.

COMMISSIONER GOODELL: So would they have done anything that was inconsistent with what you wanted with the footballs?

THE WITNESS: I don't think so, and that's why I believe they didn't do anything, because I know that, you know, how particular I am with the way that the ball feels. So I don't think that anyone would tamper with the ball.

COMMISSIONER GOODELL: So it would be done consistent with the way you wanted balls, essentially?

THE WITNESS: Yeah. But once -- yes. Once I picked the balls, that's ultimately the ones I want to be able to play with.

COMMISSIONER GOODELL: Okay, I am good.

MR. KESSLER: Anything else?

COMMISSIONER GOODELL: Thank you, Tom. Appreciate it. Thank you.

MR. KESSLER: Should we take our lunch break now?

COMMISSIONER GOODELL: I think we should.

MR. KESSLER: Let's keep it short, I guess. I assume you guys, we have food here, so let's say a half hour?

COMMISSIONER GOODELL: Gregg can handle that.

MR. LEVY: Yeah. How much time would you like?

MR. NASH: Whatever is your preference.

COMMISSIONER GOODELL: He's saying 30 minutes.

MR. KESSLER: Let's try a half hour just so that we can make sure –

MR. NASH: Who is your next witness?

MR. KESSLER: Well, we are going to move into evidence, our declarations and then we are going to call the expert, Mr. Snyder.

COMMISSIONER GOODELL: So let's come back at five minutes after 1:00.

(Recess taken 12:36 p.m. to 1:07 p.m.)

MR. LEVY: We are back on the record.

MR. KESSLER: So at this point, to the degree that it's required, we will move into evidence. The Declaration of Robert Kraft, which I think speaks for itself. And we do urge you, Commissioner, to read that declaration.

Essentially, it's Mr. Kraft telling you about his experience with Mr. Brady and what Mr. Brady has told him about this situation, which is essentially what he told you under oath today and how Mr. Kraft values his honesty and integrity in this matter. And so we move that declaration in.

And then the second declaration is -- two declarations from Mr. Maryman, which are the declarations that explain how the e-mail search was done on Mr. Brady's computers, and no incriminating files were found, although the search was done in exactly the way it was requested by Mr. Wells. And what was done forensically for the two telephones that existed and, in addition, the telephone logs which have been moved into evidence. So that now all should go before you.

MR. LEVY: Hearing no objection, they will be admitted into evidence.

MR. KESSLER: Thank you. I'm now going to pass the baton to Mr. Greenspan who is going to present the testimony of Mr. Snyder.

MR. GREENSPAN: The NFLPA calls as its next witness, Edward Snyder.

Testimony of Edward Snyder

Direct Examination by Mr. Greenspan

Q. Would you state your full name for the record.

A. My name is Edward A. Snyder.

Q. And your current position? A. I am Dean of the Yale School of Management. I am also a professor of economics and management at Yale.

Q. And your position prior to your time at Yale? A. I have been at Yale for four years, and prior to that, the previous ten years, I was at University of Chicago, where I was also Dean and I was the George Schultz Professor of Economics.

Q. And prior to the University of Chicago, where did you work?

A. I was Dean at University of Virginia, Darden School, and previously to that, I was at University of Michigan Business School where I was Senior Associate Dean.

Q. And what has been the focus of your teaching and your scholarship, Dean Snyder?

A. Well, I'm an economist. And I have a specialty in what's called industrial organization. And throughout my academic career, I've done a lot of empirical work and with that empirical work, I study data, collect data and apply statistical models and analyses to data.

Q. Let me stop you and focus on your statistical work, your statistical experience. And if you could elaborate in terms of the type of work you've done, type of industries you've covered.

A. Well, the type of work I did, to take the first part of this, it started when I did my Ph.D. thesis. I studied criminal antitrust enforcement and I collected data on the change in criminal penalties from the misdemeanor level to the felony level. These were original data. And I collected all the -- all the enforcement data over two decades and applied statistical analyses to them.

And then after that, I worked with former Assistant Attorney General of the U.S. Department of Justice's Antitrust Division, Tom Kuiper. We did three studies involving analysis of private antitrust enforcement, also original data application of statistical analysis to those data. In terms of the industries, the other part of your question, I've studied virtually -- well, it's a real wide range of industries, and in large part through my consulting.

Q. Let me ask you, have you taught classes involving study of data, application of statistics?

A. Yes. One of the ones that is noteworthy is when I was at Chicago, over a nine-year period I co-taught with Gary Becker, Nobel Prize winner in economics, and Kevin Murphy, Clark Medalist in economics. That's the award given to the top economist under 40. Obviously I was -- I enjoyed teaching with those two luminaries. But the nature of that course was what I call a project course. And we supervised teams of Master's students who went out and collected data. And over the course of that nine-year period, we supervised about 100 Master's-level projects that involved the collection of data and the application of statistical analysis to data for the purpose of developing insights on public policy and business.

Q. Okay. How about work in litigation? Have you served as an expert witness previously?

A. Yes. I left the antitrust division in 1985 and since then, so it's been about 30 years, I've done about one major litigation a year. So it adds up to about 30.

Q. And through the course of those litigation, you mentioned consulting work; would you identify just sort of a broad brush overview of some specific industries in which you've examined data, dealt with statistical analyses?

A. Sure. It's a wide range. It's pharmaceuticals. It's steel. It's paper, publication paper. It's infant formula. It's the LCD screens that we all use now. It's computer chips. It's stock exchanges. It's financial data. It's vitamins, virtually all these different slices of the economy. And each one of those engagements involves data.

Q. Let's talk for a moment about your work as dean. You have been a business school dean for about 20 years. What do your responsibilities -- what have your responsibilities as dean entailed?

A. As dean, I, of course, represent the institution. I am responsible for the people and programs. I view myself as sort of the person who develops the strategy for the school and I'm responsible for the finances of the school. And I keep in mind the quality of the work that's done and the integrity of the institution.

Q. You mentioned you have responsibility for the people of the school. If you could speak more about those responsibilities as dean.

A. Well, I'm an HR person, too. So the school connects with a lot of people. The ones who were immediate to the community are the students and the faculty and the professional staff. And, of course, people come and go, so there's a question of who gets admitted, who gets fired, who gets let go, who gets promoted, who gets evaluated positively, who gets evaluated negatively. In some cases there are disciplinary actions and all those things, I'm not involved in every decision, but I have to manage the processes associated with those and in some cases, they do come up to me.

Q. Thanks. So turning to the matter at hand, what were you asked to do? What was your assignment in this matter?

A. My assignment focuses on the work done by Exponent, the science firm brought in to evaluate the question of potential deflation of the Patriots' balls during the AFC Championship Game.

Q. Okay. Did you have any help, anyone work with you on this assignment?

A. Yes. I had a team. Professor Michael Moore from Northwestern University, a long-time colleague of mine, Pierre Cremieux, Principal Manager at Analysis Group, other members of the Analysis Group people, Dr. Jimmy Royer, Mr. Paul Greenberg, and that constituted the team.

COMMISSIONER GOODELL: Were these people in your consultancy group or were these selected by you?

THE WITNESS: It's an interesting question. I'm not sure how much information you want, Mr. Commissioner.

COMMISSIONER GOODELL: Not a lot. I was hoping for "yes" or "no."

THE WITNESS: Professor Moore and I started doing this really just out of our own interest. And then we got linked up to Analysis Group and they were doing some work independently. And I don't –

COMMISSIONER GOODELL: So you have worked together before?

THE WITNESS: I have worked with Analysis Group and I have known Professor Moore for 35 years.

Q. So these individuals, do they have experience in statistical work?

A. Yes, it's a deep, deep bench in terms of expertise.

Q. Was there anyone else that you consulted with in the course of this project?

A. Yes. I consulted with Mr. Dirk Duffner. He has a Master's Degree from Stanford. He's a former Exponent employee, worked there for decades. And now he runs his own firm.

Q. And this is Exhibit 196 we have up. What was the purpose of your consulting with Mr. Duffner?

A. Let me just preface that by saying the following: Exponent did both scientific analyses, as well as statistical analyses. I was not hired or retained and my assignment doesn't deal with the science. I took my science as a given, their scientific framework as a given. I focused on the statistics. In the course of making adjustments to the statistics, and correcting for errors, and evaluating alternative assumptions, however, I wanted to make sure that I wasn't doing anything wrong in terms of scientific principles. So out of an abundance of caution, I checked with Mr. Duffner to make sure that indeed what I was doing was consistent with scientific principles.

Q. How did you go about evaluating Exponent's work? And by that, what I mean in general terms, what did you do?

A. Well, in very general terms, I identified what data they had collected, how they had organized the data and rearranged the data. And I will explain this, I identified their major statistical analyses. One has already been referred to earlier today, the focuses on the question of the difference in the extent of average pressure drops. So I identified these major statistical analyses. I then identified how they did the analyses. Did they make any errors, what assumptions were they making when they conducted these analyses. I just pause on the last point. I was particularly focused on that last point because it's important for me as a researcher and evaluator of data when I see alternative assumptions, plausible alternatives, if the findings change, then the results are not reliable. So I paid attention to all those steps.

Q. So having done that work, having applied that principle, and again in general terms, what was your conclusion about the work performed, the statistical work performed by Exponent?

A. Right, given the scientific framework that they provided, I can follow what they've done. Our team actually replicated their key findings. They made errors. When I evaluate alternative assumptions, their findings change, so the bottom line is their results are simply not reliable.

Q. Okay. So let's go, let's start with your slide deck. The first slide shows your three key findings. And if you could just sort of walk the Commissioner through each of the three key findings that you made and that we will elaborate on.

A. So first finding is that their analysis of the difference in differences, the analysis of the pressure drops and the difference in the average pressure drops is wrong because Exponent did not include timing and the effects of timing in that analysis. Secondly, Exponent looked at the variation and the measurements between the Patriots' balls and the Colts' balls at halftime. They compared the variances. And despite conceding that there was no statistically significant difference between the two, they went ahead and drew conclusions, but those conclusions are improper. And, last, and this goes to the issue of alternative assumptions, as well as error, if the logo gauge was used to measure the Patriots' balls before the game, then given what the framework that Exponent provides us with scientifically, and if the analysis is done correctly, eight of the eleven Patriots' balls are above the relevant scientific threshold.

Q. Let's turn to your first finding. We will go to the next slide and start at the beginning, which is the raw data. And if you would explain, what do we see here on this table, which is Exponent's Table 1.

A. This is -- this is Exponent. This is taken directly from the Exponent report. These are the halftime data. And you will see that there were eleven Patriots' balls that were measured. They were measured by Official Blakeman and Official Prioleau. There were four Colts' balls measured, again, by those two officials, and those are the data that they focused on.

Q. What do we know about the sequence of the measurements and the sequence of events at halftime?

A. After the balls were brought in, the Patriots' balls were measured first and the Colts' balls were measured after. How much after, there's uncertainty about.

Q. Let's take a look at the next slide, this is Exponent's Table 2. And you will see here, Dean Snyder, the differences. There's a row inserted "Patriots average" and "Colts average." If you could discuss the importance of those figures to the analysis here.

A. Well, this is sort of a baby step along the way in doing the analysis of difference in differences. One thing to note, though, and this motivated Exponent to make some assumptions and reorganize the data, you will see that the Patriots average on the right-hand column exceeds the left-hand column, 11.49 compared to 11.11. For the Colts average, it's reversed. This column exceeds this column (indicating). This led Exponent to believe that the two officials switched gauges between the time that they measured the Patriots' balls and when they measured the Colts' balls. So one of the things that Exponent did going back to the raw data was that they then said, well, maybe it's better to organize the data by what they presume to be the measurements by gauge.

Q. Let's take a look at the next slide, which is Exponent's Scenario 3. It's their Table 5. And what's happening here in Scenario 3 relative to that raw data?

A. Well, now, they have organized the data by gauge. And the Patriots averages don't change. They have also made one more adjustment. They believe that Colts ball number 3, the measurement was transcribed incorrectly. So if you imagine the two officials calling out the numbers, somehow the person writing down the numbers put them in the wrong column. So they switched those. And now we have got revised averages for the Colts. And 12.95 for what they presume to be all the logo measurements compared to 12.5 for the non-logo. And one of the things I should point out here is there is a belief that the logo gauge, and this was supported by further testing by Exponent, reads higher. It consistently reads higher. And that's how they have organized the these data into what they call their data Scenario Number 3.

Q. Why have you chosen to focus on their data Scenario Number 3?

A. Well, the short answer is they do. This is the data scenario that they pay the most attention to.

Q. Okay. Let's look at the next slide. And just taking a look at the quote at the top of the page, this is from the Exponent report. What does that tell you about the place of this analysis within the overall Exponent work?

A. Well, when they say, "This is the most significant," what they are saying is of all the work that they have done to analyze these results, this is what I call their core analysis, this is their most significant analysis. And it goes to this basic question, did the Patriots' balls have a bigger drop in pressure than the Colts' balls?

Q. Table 6, this is also at the bottom of your slide, this is from the Exponent report. If you could again walk us through the table and tell us what Exponent is looking at with those figures.

A. So you have got the averages now based on the different gauges. What they do is identify the drop compared to the starting values, the pre-game starting values that are presumed to be for the Colts' balls, 13.0 psi and 12.5

for the Patriots' psi. And compared to those starting values, you can then identify the difference in the drops by gauge. And those two numbers, about .7 psi says that the Patriots' balls dropped by .7 psi more than the Colts' balls.

Q. Okay. Let's go to the next slide. And if here, if you could describe the approach taken by Exponent in comparing the relative drops in pressure of the Patriots' balls and the Colts' balls.

A. Okay. So here is their approach. It's called a difference in differences analysis. It's a standard kind of statistical approach. Here it really could be difference in average drops, just to put it in the context of what we are studying. And we have already covered the first bullet point. They have identified the differences between pre-game and average halftime psi's. The second bullet point should be emphasized here. The theory of the Exponent analysis, their most significant analysis is that the Colts' balls are a control for the Patriots' balls.

Q. What does that mean, "a control"?

A. Well, let's just go slowly. I mean, it's the Patriots' balls that are being suspected of being deflated outside the rules. The Colts' balls are not being suspected of being deflated outside the rules. So the Colts' balls end up being a reference or a benchmark for what would have happened naturally. That's the idea of a control.

Q. Okay. And Exponent continues. They inquire whether your slide continues. They look at whether the greater drop was statistically significant. Could you explain the concept of "statistical significance."

A. These terms don't role off the tongue. Statistical significance here is, okay, you may see a difference in these averages, but you also realize, you have got a really puny control group. It's four Colts' balls. We have got measurement of them. We can't just say any time there's a difference, it's reliable. So what Exponent did was that they adopted the standard, which is statistical significance at the five-percent level. It's common in science. It's common in social science. That's the standard that Exponent did. It basically says, when we see a difference, when we see a difference, we want to make sure it's not due to chance.

Q. In your experience, if a statistical threshold, here, the .05 is chosen, and the analysis doesn't have results that cross that threshold, what does that tell you about the analysis?

A. It's not an analysis on which you should derive findings, reach conclusions. It's not statistically significant. It doesn't -- what you see in scientific studies and whether it's testing by the FDA or careful protocols, you have statistical significance as the step that then is the basis for conclusions.

Q. What if the statistical significance is really close to that .05, but it doesn't cross that threshold, but it's on the margins?

A. You can't -- you can't go down that path, because then you keep saying, what if it's sort of close? Then you keep moving the standard. It's, you know, it's the standard. Since we are in this group, I will say it's like you don't score a touchdown unless you break the plane. You can't say it's close.

Q. Let's take a look at the next slide. And this is now Exponent's conclusions about statistical significance. And could you explain what's happening here including what a p-value is.

A. So this, again, is Exponent's table, Table 8. They are reporting the results, focusing on the question of statistical significance for four different data scenarios. Three is their preferred, but here they are reporting all of them. And in the table you see referred to here, the p-value's calculated using Exponent's statistical model. They developed a statistical model to evaluate the difference in difference. And they are saying-based on our statistical model, the difference in average pressure drops is statistically significant. So the p-values that they report are well below .05; .05 is the five percent benchmark. And they are saying our results are statistically significant.

Q. Because they are smaller than -- the p-value is smaller than .05?

A. Correct.

Q. And what is the conclusion that they draw from this statistical significance?

A. This is the standard protocol. When you get statistically significant results, then you draw conclusions. So what's bolded here is, okay, we have significant results. We now say the following, "In all cases studied, the additional pressure drop exhibited by the Patriots' footballs is unlikely to have occurred by chance."

Q. What did you conclude about Exponent's difference in differences work?

A. Well, it's wrong. It goes back to their basic theory, the basic idea that the Colts' balls a control. If you want -- and I understand the idea of using the Colts' balls as a control, but they have to be a good control. If they are a good control, then you can isolate on whether the question of whether the additional pressure drop exhibited by the Patriots' footballs is or is not likely to have occurred by chance.

Q. And what was your conclusion as to whether the Colts' balls served as good controls in their analysis?

A. They didn't, because I mentioned this earlier. There was a sequence of events at halftime. And the sequence of events at halftime was that the Patriots' balls were measured first. The Colts' balls were measured second, or even later, depending on the sequence of halftime events.

COMMISSIONER GOODELL: What would be the significant time period where it becomes important it exceeded that amount?

THE WITNESS: I am going to cover that, Mr. Commissioner. But basically even if you take the minimum sort of bump, three and a half minutes, this p-value goes above the key threshold.

COMMISSIONER GOODELL: Three-and-a-half minutes from the first ball to the last ball, from Patriots to Colts?

THE WITNESS: Yeah. If you just say we are going to make the Colts' balls, which are a little bit warmer and a little bit dryer, and say, well, what if they were, in effect, adjusted for that, and they were measured when the Patriots' balls were measured, this result goes away.

COMMISSIONER GOODELL: And who says they are dryer? "Three-and-a-half minutes they get dryer."

THE WITNESS: Well, you can leave out dry. Just do warm. In fact, that's the case I am going to turn to next.

Q. Let's focus on that and go to the next slide. And what does Exponent tell us about the importance of time?

A. Well, the Exponent report is full of scientific guidance that says timing is important. And they refer to basic thermodynamics. They say it's completely expected, this top bullet point, that a football is brought from a warmer environment into a colder environment and then when it's brought back into a warmer environment, that the psi will change. It will go, it will start high, go down and then come up. And these variations in temperature and pressure are time-dependent in the time ranges at issue in the present investigation. And then the second bullet point, especially the bolded point, "A key factor in explaining the difference in measurements between the Patriots' and Colts' balls is timing." These are Exponent quotes.

Q. And let's jump to Exponent's table. This is their Figure 22. And if you could sort of walk us through this figure and what it shows us about the importance of time.

A. Okay. So along the horizontal axis here is time, minute by minute. And it starts at 2:38. So there is a lot happening with the game before of this focus.

Q. 2:38 prior to halftime?

A. Right. That's when the balls are being brought off the field and then the locker room period begins at minute 2:40 and it lasts –

COMMISSIONER GOODELL: I'm sorry; what was that 2:38 starts when, at the beginning of the game?

THE WITNESS: No, that is my understanding of when the balls are being brought off the field into the locker room.

COMMISSIONER GOODELL: What happens from zero to 2:37, I guess is a better –

THE WITNESS: First half is playing.

COMMISSIONER GOODELL: Zero is the start of game?

THE WITNESS: Yes, or some pre-game activity, yes. That's a good question. It may be when the balls are brought onto the field; I'm not sure.

COMMISSIONER GOODELL: That's important, wouldn't you say?

THE WITNESS: Well, there's plenty of time according to Exponent. I'm not here to question that, but there's plenty of time for the balls -- you take the assumption that the Colts' balls were at 13.0. There's plenty of time, whether it's 2:38 or 2:10 or 2:00 or 2:50 for the Colts' balls to equilibrate to basically this level, assuming that they are dry (indicating) or this level assuming they are wet, and the same thing for the Patriots' balls, to equilibrate.

Q. Dean Snyder, what's happening with the psi of the balls right before they are brought into the locker room, so between minute 2:38 and minute 2:40?

A. Nothing, really.

Q. Okay. And then what do we see happens to the pressure of the balls once they are brought into the locker room at minute 2:40?

A. Well, they warm up. So going back to the Commissioner's question, let's put aside the issue of moisture and just focus on the dry schedules. The top one is 13.0 psi dry. That would correspond to a Colts' ball that's dry. And it comes into the locker room right here (indicating). It's at this level and then it warms up. It follows this transition curve. And a Patriots' ball that's dry comes in lower and follows this curve (indicating).

Q. Let's take a look at, it's our Slide 10, this is another quote from Exponent. And if you could talk about the significance of the bolded language, again, in terms of your analysis of the importance of timing at halftime.

A. Well, there's a strong dependence on time. (Reading): "Specifically, the pressure in a football measured immediately" -- here I'm quoting -- "Specifically, the pressure in a football measured immediately after coming into the locker room will be significantly lower as compared to the pressure measured in the same football once it has sat and warmed up in the locker room for several minutes." That's from Exponent.

Q. So let's go to our Slide 12. And what is this showing?

A. This takes the earlier Figure 22, and I will refer to that again. It takes the top schedule, what Exponent calls their transient analysis, that's their scientific framework. It says, okay, you bring in a Colts' ball. It was pre-game at 13. It's brought right into the locker room. It's going to be 11.87. This is, like, so 2:40 is, like, in locker room terms, it's minute zero. And then 12 minutes later, it's warmed up and it's roughly 1.1 psi greater in 12 minutes.

Q. The same ball? A. The same ball.

Q. What did Exponent do in its difference in difference analysis to account for time?

A. Nothing.

Q. How do you know?

A. Absolutely nothing. If you look at their difference in difference equation in their appendix and you look at Table A3, where they report their results, they have explanatory variables for their difference in difference analysis and time is not an explanatory variable. You can read the Exponent report forwards, backwards, upside down. You see time referred to again and again and again and again. However, you have to look at what they actually did, the statistical analysis that they actually did. They left time out of the analysis that they said was the most important.

Q. Were you and your team able to account for time in trying to replicate their difference in differences work?

A. I took their scientific guidance and said, let's adjust for time.

Q. Let's go to the next slide and let's just focus here. We are going to go through these three cases. Let's focus on case 1 and what you and your team tried to do.

A. Case 1 is what I would call the minimum bump, the minimum adjustment for time, assuming that the Colts' balls were measured immediately after the Patriots' balls, no moisture effect.

Q. Let's go to the next slide. What's happening here? This is your slide. What are you showing in your case 1?

A. Well, it's my slide, but it's Exponent's transition graph. This is -- the top part of that is right off of Exponent figure 22. And if it's okay, let me just explain what's happening here. This is the average psi of the Colts' balls (indicating), okay. And under this assumption about when they were measured, this occurs right at this point in time. So this is a given. And none of these analyses are going to change the observed average measurements for the Colts' balls. Those are the starting values. If we drop a line down here, this is when the Patriots' balls were measured. So I'm going through basically an adjustment that says if the Patriots' balls are measured here, what if we said and adjusted for time and, in effect, moved that measurement in this direction just three-and-a-half minutes? And we use Exponent's transition analysis to tell us how much of an adjustment that would have minute by minute on the height of this. And the difference in the height of this and this looks to be about this amount right here (indicating). That's the adjustment in time. That's the difference in psi.

Q. Let's go to your next slide to see the impact on statistical significance.

A. Well, again, just for reference, this is Exponent's analysis, except that there is a difference in difference that couldn't be explained of about .7. I am going to do rounding here. And it's statistically significant. If we do this minimum bump, that difference in psi that's, quote, "unexplained" goes from .7 to .4 psi. And critically, the statistical significance is now eliminated. We now go from under .05 to above .05.

Q. What is the importance of that finding? A. This is, well, Exponent adopted statistical significance for a reason. We have a very small sample. We have measurement error. We have other factors. You adopt a standard of statistical significance for a reason. And the importance now is this is not a result on which you go from statistical significance to conclusions. You don't -- you stop there.

Q. You did it. You did a second case. What adjustment, what were you trying to account for in Case Number 2?

A. Well, Case Number 2, here's the sequence of events that was basically -- we will call it halftime sequence number 1. And the Patriots' balls are measured first. The Colts' balls are measured second. And then the Patriots' balls were reinflated. This is in the Wells report. What's acknowledged here, though, is there remains uncertainty about the order of the last two events, not uncertainty about the Patriots being first, but uncertainty about these two. So what if you just evaluate that uncertainty and flip these? So it's Patriots' measurement, Patriots' reinflation, and then Colts' measurement.

Q. Let's go to the next slide.

A. Basically it's the same analysis. Instead of a three-and-a-half-minute adjustment for time, it's now a seven-and-a-half-minute adjustment for time.

Q. And let's go to the next slide and see what happens.

COMMISSIONER GOODELL: Just so I'm clear, you are saying it would take four minutes for eleven balls to be properly inflated? That's your analysis or whose analysis is that?

THE WITNESS: That's in the Exponent report and the Wells report. They have a range, time ranges for those sequences of events.

Q. And what happens to the p-value and more generally, if you could speak to the significance of the p-value in statistical terms once you make an adjustment?

A. Well, again, I think it's good to just always refer back to what was the so-called unexplained difference in drops. According to Exponent, it was about .7 psi. Now, if you consider this alternative sequence with a time difference of seven and a half minutes, on average, the difference in psi now goes to under .3 and the p-value goes to .2. This is a kind of range of a p-value where you say, I don't know whether there was anything at all.

COMMISSIONER GOODELL: What do you mean by that?

THE WITNESS: I mean by that when you set up a test like that, you are trying to accept or reject hypotheses. And when you see something like this, you say, I don't know what's going on. I don't know if there's any significant difference in difference from which to draw conclusions.

Q. Let's talk about your third case and what you tried to test for here.

A. Well, the third case, again, goes back to the idea of a control. And the concern that motivates this is that Exponent was testing balls at two different points in time. And the Patriots' balls not only would be colder, they could be wetter compared to the Colts' balls, which would be warmer and dryer. That's not apples to apples. So you want to make an adjustment for time that affects both warmth and moisture to see, not to say you know exactly how wet they were, because I don't know. But what if there is a moisture effect as well as a warmth effect?

Q. Let me ask you a question. You said, "What if there's a moisture effect?" Was this an issue that you discussed with Mr. Duffner?

A. Yes.

Q. What did he say?

A. He said it's definitely the kind of thing that should be explored. Balls come in wet. They get dry over this time period. So this keeps the seven and a half minutes the same, but also takes the Colts' balls back, it says, well, what if there is a moisture effect.

Q. And what happens to the p-value when you do this analysis?

A. Well, the p-value goes even higher. And with respect to this unexplained difference in difference, .7 now goes to .07. 90 percent of the difference in difference is now explained.

Q. What's your takeaway from your first finding, your analysis of their difference in differences work?

A. Timing needs to be included in the analysis. When you include timing, the results shift from being statistically significant to insignificant. The unexplained difference in difference falls and under plausible assumptions goes to a de minimus level.

Q. Let's talk about your second finding and another aspect –

COMMISSIONER GOODELL: Could I just hear what his plausible assumptions are. What are your plausible assumptions?

THE WITNESS: Plausible assumptions is that, in addition to considering the minimum time adjustment, if you consider the alternative time sequence, and I'm not here to say it's one or the other, but you had two time sequences at halftime that I believe should be considered. One is Patriots, Colts measurement –

COMMISSIONER GOODELL: Your 1, 2, 3, right?

THE WITNESS: Yes.

COMMISSIONER GOODELL: That's your plausible assumptions?

THE WITNESS: Yeah, just saying that there was a greater –

COMMISSIONER GOODELL: What about dry time?

THE WITNESS: Yes, and what if there is a moisture effect.

COMMISSIONER GOODELL: But that's a what-if, right?

THE WITNESS: Yes, it is a what-if, yes, sir.

Q. What did Exponent do in its, what you call statistical variability analysis? And if you have an understanding as to why they did this analysis?

A. Well, this is a relatively brief commentary. My belief is, and this is a bit of a speculation, is that they wanted to look at the variants, the dispersion in the measurements between the Colts' balls at halftime and the Patriots' balls at halftime to see if there was a contrast. And if there was a contrast so that the Patriots' balls had more dispersion, more variance in their measurements, that would lend support to the idea that they didn't have a common starting value. Why wouldn't they have a common starting value? Hasty deflation.

Q. Let's go to the next slide. And what did Exponent conclude as a statistical matter about variability?

A. No statistical -- no statistically significant difference.

Q. Did they stop there?

A. No. They continued, which is striking, because, whereas in the difference in difference analysis, they adopted the standard five percent as the benchmark, here, they said, no, we will just continue on and reach conclusions. And it's right here at the bottom. So without having found anything that's statistically significant, nevertheless they have a statement that begins in their report, "therefore."

Q. And in your experience, as a statistical matter, is it a sound practice to draw conclusions from an analysis which doesn't reach statistical significance?

A. No.

Q. Even putting aside the fact that Exponent's results were not statistically significant, are you aware of any explanation for greater variability among Patriots' balls compared to Colts' balls?

A. I'm not here to offer scientific insights. I don't know if the first-half conditions could lead to more variance. I'm just going to focus on the scientific guidance provided by Exponent. And recognizing that the Colts' balls were measured some time in here (indicating). They are measured at a relatively flat part of the curve (indicating). And if you sample from a relatively flat part of the curve, you get less variance. And this was not considered by Exponent when they made this comparison and reached the "therefore" conclusion.

Q. Was this issue of the impact of time on variance something you discussed with Mr. Duffner?

A. Yes. I asked him if the insight that we had developed on this was correct, and he said -- he said, definitely. I mean, we were basically finishing each other's sentences. He said -- I said the curve flattens and that's going to lead to less variance. And he used a different term. He said "curve asymptotes," a more technical term, but he said the same thing.

Q. Let's go to your finding number 3. What's the bottom-line conclusion here?

A. Exponent did an analysis to establish what you might say is a scientific benchmark, a threshold to say should the Patriots' balls or are the Patriots' balls above this threshold? And my finding is that if you consider as a plausible assumption that the logo gauge was used pre-game by Mr. Walt Anderson, I'm not saying it's true, I'm just saying if you entertain that assumption, given the uncertainty, and you execute Exponent's analysis correctly, then eight out of the eleven Patriots' balls are above this relevant scientific threshold.

Q. Let's go to the next slide and the beginning of Exponent's analysis. Their comparison of the Patriots' balls halftime measurements to the Ideal Gas Law Formula. If you could describe, what did Exponent do? A. Well, they applied the Ideal Gas Formula. They have parameters here of a starting temperature between 67 and 71 when that initial psi of 12.5 was established and then a final temperature of 48. And then they are saying, well, what if they are brought into the locker room right then, what should they measure? And the key number here is that they identified this as their scientific threshold (indicating), and they say the balls have not been deflated. The measurement should be above 11.32.

Q. Okay. Let's go to the next slide. And if you could explain, how did Exponent do this? How did they go about this comparison?

A. Well, it gets into some additional math. In addition to the Ideal Gas Law math, they also recognize that the two gauges have this tendency to read differently. The logo gauge reads about .3 to .4 higher than the non-logo gauge. So what they did was carefully, according to their report, establish how you convert readings into a so-called master gauge well-calibrated, accurate master gauge for both the logo readings and the non-logo readings.

Q. And how do they do this conversion?

A. You mean in terms of the actual test? Q. Yes, how they execute.

A. Well, they basically say, well, if you say it's the master -- excuse me, if it's the logo gauge used, well then, you should convert the readings, the halftime measurements and adjust them to the master gauge readings.

Q. And that's a mathematical formula?

A. It's just a crunching of the -- through the master gauge adjustment.

Q. And when Exponent did these conversions, what conclusion did they reach about how the Patriots' balls compared to that range or the bottom end of the range you talked about in the prior slide?

A. They found that eight of the Patriots' balls were below this critical scientific threshold.

Q. Did you find any errors in Exponent's conversion work?

A. Yeah, yes. They made a very basic mistake. They have the master gauge conversion adjustment, and they converted the halftime readings for the master gauge conversion, but they did not convert the starting values for the master gauge conversion.

Q. Does that make a difference here? Does that make a difference in the outcome?

A. It does under one of two assumptions. And there are only two assumptions to make. Pre-game, it was either Mr. Anderson used the logo gauge, his recollection, or he used the non-logo gauge. It turns out that the master gauge conversion is not a very big adjustment at all for the non-logo gauge. So this error doesn't play out to have any significant effect on the Exponent findings if the non-logo gauge was used. However, because that logo gauge measures a lot higher, you have to make the adjustments consistently, both to the starting values and the halftime values.

Q. So let's put a pin in the conversion error and take a look at and describe what we know about the possibility that the logo gauge was used for the pre-game measurements.

A. Well, without reading this, I mean, as a researcher, here, the key point for me is that both assumptions should be evaluated in terms of whether Mr. Anderson used the logo gauge or the non-logo gauge.

Q. Was there evidence before Exponent that the logo gauge being used for a pre-game measurement was a plausible possibility here?

A. Yes.

Q. Let's go to the next slide. And were you able to correct for that inconsistency that you described in Exponent's master gauge conversion?

A. Yes. Now, the effective starting value is not 12.5, it's 12.17.

Q. How do you get the 12.17?

A. You apply the master gauge conversion consistently to both halftime measurements, as well as the starting value.

Q. Okay. And let's go to the next slide. And what is the impact of making that correction on the results?

A. Now eight of the Patriots' balls are above the critical threshold predicted by Exponent, three are below.

Q. We've talked about uncertainty in the gauges, uncertainty in the sequence of events at halftime, among other things. In statistical work, what is the statistician to do when faced with uncertainties in the data?

A. Well, in this case, there are only two options: There is the logo gauge and the non-logo gauge. And my view is you should entertain both options. You should explore what happens to your findings, assuming that Mr. Anderson used one and then the other.

Q. Do you see throughout Exponent's report, do you see that in all cases, they are testing for all possibilities?

A. No. I see instead rather than saying neutrally, let's look at assumptions and see if our results are consistent, as they did here, they basically argued against the likelihood that the logo gauge was used.

Q. By the way, the conclusion that you reached that eight out of the eleven balls were actually above the bottom end of the Ideal Gas Law formula prediction, are you the only person who's come to that conclusion?

A. No. There are multiple people who have come to that conclusion. The AEI report came to that conclusion. There's a Nobel Prize winner who has come to that conclusion. A Ph.D. in physics has come to that conclusion. I think there's a math teacher in Maine who has come to that conclusion.

Q. All right. Dean Snyder, a few final questions. Did you make any conclusions about the way the data was collected the day of the AFC Championship Game?

A. I think it's one of the most intriguing things here is that the officials, I think they had, actually, very good intuition about what to try to do. They didn't just measure the Patriots' balls. They measured the Colts' balls. They had the idea of a control. They had the idea of measuring both sets of balls with two gauges. But -- but their intuition only carried them so far. There were so many things that they didn't have in mind. Now everybody is talking about the Ideal Gas Law. I don't think they had the Ideal Gas Law in mind when they brought the balls into the locker room and measured them at different times. They didn't record the timing of those measurements. They didn't record the temperatures. They didn't make sure which gauge was being used. They didn't retain -- find all the gauges.

COMMISSIONER GOODELL: They didn't what?

THE WITNESS: They didn't find all the gauges for the pre-game and the -- my reading of the report is that there are gauges that were set by the Patriots and the Colts in the process described earlier that aren't available.

A. And the moisture point that you raised, I don't think anybody tracked what balls were wet, how many of them were wet, whether they were in bags. And they didn't track what was happening during the first half. So I would give the officials credit for developing a protocol, but the bottom line is that it's an impromptu protocol that leaves a lot of factors out and not controlled for.

Q. Are there steps that could be taken going forward to ensure the reliability of measurements taken on game-day if people want to evaluate the measurements to draw conclusions about them?

A. Well, I'm not here to offer views about protocols, but I'm sure that protocols could be developed along those lines if the League decided that was important.

Q. Dean Snyder, did you reach any conclusions about the number of assumptions in Exponent's analysis?

A. A lot of assumptions along the way, just saying we are going to switch the data, we are going to switch Colts' ball number 3 -- I mean, the Colts' data and line them up the way they did, sequencing. It's a very large number of assumptions relative to actual data observations.

Q. Did Exponent consider all of the data available to it?

A. No, they did not.

Q. Would you be more specific.

A. Let me give two specifics. The 12th ball, the ball intercepted by D'Qwell Jackson during the first half, it was measured by, according to the report, someone on the Colts' sideline, and then it was measured by the NFL Official, Mr. Daniel or Daniels, I believe. And he, interestingly, he measured that ball three times with the same gauge and wrote the results on the ball.

Q. Do you remember what the results were?

A. Well, I think the results -- if you included it in the analysis, it would be favorable to the view that there was not deflation, first of all. But the other thing that I found particularly important was, to my knowledge, this was the only time during the game that officials used the same gauge and recorded three measurements. Why is that important? Well, here, you get a sense of potential measurement error. People who are not trained to take these gauges, put them in the footballs and record temperature -- psi. So what do you see? You see three measurements on the 12th ball and they differ by .4 psi; .4 psi is huge. So the measurement error that we are dealing with in this environment is the combination of that and the protocol. I mean, it just, it really was striking to me. And Exponent said we are not going to pay attention to the 12th ball.

COMMISSIONER GOODELL: Who is Mr. Daniels, James Daniel? Not a game official?

MR. REISNER: No.

Q. Other data?

A. I didn't mean "official" in the sense of officiating.

Q. You had said that there was another set of data not considered by Exponent. What was that?

A. The other data, and this goes back to the officials having some sense of the protocol, they measured post-game. They measured four Colts' balls. They measured four Patriots' balls. When I saw that, I said to myself, wow, now you've got more control data. There's no possibility that between halftime and the end of the game you would have tampering with either sets of balls. So now we have, in addition to the four Colts' balls at halftime, which I described unscientifically as a puny control group, now you have the ability to triple that with the end of the game data; excuse me; the end of the game data. But Exponent said we're not going to look at those, either.

Q. Do you remember anything about the measurements of the Patriots' balls post-game relative to the measurements of the protocols -- sorry -- measurements of the Patriots' balls post-game compared to their reinflation level at halftime?

A. Yes. There was a statement that they were inflated at halftime to, as I recall, 13. The post-game measurements were above 13. Again -- well, I shouldn't say "again." It's a finding, it's a result that just underscores it's so difficult to understand what's going on. Exponent made a lot of assumptions to navigate through the halftime data. I don't know what assumptions you would have to make to navigate through the post-game data.

Q. Dean Snyder, last question. What is your bottom-line takeaway from the work of the -- the statistical work of Exponent?

A. It's just not -- it's partly the setting, it's partly the impromptu protocol, but it's also the work that they have done statistically. The combination is it's not something that leads to reliable conclusions. And, certainly, it's certainly not the kind of scientific work that I would be comfortable with reaching judgments about people. I'm in a very different situation from the Commissioner, but these are -- these are not reliable findings.

MR. GREENSPAN: Thank you.

MR. KESSLER: Should we take a little break before we do cross?

MR. REISNER: Take five minutes, maybe?

COMMISSIONER GOODELL: Sure.

(Recess taken 2:17 p.m. to 2:28 p.m.)

Cross-Examination by Mr. Reisner

Q. Good afternoon, Dean Snyder. Dean Snyder, do you have a degree in statistics?

A. No.

Q. Are you a member of the American Statistical Association?

A. No.

Q. To your knowledge, is any member of your team a member of the American Statistical Association?

A. I don't know one way or the other.

Q. As far as you know, no member of your team is a member of the American Statistical Association, correct?

A. Correct.

Q. Now, you were assisted in your work here by members of the Analysis Group, correct?

A. Yes, and as well as by Professor Moore.

Q. And the Analysis Group, that's a consulting firm, right?

A. Yes.

Q. Very much like Exponent is a consulting firm, correct?

A. Well, they're different, but they are both consulting firms.

Q. And Analysis Group frequently works with lawyers involved in litigation, correct?

A. Yes.

Q. And Exponent frequently works with lawyers involved in litigation, correct?

A. I believe so.

Q. And how many times have you worked with the Analysis Group in the past?

A. I've been working with them for about seven years, and depends on how you count cases. Sometimes cases have different aspect of them. So you take, for example, the litigation involving LCD panels. That's one litigation in some people's minds, but it involves a lot of cases in other people's minds. So it's a little hard to count, but I have worked with them for the past seven years.

Q. Is it fair to say you have worked with them on at least a dozen cases over those seven years?

A. That's probably -- I wouldn't -- I haven't counted, but I think that -- I wouldn't disagree with that.

Q. And you receive payment in connection with the work that you do at the Analysis Group, correct?

A. Yes.

Q. That payment is separate and apart from the compensation you receive in connection with your duties at Yale, correct?

A. Yes.

Q. Now, before your testimony today, and in connection with the work that you did, did you read the entire Exponent report in connection with your analysis?

A. Yes.

Q. And so are you aware that, in addition to the analysis of statistical significance and the difference between the pressure drops in the Colts' and the Patriots' balls, Exponent separately conducted a series of other tests and experiments, correct?

A. Yes.

Q. And among those tests were transient experiments, yes?

A. Yes.

Q. And among those tests were game-day simulations, correct?

A. Yes.

Q. I want to focus first on your Finding 1. And I'm referring to what's in evidence as Exhibit 191. It's the low-tech version of your deck that you just presented. And Finding 1 is, "Exponent's statistical analysis of the difference in average pressure drops is wrong because it ignores timing," correct?

A. Correct.

Q. And that criticism focuses solely on the statistical analysis performed, right?

A. What they reported, as I said, in Table A3, their statistical analysis of difference in difference.

Q. This criticism didn't go to the transient tests that they performed, right?

A. I'm not sure what you are asking me. The transient test as reflected in Figure 1, those are the transient curves that show timing, something important.

Q. But your criticism is directed to their analysis of statistical significance, correct?

A. No, it's their model. Their model did not include timing. When you go to the Table A3 and you look at the variables they included in their model, they left timing out.

Q. And when you refer to "their model," you are referring to the model used in connection with their statistical significance analysis, right? A. I don't understand your question. The model did not include timing.

MR. REISNER: Can we hand the witness a copy of the Exponent report.

MS. GOLD: It's Tab 1 (handing).

Q. So you understand that the Exponent report consisted of at least three components: A statistical significance analysis, a transient analysis and game-day simulations?

A. I don't -- I don't understand your first characterization. They did an analysis of the difference in difference. They tried to explain it and they didn't include timing. That's not the first -- that's not how I would characterize the first component of their work. That's what they said was their most significant work. I think --

Q. Show me where in the report it says that's their most significant work.

A. I think it's in my slides.

Q. I didn't ask you about your slides. Where in their report does it say it's their most significant work?

A. It's the quote on my slide that identifies the difference in average pressure drops, Exponent Scenario 2. It says, "What is most significant about the halftime measurements is that the magnitude of the reduction in average pressure was greater for the Patriots football."

Q. So your testimony is that that quote says that's the most important part of their analysis?

A. Well, I think most people would agree that that is the most important. I mean, you heard Mr. Nash's questions and opening. And he focused on the difference in difference. The difference in difference is the key to the case.

Q. Is it a fairer way to describe the Exponent work as that they looked at the statistical significance analysis as the starting point to see whether there was more to study? Isn't that a fairer way to describe the Exponent report?

A. I don't think so.

Q. Let me direct your attention to the Exponent report at page X, Roman X. And the second-to-last paragraph reads, "It also appears that the Patriots' game balls exhibit a greater average pressure drop than did the Colts' game balls. This difference in the magnitude of the decrease in average pressure between the Patriots and the Colts footballs as measured at halftime was determined to be statistically significant, regardless of which gauges were used pre-game and at halftime. Therefore, the reasons for this difference were an appropriate subject for further investigation." Does that refresh your recollection that the entire model of the Exponent study was to look at statistical significance first to see whether there was something to be studied further and then to conduct experiments?

A. If that's the logic, I just don't understand it. I mean, you read the Exponent report. I gave you the quotes. They say that timing, minute by minute, matters. But when they decide whether they have a significant result or not, and they base conclusions on it, their own model, you just read the first page of the appendix and they didn't include it as an explanatory variable in their own model. Just look at Table A3. Look at their equation. If you can show me -- if anybody can show me that in their statistical model that they used timing after stating and proving to the world that timing matters, then I will change my view. But the basic thing, and you don't have to be an expert in anything other than statistics or econometrics to know this.

Q. You did not read the report as structured, first, let's see whether there is a statistically significant difference? Without –

A. Without taking into account timing –

Q. Let me just finish my question.

A. Oh, I'm sorry.

Q. If, yes, then let's conduct experiments to see what is responsible for the difference. That's not the way you read the report?

A. Your characterization is incorrect.

Q. I'm just asking whether you read the report.

A. Excuse me. You are saying they first did a model to figure out if it was statistically significant. The model didn't include timing. It's not like they said we have a statistically significant result independent of a model. They included variables to explain it, right? That's what their model does and they left timing out. So they only got to, I think we agree they only got to a statistically significant result by excluding timing.

Q. We don't agree. And A3 and the model that you are referring to, that's included in Appendix A to their report, correct?

A. That's their model. That's the model they ran.

Q. But my question is: That's included as Appendix A to their report, correct?

A. Yes, A3, yes, that identifies the model that they ran that generated their so-called statistically significant result.

Q. And that appendix is referenced in connection with their statistical significance analysis, right?

A. No. That's their model. That's their model to explain the difference in difference.

Q. And your criticism is that Exponent didn't take into account timing appropriately, right?

A. When they tested -- when they did their difference in difference analysis, you look at the equations. If I could refer you to the appendix.

Q. It would be better if you could answer my question.

MR. GREENSPAN: And I would ask you to just let him answer the question.

MR. LEVY: Knock it off.

A. When you say their analysis of statistical significance, that's an error. That's simply an error, okay? They do an analysis to explain the difference in difference and they don't include timing. And on that basis, they conclude that it is statistically significant and then they say that there's a finding that follows that. It's a finding that is flawed.

Q. But they included timing in other aspects of their work, didn't they?

A. I'm sorry. Yes, they did side analyses throughout.

Q. What makes you call them "side analyses"? Where are they called side analyses in the report?

A. That's my characterization.

Q. Okay.

A. And I believe -- I believe -- it's a fair point. I believe that the core analysis here is the difference in difference analysis. I think any fair reading of their report indicates that the difference in difference analysis is the core and their model excluded timing.

Q. And you understand that they conducted transient experiments, right?

A. Transient experiments is what generated Figure 22, which tells you timing should be included.

Q. And the purpose of the transient experiments was to determine the impact of timing of the halftime measurements on air pressure levels, correct?

A. Yes.

Q. And from reading the Exponent report, you understood that the main focus of the transient experiments was to determine whether the timing of the halftime measurements could explain the difference in the pressure drops observed between the Patriots' balls and the Colts' balls? That was your understanding from reading the report, right?

A. I couldn't tell what they were doing with that. And when you say "explain," there was language to the effect could they explain fully, under certain parameters. So I think, I think you would have to ask Exponent what they were trying to do and if they were trying to set up an experiment that used timing to explain everything. But it was different, I agree, from the difference in difference analysis that was featured in their report on which they claim they had statistically significant results.

Q. Okay. So let me ask you to turn to page 43 of the Exponent report. And fourth paragraph down, second sentence, third sentence referring to the transient experiments, "Therefore, the main focus of the transient experiments was to determine if variation in measurement timing was sufficient to explain the variation in the observed differences than the average pressure drops between the teams given the range of likely environmental factors present on game day and the realistic timing of measurements given the sequencing and duration of the various events known to have occurred at halftime." So was it your understanding that the purpose of the transient experiments was to determine whether the timing of the halftime measurements could explain the difference in the pressure drops observed between the Patriots' balls and the Colts' balls?

A. I think a fairer reading of this statement, which I think is revealing, is that they were trying to do these other analyses and determine whether these transient analyses were sufficient on their own to explain the difference in difference.

Q. That's your interpretation or that's what it says in the report?

A. Well, it says right here, "The main focus of the transient experiments was to determine if variation and measurement timing was sufficient to explain." It doesn't say "partially explain" or whether it's a relevant variable. It doesn't say whether timing should be included in the analysis. It doesn't say because it's not sufficient, we are going to exclude it. It just says we are going to do this test to see if timing is sufficient to explain, and I think it's a fair reading –

Q. Yes.

A. -- everything.

Q. And so you are not suggesting, Dean Snyder, that Exponent failed in its work to identify and consider the timing of the measurements as a factor to be considered? You are not suggesting that, right?

A. In their core analysis, exactly.

Q. You are calling it a core analysis, but in their statistical significance analysis, correct?

A. That's not the right term. I'm sorry to -- to -- to correct you on this. They had a difference in difference analysis on which they reached their core findings that there was this -- this didn't happen by chance.

Q. Did they use their statistical significance analysis to reach conclusions as to the likelihood of tampering?

A. Well, I think I have it in my slides.

Q. Can you answer my question without looking at your slides?

A. No, I can't, because I spent a lot of time trying to get this right. And it's very clear that their finding on statistical significance is what leads to their "therefore" statement. So you might as well just refer to the slides. I think you get the best -- the best guidance.

Q. Well, I think, frankly, the best guidance comes from the Exponent report and not your slides as to what Exponent studied. And the question is --

A. It's a quote from Exponent.

Q. -- did Exponent rely on their statistical analysis of the data to reach conclusions as to the likelihood of tampering, or did they rely on other aspects of their experimental work, if you know?

A. I will just read what Exponent stated based on their difference in difference analysis.

Q. Do you have a page number for what you are reading?

A. Yes, Exponent report, Table 8 on page 11. Quote, "In other words, in all cases studied, the additional pressure drop exhibited by the Patriots' footballs is unlikely to have occurred by chance."

Q. "Unlikely to have occurred by chance," doesn't say anything there about likelihood of tampering or human intervention, does it?

A. I will let -- I will let other people figure out what they were intending to state there.

Q. I think what they were intending to state is what they stated, and it doesn't refer to likelihood of tampering, does it? Does it refer to likelihood of tampering?

A. I don't have an answer to that one.

Q. Are there other aspects of the Exponent report that do directly address likelihood of tampering based on experiments conducted and analyses of data generated based on those experiments? A. I don't know what you are asking me.

Q. I'm asking you just what I asked you.

A. It's just a general question.

Q. It's really not a general question. I'm asking: Do you know based on your review of the Exponent report whether there are other portions in their report in which they do draw conclusions about likelihood or probability of tampering based on experimental results?

A. I don't think.

Q. You don't remember?

A. I don't know what -- I don't know what -- I don't even understand the question. I view this as the standard approach when you find statistically significant results to draw conclusions. And I think this is exactly the conclusion that they were drawing. And I think any reasonable reading of it speaks to the issue of whether this extra deflation was the result of chance or something else. You are telling me, well, it doesn't say "tampering." I understand that. But I will just let other people read this.

Q. But something else could be timing, right?

A. Does it say "timing"?

Q. It says, "It is unlikely to have occurred by chance and further study is warranted." And timing was studied, right?

A. And why not include timing in the original model? They have a list of variables that they include in their original model, but they excluded timing. Isn't that the key thing here? Why go to a side analysis and say timing is sufficient to explain everything? Put it in your original model. Come on. And, yes, I'm a member of the Econometrics Society in the past. Any graduate student in statistics or econometrics would know this is wrong. This is a restriction. This is saying timing is unimportant despite reading the Exponent report. It's timing all over the place.

Q. Well, I would move to strike if this were in real court, but I won't move to strike. But I'm sure Exponent will not describe their other work as a side analysis and would describe their work quite differently than you are describing it. And I think we will have the opportunity to hear from them. Didn't even the statistical significance analysis used by Exponent incorporate something called an order effect to account for the timing of the ball measurements at halftime?

A. When you talk about the analysis on which they reached their conclusions, no. They did do a separate analysis to which they referred, I think, in the appendix in a particular footnote at the very end where, instead of evaluating timing, they took the order of the balls and they discussed unreported results.

Q. And what you referred to as their appendix at the very end, right now in your answer is what you previously described as the core of their work in Appendix A, right?

A. Well, the core of their work in Appendix A explains how they -- the details of their model, which is discussed at length. In the appendix, they also refer to unreported results in a footnote. I think you are talking about a footnote where they discuss unreported results. There is no equation. There is no table and it's not timing. It's order of football measurement. And I would be happy to find it. It actually is a very interesting statement on their part.

Q. It's at Page A3 of their appendix and it's at Footnote 49. And when you look at that footnote, isn't it a fact that, "Exponent explicitly took account of time effect in their statistical analysis by incorporating an order effect into their model to determine whether any portion of observed ball-to-ball variation and pressure was explained by the order of measurements"? Isn't that right?

A. Here's the —

Q. Is that right? Is that what that footnote says?

A. You said "timing" in your question. That's not timing. It's order of measurements.

Q. It says "timing." It says, "To account for any time effect in our statistical analysis, we incorporated an order effect into our statistical model to determine whether any portion of the observed ball-to-ball variation in pressure was explained by the order of measurements."

A. Are you just asking me is that what it states?

Q. Well, is that what it states?

A. It is. That's what they've stated.

Q. And that incorporated the concept of timing into their statistical model, didn't it?

A. No. Here's what this did.

Q. That's fine. I will just leave it right there.

A. I would like to explain. It's an important point. It's not timing. It's order of ball measurement. That's the so-called explanatory variable. And the variable that they are trying to explain, the so-called dependent variable, is not the difference in average pressure drop. It's not the difference in difference analysis. It's ball-to-ball variation, which we know is subject to so much measurement error that I'm not surprised it doesn't explain that.

Q. But it takes time to measure ball 1 through ball 15, correct?

A. Are ball 1 and 15 all measured at the same increments in time? That embodies an assumption.

Q. My question is, did it take time to measure ball 1 through ball 15?

A. Yes.

Q. Do you know, based on the report, approximately how much time it took to measure from ball 1 through ball 15?

A. Well, there's uncertainty. That's what the -- that's what the report says. We don't know.

Q. And there are estimates in the report about how long it took, correct?

A. Under certain assumptions. And this, this analysis does not play it out. They don't explain whether they took those different assumptions into account.

Q. But you will agree, won't you, that it had to take some time to gauge 15 balls going from ball 1 –

A. Yes.

Q. -- to ball 15, correct?

A. Yes.

Q. So whatever time it took, you would expect it to be reflected in the ball data, correct?

A. Well, certainly time, it takes time to gauge balls. But again, the dependent variable here has nothing to do with a difference in difference analysis. It has to do with the ball-to-ball differences. That's what -- I can read it again, but you've already put it into the record. It's not -- it's not a test of -- it's not a check on their difference in difference analysis.

Q. And in their -- in their transient analysis, Exponent expressly took account of the full period of halftime and expected psi levels of the Colts' balls and the Patriots' balls based on the testing that they performed, didn't they?

A. Yes.

Q. Now I want to focus your attention on Finding 3 in your deck. Finding 3 says, "If the logo gauge was used to measure the Patriots' balls before the game, then eight of the eleven were above Exponent's expected outcome. Now, to reach this conclusion, your analysis assumes that the actual or true pressure of the game balls delivered to the referee by the Patriots was 12.17 psi, right?

A. This is just consistently applying the master gauge correction to both the halftime measurements of the game balls and to the starting value, which does have the effect that you just described.

Q. So your assumption is that, the assumption in your analysis is when the balls were delivered by the Patriots to the refs pre-game, that the psi measurement of the balls was 12.17, correct? A. It's a little -- there are a few side issues. I'm not going to quibble too much. It's basically right. There were some adjustments by Mr. Anderson –

Q. Yes.

A. -- to get the balls using one of the gauges to what he thought was about, according to the record, about 12.5. What this means is, if he used the logo gauge, this is just sort of basic subtraction, if he used the logo gauge to get those Patriots' balls calibrated to 12.5, and that logo gauge reads about .3, a little bit more than .3 above 12.5, then the effective starting value is what you said.

Q. 12.17, right?

A. Correct.

Q. So you understand that according to the Patriots themselves, the psi level at which they delivered game balls to the referee for the AFC Championship Game was not 12.17, right?

A. They used a gauge and we don't know what gauge they used and we don't know if their gauge had the same kind of differential that the logo gauge had versus the non-logo gauge.

Q. My question really went to your understanding of the psi level that the Patriots said they delivered the ball to the ref pre-game. And my question is, do you understand that the Patriots say that the psi level that they set the balls to before the game was 12.5 or 12.6? Is that your understanding of the Patriots' position?

A. With their -- with whatever gauge they used, that's their understanding, you are right.

Q. So the answer to my question is yes, that's your understanding?

A. Yes, but we don't know what that gauge was. We don't know if that was giving accurate measures or not.

Q. The Patriots didn't say that they delivered the balls to the ref at 12.17, right?

A. Correct. And we don't have -- correct.

Q. And you know that the NFL playing rules require that balls be between 12.5 and 13.5 psi, correct?

A. Correct.

Q. So your analysis basically assumes that the Patriots delivered game balls to the referee before the game that were underinflated in violation of the rules?

A. No. It means that if they used a gauge that was like the logo gauge, they would have delivered balls that were 12.5 and they didn't know it.

Q. How about if they used a gauge that was like the dozens and dozens and dozens of gauges that Exponent studied as part of its work in this case, all of which read relatively close to the master calibrated gauge? What if they used one of those dozens and dozens and dozens and dozens of gauges? Would the reading have been 12.17 or would the reading have been 12.5 or 12.6?

A. Clearly if they used the new gauges bought by Exponent through particular sources that were all alike, that would be true. But we don't know what Patriots' gauge was used and there is no basis in the report. And this is just part of the problem that you get into when you go down these rabbit holes. You don't have the Patriots' gauge. You don't know if that was an older gauge. There's evidence to indicate that older gauges read higher than new gauges. Exponent collected a bunch of new gauges and said, oh, new gauges, fine. No surprise there. I'm not -- I'm not quarreling with this. It's just the major point here is there are just so many uncertainties.

Q. Again, I just can't resist to move to strike, but I don't know whether that's applicable in this proceeding or not. Part of your analysis in your finding or criticism 3 is an application of the Ideal Gas Law, right?

A. No. I think that's just math. They are just doing math there.

Q. But the math is plugging numbers into the Ideal Gas Law formula, isn't it?

A. I'm not quarreling with the math on the Ideal Gas Law formula, I'm only quarreling with their inconsistency in applying the master gauge conversion.

Q. In your conclusion that, "Eight out of eleven were above Exponent's expected outcome," "expected outcome" means based on an application of the Ideal Gas Law, correct?

A. And if they –

Q. Can you answer that question "yes" or "no"?

A. No, I can't, because there are two parts to establishing the relevant scientific threshold given Exponent's own methodology. One is to do the math on the Ideal Gas Law correctly. The other is to do the math on the conversion consistently. They didn't do the latter. I'm just correcting the latter.

Q. Would you agree that the Ideal Gas Law is not, in practice, going to yield a directly relevant measure because the balls were not tested on the field at 48 or 50 degrees, but tested subsequently in the locker room at a warmer temperature?

A. I think that's true. I don't think anybody, prior to this whole issue, understood -- they understood the Ideal Gas Law, but that's a sort of abstract law. How that law actually applies to footballs being brought in from the field, that's all, you know, Exponent had to do the transient analysis to understand how footballs would react when they were brought in and warm up and dry.

Q. Exactly, which is why the Ideal Gas Law itself only has theoretical applicability to this problem and not practical applicability, because the balls were not measured at some frozen temperature at the end of halftime outside, but had an opportunity to warm to some degree, fair?

A. I think that's a fair point.

Q. In any event, you concede that if the non-logo gauge was used pre-game, application of the Ideal Gas Law cannot account entirely for the pressure drops observed in the Patriots halftime measurements, correct?

A. You are talking about the analog to -- I just want to be clear -- the analog to –

Q. Your criticism doesn't apply to the use of the non-logo gauges used pre-game, correct?

A. That's correct. This is their structure. The mistake on the inconsistent master gauge conversion is only substantively important under the assumption that the logo gauge was used, not under the assumption that the non-logo gauge was used.

Q. And just flipping back for a moment to your criticism 1, what you call Case 1.

COMMISSIONER GOODELL: Where?

MR. REISNER: This is at page 3437, Bates Number 3437 in this deck.

Q. When you recalculate the statistical significance analysis by Exponent, you yield a p-value of .067, correct?

A. Yes.

Q. And is it fair to say that that p-value means that there's a 6.7 percent likelihood that chance explains the variation and a 92.3 percent chance or likelihood that chance does not explain the outcome?

A. Correct.

Q. Just a couple of questions about your finding Number 2, which looking at the front page of your deck says, "Exponent improperly draws conclusions based on the variability in halftime pressure measurements despite conceding that variability is statistically significant." The conclusion that you are challenging, Dr. Snyder, is the statement by Exponent at page 62 of its report that, "Therefore, subject to the discovery of an as-yet unidentified and unexamined factor, the most plausible explanation for the variability in the Patriots halftime measurements is that the eleven Patriots' footballs measured by the officials at halftime did not all start the game at or near the same pressure," right?

A. Well, that's true.

Q. Is that the conclusion that you are challenging?

A. Well, it's two things. One, is they proceed with a conclusion without having found a statistically significant difference. And then, secondly, when they say, "As-yet unidentified and unexamined factor," they examined timing. It was right there in their own Figure 22. They just didn't bring it up.

Q. Well, but that's not really fair. When they determined absence of statistical significance as to variability, they were just looking at the raw data, right?

A. I don't know why that's not –

Q. Can you answer?

A. What I said was fair. It's exactly fair. They set up statistical significance as a standard. They used it in their difference and difference analysis and then they dropped it for this and they went on to make an inappropriate conclusion and they ignored timing.

Q. Okay. When they made their lack of statistical significance finding with respect to variability, they were doing it based on the raw data, correct?

A. I don't even know what that means, "on the raw data."

Q. Based on the halftime measurements and only the halftime measurements.

A. I'm just lost. They compared the variance and they didn't find a statistically significant difference, even after they had flipped the Colts' ball number 3, which reduced the variance in the Colts' balls measurements.

Q. And when they reported their observations on variability later in the report on page 62, they weren't just relying on the raw halftime data; they were also relying on learning from the transient experiments that they performed, correct?

A. I'm not sure if I am following your question. I'm happy to look at page 62.

Q. Look at page 62 of the report. Page 62 last paragraph, first sentence, "The fluctuations in pressures" –

A. I'm sorry, sir, sorry to interrupt. I see. I was on the wrong page. If you could just pause a second; yes.

Q. Reading at the first sentence in the last paragraph on page 62, "The fluctuations in pressures between the pairs of Patriots' football measurements highlighted in Table 15 exceed those expected based on the transient curves." Does that refresh your recollection that in making their conclusions and stating their observations as to variability later in the report, they didn't rely simply on the raw halftime data, but also on the learning that they obtained based on their transient experiments?

A. I guess you would have to ask them exactly what their bases were and if they were willing to say we didn't find this statistically significant difference, but then for some other work that they did, they were willing to reach this conclusion.

Q. Okay. We'll do that.

MR. REISNER: Nothing further at this time.

MR. GREENSPAN: Nothing from me.

COMMISSIONER GOODELL: Thank you. Appreciate your time.

THE WITNESS: Thanks, Mr. Commissioner.

MR. KESSLER: Let me just do some housekeeping. Mr. Levy indicated to me that you didn't have copies of the Declaration of Robert Kraft and the two declarations of Mr. Maryman, so let me just identify that. The Kraft Declaration is NFLPA 168 and the Maryman Declaration is NFLPA 4 and NFLPA 6. And the next witness we would call is Mr. Vincent, if you want to proceed right to that.

COMMISSIONER GOODELL: Yes.

MR. KESSLER: I'm just going to note for the record, we have been keeping count. We have the NFL at one hour and 45 minutes out of their two-hours' allotment that you gave to them. And what do we have for ours, Heather? We will tell you ours in a second to see if we are correct.

MR. LEVY: I think it's two hours and 42 minutes, but I am keeping track. But as noted in my correspondence, the Commissioner is inclined to grant at least another hour on the end and is willing to show flexibility at the end of that hour. So we should continue to proceed ahead here.

MR. KESSLER: I just want to be clear about this because I have been planning my examination based on that I would have to make some good cause showing as you indicated for something else, and there are additional witnesses that I would call. If I'm going to just automatically be granted, you know, an hour, at least, then I have got more people to call about this. I'd just like to be advised about what my rules are. That's, I think that's fair.

MR. LEVY: You have got at least another hour, and we will be flexible beyond that. If you have got other witnesses to call, have them available.

MR. KESSLER: Okay. Well, I've already asked that I would like two additional witnesses I mentioned, and so I assume they are here, so I will call them if I now have the time to do it. Let me see how it proceeds with Mr. Vincent and Mr. Wells and I will see how much time I have used up.

MR. LEVY: Jeffrey, who are the two additional witnesses?

MR. KESSLER: Dr. Marlow and Mr. Gardi, both of whom I believe are here.

COMMISSIONER GOODELL: Go ahead, please.

Testimony of Troy Vincent

Direct Examination by Mr. Kessler

Q. Mr. Vincent, would you please state your name for the record.

A. Troy Vincent.

Q. And, Mr. Vincent, what is your current occupation?

A. I am the Executive Vice President of Football Operations here at the National Football League.

Q. Could you please tell us what are your responsibilities as the Vice President For Football Operations?

A. My responsibility and our department is charged with preserving the integrity of the game, overseeing all of football operations, day of the game, uniform violations.

Q. So that would include basically everything that happens on game-day; is that fair?

A. It's fair.

Q. And that would include the referees' testing of footballs? That would be something within your personal jurisdiction; isn't that correct?

A. Yes, sir.

Q. And would you be the most senior person, short of the Commissioner, who is responsible for that particular set of activities?

A. Dean Blandino would be the other.

Q. I'm sorry; who was that?

A. Dean Blandino, head of officiating.

Q. Does he report to you?

A. Yes, sir.

Q. Okay. So again, I'm just trying to think, there is no one more senior to you responsible for how the officials would test game balls than possibly the Commissioner; isn't that correct?

A. That's correct.

Q. Okay. So let me ask you first, Mr. Vincent, how did you first learn that there was any issue or allegation about the footballs that the Patriots were using in the AFC Championship Game?

A. It was first brought to my knowledge approximately six or seven minutes remaining in the second half [sic] of the AFC Championship Game. There was a knock on the door by the General Manager from the Indianapolis Colts, Ryan Grigson. He proceeded in the room and he brought to myself, and Mike Kensil was actually sitting to my left, and said, "We are playing with a small ball." That was my first knowledge of the situation.

Q. You had never heard anything about the Colts having made allegations before the game started prior to that time?

A. No, sir.

Q. Okay. And what did you do after –

COMMISSIONER GOODELL: Did you say "second half"?

THE WITNESS: It was second quarter.

COMMISSIONER GOODELL: Second quarter.

Q. What did you do after you received this allegation from the Colts in the second quarter of the game?

A. So immediately as Ryan stepped out of the room, I turned to my left and I just told Mike that during halftime we should probably look at testing all of the balls from both sidelines. And at that particular time, he was on the phone with our sideline officials putting steps in order.

Q. So you were the one who made that decision for that testing to be done?

A. From inside the box, both Mike and I, we both agreed that this should take place, yes, sir.

Q. Okay. Now, prior to this time, when this happened, were you familiar at all with the procedures that the officials utilized for testing pressure in footballs at games? Was that something you were familiar with or was this the first time you became familiar with that?

A. No, I'm actually familiar, I was familiar with the game-day process of the testing of game balls on game day, yes, sir.

Q. Okay. So prior to this game, okay, had you ever heard of the Ideal Gas Law?

A. No, sir.

Q. Do you know if anyone in the NFL Game-Day Operations had ever discussed the impact of the Ideal Gas Law in testing footballs?

A. Not with me.

Q. You had never heard of that?

A. I hadn't.

Q. Okay. Now, in the procedures that were set up prior to this game, okay, were there ever any procedures where the referees were told they should record temperature inside the room while they were testing each football? Do you know if that was ever an instruction given to the referees that they should write down temperature or take temperature?

A. No, sir.

Q. Okay. That was not done?

A. No, sir.

Q. Okay. How about recording? Did you know that they used multiple gauges sometimes, different types of gauges to test footballs prior to this game?

A. There's one gauge, yes, sir.

Q. There is one gauge or multiple gauges?

A. Well, there's two, two gauges, but they use -- they use the one gauge to test.

Q. Right. But you knew there were two types of gauges that could be used?

A. Not types. I know that there are two gauges that are on the premises.

Q. The logo gauge and what we are calling the non-logo gauge?

A. Yes.

Q. Did officials have instructions prior to this game as to whether they should use a logo gauge or a non-logo gauge to test?

A. Not to my knowledge.

Q. Okay. Were they asked to record anywhere in writing which gauge they used when they were doing testing?

A. Not to my knowledge.

Q. Okay. Were there any steps taken to preserve gauges as they were utilized to keep them somewhere?

A. The referee usually keeps them. Q. The referee usually keeps his own gauges?

A. Yes.

Q. Now, with respect to whether the balls were wet or dry, do you know if there were any procedures prior to this to record if a ball was wet or dry at the time it was being tested for pressure?

A. No, sir.

Q. Okay. How about the timing of when the testing was done? Was it ever instructed you should record what minutes the test was done so you could see how long the ball was in the room at the time of testing?

A. No, sir.

Q. Okay.

COMMISSIONER GOODELL: Mr. Kessler, just so I'm clear, are you talking about pre-game?

MR. KESSLER: Yes, I'm talking about pre -- about the whole game.

Q. My questions apply to the whole game. You understand that?

A. Okay.

Q. In fact, let me ask you, prior to this game, was it routine or required for balls to be tested again at halftime, or was that only for this game?

A. No, there was no routine. It was just protocol was to test two hours and 15 minutes prior, but it was brought to our knowledge that potentially there could have been a violation.

Q. Okay. So in all other NFL games generally, there is no testing at halftime at all, correct?

A. No, because we typically don't have a breach with a game ball violation.

Q. Okay. And there is typically no testing after the end of the game regarding footballs, either, correct?

A. No, sir.

Q. So the only testing the NFL had in place was the testing before the game started as a routine matter?

A. Protocol, before the game.

Q. Now, at the time that was true, did you know that the footballs were automatically going to lose pressure if it was cold outside compared to how warm it was inside? Was that ever something you thought about prior to this game?

A. No, sir.

Q. Okay. Now we then get to the halftime. You were present for the halftime testing, correct?

A. Yes, sir.

Q. And is it fair to say you did not tell anybody to record the temperature in the room at the halftime testing, correct?

A. No, sir.

Q. And nobody recorded the temperature in the room at the halftime testing, correct?

A. Not to my knowledge.

Q. Right. You didn't tell anybody to record the exact time when different balls were tested at the halftime, correct?

A. No, sir.

Q. And to your knowledge, nobody recorded that?

A. Not to my knowledge.

Q. You didn't tell anybody to record whether or not the balls were tested on the Colts before reinflating the Patriots' balls or after? You didn't instruct anybody to record that anywhere, correct?

A. No, sir.

Q. And to your knowledge, it was not recorded anywhere?

A. Not to my knowledge.

Q. Okay. You didn't instruct anyone to indicate whether the balls were wet or dry at the time they were being tested, correct?

A. No, but most were wet.

Q. Most of the balls were wet? Let me ask you about that. Do you recall during the game that in the second quarter, the Patriots had the football time in possession for a much longer period of time than the Colts?

A. No, sir, I don't recall that.

Q. Let me represent to you, according to League official statistics, the Patriots had the ball for 10:18 and the Colts had it only for 4:42, okay? So let's assume that the League statistics are correct, okay? You are a former player, correct?

A. That's what they say.

Q. Based on your years of experience as a player, okay, is it correct that when the team has the ball in offense, okay, the ball is out of the bag and being used, but when you are on defense on a rainy day, the balls are generally kept in the bag; is that fair?

A. My understanding, yes.

Q. Okay. So is it also fair based on your experience that if the Patriots had their balls in play for ten minutes and 18 seconds while the Colts only had their balls in play for four minutes and 42 seconds in the second quarter, it was very likely that the Patriots' balls were going to be wetter than the Colts' balls; is that fair?

A. Possibly, yes.

Q. Okay. And it's also true that some balls may stay in the bag the whole time for both teams and just be dry because they never came out of the bags, right?

A. Possible.

Q. And when this testing was done, no one told the referees, hey, see if it's a dry ball and note that or if it's a wet ball, right? No one was asked to record that?

A. Not to my knowledge.

Q. And the reason for no one doing this is because neither you nor anyone else was thinking about the Ideal Gas Law or how time or temperature or wetness my affect these readings, right?

A. Correct.

Q. Okay. Now, let me show you the following, which is NFLPA Exhibit 136. You will recognize what's attached to this is a letter from Mr. Gardi sent to Mr. Kraft on 19th. Do you see that?

A. Mm-hmm.

Q. Now, did Mr. Gardi do this on his own, make this decision, or did you participate in the decision to start this investigation by NFL security that is described here?

A. We spoke about this prior to game time on my way back to the hotel that we tested game balls during halftime. And because the Patriots had eleven game balls that were under compliance, that this may -- we may need to do potential further investigation. So Dave and I and others on our staff, we came to the conclusion that we probably need to do some additional follow-up.

Q. Now, when you say, "They had eleven balls under compliance," what you meant is that they had eleven balls that were below 12.5 being measured, correct?

A. Yes.

Q. But at the time, you didn't know that some of that reduction could happen just because of cold or wetness or other factors, right? That just wasn't something you were aware of, correct?

A. I didn't include science, no, sir.

Q. Okay. Let me ask you this. If you look at this letter on the second page, it talks about the fact that one of the game balls was inflated to 10.1 psi. Do you see that?

A. Yes, sir.

Q. Now, I am going to give you another exhibit, which is NFL 14. And you will see these are notes, I believe, that were taken when the testing was done. And you signed them in several places. If you will look at page 256, I think it's the first time your signature appears; is that correct?

A. Yes, sir.

Q. And you signed this as a witness of the halftime testing; is that correct?

A. That's correct.

Q. Okay. And if you look at the listing of the pressures that are written down for the Patriots' eleven balls, none of them are as low as 10.1; is that correct?

A. That's correct.

Q. Okay. So do you know why Mr. Gardi thought that a ball was as low as 10.1 when none of those measures were here?

A. No.

Q. Okay. Let me ask you another one. His next sentence says, "In contrast, each of the Colts game ball that was inspected met the requirements set forth above and that requirement was 12 and a half to 13 and a half," correct?

A. Correct.

Q. Well, let's look at the Colts ball measurements. If you look at the Colts ball measurements which you signed, I believe that is on page 266. And that's also your signature, correct?

A. Correct.

Q. And, in fact, if you look at the Colts ball measurements on the right-hand side, the ones by Mr. Prioleau? Do you see that?

A. Yes.

Q. You will see that three out of the four Colts' balls are below the 12.5, correct?

A. Correct.

Q. Okay. So do you know why Mr. Gardi thought that the Colts game balls all met the requirements when on one of the gauges, three out of the four didn't go to 12.5?

A. Well, here it is -- he's specifying that one of the two gauges -- that's how we looked at the Colts -- I mean, the Patriots' ball as well, neither of the gauges none or both gauges with the Colts' ball, none of them were in compliance. Or at least here with the Colts' ball, what we saw was that at least one of the gauges, they all were in compliance.

Q. The letter doesn't say that, one gauge versus two gauges, right? It doesn't reference it? Mr. Gardi's letter doesn't say it was on one gauge versus the other, correct?

A. Correct.

Q. Now, at the time that you were looking at this, you had no idea what gauge had been used pre-game by the official to measure the balls, Mr. Anderson? You didn't know whether it was the logo gauge or the non-logo gauge, correct?

A. That's correct.

Q. Is it fair to say, Mr. Vincent, that there was a lot of confusion about what these numbers were, that Mr. Gardi didn't even know what the numbers were correctly at this time?

A. Not at all.

Q. You think it was very clear?

A. I think it was clear.

Q. So do you have any explanation -- is Mr. Gardi a lawyer?

A. Yes.

Q. Is he a careful lawyer?

A. Yes.

Q. If it was so clear, do you have any explanation as to how he could have "10.1" written down as the figure and it was not one of the figures?

A. I can't speak for David.

Q. So it wasn't clear for Mr. Gardi at least? Would you give me that?

A. Based on his letter, no.

Q. You, in the discipline letter that you wrote in this case, let's go to that. This is NFLPA Exhibit 10. This was the discipline letter that you sent out in this case; is that correct?

A. Yes, sir.

Q. Okay. And I note there has been a ruling that I cannot ask you about delegation issues, so I'm just noting that if not for that ruling, I would be asking now at this point about that.

MR. KESSLER: But since you've ruled that I'm not allowed to ask those questions, that's the reason why I'm not going to waste our time and ask questions which you said I can't ask. So I assume that ruling stands?

MR. LEVY: The ruling stands. Let's move on.

MR. KESSLER: That's fine. I just want to make sure the ruling stands. Okay.

Q. In the third paragraph, it says here, look at the first paragraph. I am so sorry, in the third paragraph, it says, "With respect to your particular involvement, the report established that there is substantial and credible evidence to conclude you were at least generally aware of the actions of the Patriots employees involved in the deflation of the footballs and that it was unlikely that their actions were done without your knowledge." Do you see that?

A. Yes, sir.

Q. Is that the finding of the Wells report that you relied on in order to impose discipline in this matter?

A. Yes, sir.

MR. NASH: Objection to the form of that question. A. This is what we derived from the Wells report on information that was -- but we didn't impose discipline.

Q. Who imposed discipline?

A. The Commissioner. We made recommendations to our unit.

Q. You made your recommendation based on this particular finding in the Wells report that's identified here?

A. No. This is one factor that was included.

Q. Okay. Did you personally read any of the interview reports of the people that Mr. Wells interviewed?

A. Yes.

Q. Okay. You did?

A. In the Wells report?

Q. Yes.

A. Yes, sir.

Q. So you had full access to the interview reports that Mr. Wells did of different people in making your decision?

A. The report that was public, I read that report, yes, sir.

Q. Not the report, okay.

A. I'm sorry; I'm sorry.

Q. Let me be clear. Mr. Wells conducted a lot of interviews and he made his own notes or reports of his interviews, memoranda; did you read any of those or did you just read the report?

A. Oh, no, sir, no; I'm sorry. I didn't have access to those.

Q. So you based your recommendations of discipline in this letter solely upon reading the Wells report? That's what I wanted to establish.

A. Yes.

Q. You didn't read any other documents?

A. Didn't have any other documents to read.

Q. Okay. You didn't interview any other people yourself?

A. Oh, no, sir.

Q. You didn't do any review of other documents other than reading the Wells report? That's what I want to be sure of.

A. Looked at some previous cases.

Q. Previous decisions?

A. Mm-hmm.

Q. Of discipline, correct?

A. Well, of violations, more so violations in this particular area.

Q. Okay. Well, that's going to get to another question I am going to ask. Did you look at any previous examples of any player being disciplined for a violation like this?

A. No. I looked very hard and I was just thinking about my time as a former player, a Union representative, I just couldn't find -- we just didn't see actions, this kind of action from a player. You just, we didn't find this kind of action or behavior of a player.

Q. Let's look into that. Were you aware during the 2014 season that there was an incident with the Minnesota team having warm footballs?

A. Yes, sir.

Q. Okay. Would you agree with me that the quarterback of Minnesota would have been generally aware that those footballs would be warm to his touch?

A. I'm not aware of that just based off of the reading of the file. No, this was just –

Q. You were the executive vice president –

MR. NASH: Objection. Let him finish the answer, please.

Q. Finish your answer.

A. This is a game ball employee that took it upon himself to warm a football. So you had a game ball employee from the Carolina Panthers that was on the Minnesota Vikings sideline that actually took these things in his own action and thought that was the proper thing to do.

Q. Were those balls put into the game, the balls he warmed?

A. It was just one.

Q. Was that one put into the game?

A. No, sir.

Q. How do you know that?

A. Because the report would have said it.

Q. Well, do you know that personally or just assuming that?

A. I'm assuming based off the evidence that was in the report.

Q. Did you start any investigation of any player regarding that incident?

A. There was no need because it was addressed immediately. It was a natural break in the game and our office called the sidelines to ask the question and to make sure that there wasn't any other misconduct.

Q. What report are you referring to, by the way?

A. Just the actual case itself, looking at the paperwork.

Q. Was there paperwork involved in that?

A. Well, it was a follow-up from the office, yes.

MR. KESSLER: We had asked for that, and there has been nothing produced, I don't believe, on that. If I'm wrong, Dan, you can advise me.

MR. NASH: I think you have been produced with everything.

MR. KESSLER: I just represent I don't believe that has been produced to us, any kind of written report. We know about the public report, but we haven't seen any written report. So if there is one, I would ask that it be produced.

Q. Let me ask you next about the following. Are you aware -- let's take a look at NFLPA Exhibit 177. You will see this is a report quoting Aaron Rodgers that took place during the November 30th game between the Packers and the Patriots. And you will see that Mr. Rodgers was quoted as saying, "I like to push the limit to how much air we can put in the football, even go over what they allow you to do and see if the officials take air out of it." Do you see that?

A. Yes. Q. Did you or anyone in your office conduct any investigation of Mr. Rodgers for making that statement?

A. No, sir.

Q. Would you agree with me that if Mr. Rodgers was pushing the limit of how much air could be in a football, that that would be him at least being generally aware of activities to try to violate the NFL rules regarding pressure for footballs?

A. The way I'm reading, this is a post-game comment and there is no need for us to react or overreact.

Q. So this was not important enough for you to react to Mr. Rodgers saying he liked to push the limit and see if officials caught it; that was not a serious thing for you to react?

A. In a post-game interview. Because if the testing of the games (sic) pre-game and all balls were in regulation, there is no need for us to react for post-game comment.

Q. So in your view, Mr. Rodgers not even being investigated and Mr. Brady being suspended for four games for allegedly being generally aware of someone else's activities, you think that's a consistent treatment, in your mind?

A. This is a post-game comment.

Q. Okay. Let me ask you about this one. Take a look at NFL Exhibit 1597, Exhibit 73.

MR. KESSLER: If we can give that to him, please.

Q. Mr. Vincent, is this one of the incidents that you looked at to see how things were treated in the past regarding claims of tampering with footballs?

A. This was reviewed, yes, sir.

Q. Okay. And so, you can see here that the League, Mr. Hill, was he the Vice President of Football Operations before you?

A. Yes.

Q. And you will see that he suspends this employee of the Jets, Mr. Robinson, for trying to use unapproved equipment to prep a kicking ball prior to a game. Do you see that?

A. Yes, sir.

Q. Now, do you know why there was no investigation made or action taken against a kicker under the theory that he was generally aware that this attendant would have been preparing the balls for him in this manner?

A. No, sir.

Q. Now, the policy that you cite in your letter, in your discipline letter regarding Mr. Brady -- well, let me ask you this. Where do you find the policy that says that footballs can't be altered with respect to pressure? Is that going to be in the competitive integrity policy that Mr. Wells cited in his report?

A. Game-Day Operations Manual.

Q. In the manual? Okay. Is it correct, to your knowledge, that the manual is given to clubs and GMs and owners, et cetera, but the manual is not given out to players; is that correct, to your knowledge?

A. That's correct, to my knowledge.

Q. In fact, when you were a player, you were never given that manual, right?

A. No.

MR. KESSLER: I don't have any further questions. Thank you very much.

Cross-Examination by Mr. Nash

Q. Just a few questions, Mr. Vincent. You were asked about your presence during the halftime at the AFC Championship Game?

A. Yes.

Q. How would you describe the process that took place; was it an orderly process? How would you generally describe what happened in terms of the measurement of the football?

A. Very orderly. Actually, I was one of the last to enter into the locker room. Upon my entrance into the rear room where the officials were, Al Riveron was actually directing traffic in a very calm manner.

Q. From your observations, who did the measurements?

A. I think it was Clete and it was two officials, and then we had the one League security rep.

COMMISSIONER GOODELL: I'm sorry; two game officials?

THE WITNESS: Two game officials, yes, sir.

Q. Are the two game officials the people who did the measurements?

A. Yes, sir.

Q. And to your observation, were they careful in doing them?

A. Yes, sir.

Q. If I could ask you to look at NFLPA Exhibit 136, you were asked some questions about the letter to Mr. Kraft. At the time that this letter was written, had any final determinations been made about whether the Patriots or anybody associated with the Patriots had actually violated the rules?

A. No, sir.

Q. What happened following the issuance of this letter?

A. Actually, once Dave sent the letter to the club, I think there was maybe a few days later, Mr. Wells and Jeff had came in too. We felt like an independent investigation should take place.

Q. Now, Mr. Kessler asked you about whether you had been familiar with the Ideal Gas Law or other factors that could account for the decrease in the inflation in the Patriots' balls. Do you remember that?

A. Yes.

Q. Was the purpose of the investigation to look into things like that?

A. Yes, sir.

Q. Now, you were asked a few questions about other incidents. The first one you were asked about was the Vikings. Do you recall that?

A. Yes, sir.

Q. If I could turn your attention to, I think it's Exhibit 174, the NFLPA 174. Do you remember seeing this article at the time?

A. No, sir. This is the first I'm seeing it.

Q. In looking at it, does this refresh your recollection at all about the events of the Vikings game?

A. Yes.

Q. Would you say that this accurately describes your recollection of what happened at the Vikings game?

A. Yes.

Q. Did you have any information at that time or do you know of anyone at the NFL who had information of any player being involved with the ball boy warming the football for the Vikings?

A. No, sir.

Q. You were asked about Aaron Rodgers. It's NFLPA Exhibit 177. Do you have that?

A. Yes, sir.

Q. You were asked about a quote, and I note in the quote it says something about to see if the officials take the air out of it. And you were asked whether you did an investigation. Did you have any information that either Mr. Rodgers or anyone from the Packers had actually tampered with a football after the officials measured it?

A. No, sir.

Q. Did you have any information or any evidence that either Mr. Rodgers or anyone associated with the Packers actually used the football in that game or any other game in which the inflation was not properly done on the footballs after the officials had measured it?

A. No, sir.

Q. Or at any time, did you have information that the packers or Mr. Rodgers used the football that was not properly inflated?

A. Not at all.

Q. If you had such knowledge and such evidence, would you have conducted an investigation?

A. What we would have done is our normal protocol. Before games, we would have tested the ball.

MR. NASH: Thank you.

MR. KESSLER: Just a few more questions.

Redirect Examination by Mr. Kessler

Q. You just testified to Mr. Nash that NFLPA Exhibit 174 accurately described the incident with Minnesota. And so based on that, do you now recall that, in fact, it was both teams who were involved in warming footballs, plural, as stated in this article?

A. It was just, it was my knowledge that it was just the one team.

Q. Okay. So now, so even though you just testified under oath that the article accurately characterized it, it is now your new testimony that the article is mischaracterizing that?

MR. NASH: Objection; mischaracterizing what he said.

A. No, this is the first I've actually seen the article.

Q. Why did you say it characterized it correctly when your counsel just asked you that question?

A. Based off what the article represents.

Q. The article represents that both teams were warned, correct? That's what the article says?

A. Yes, sir.

Q. Were both teams warned?

A. Based off the article, yes.

Q. Okay. So if both teams were warned, that would mean that both teams were involved in the activity, right, not just one?

A. That's correct.

Q. Okay. And so both teams, it would involve more than one football, at least one football for each team, correct? A. That's not correct.

Q. Well, were both teams warming the same football?

A. Well, it was because you had National take place, you want to inform both teams that this is not prohibited.

COMMISSIONER GOODELL: Are you saying "warmed" or "warned"?

MR. KESSLER: "Warm."

COMMISSIONER GOODELL: "Warm"?

MR. KESSLER: "Warm," W-A-R-M is what the article said.

Q. This was a game that was played in minus seven degrees; is that correct? That is what the article says?

A. Yes.

Q. So it was a very, very cold game. And what was happening, according to the article, is sideline attendants were using heaters to warm the footballs, right?

A. Correct.

Q. And would you agree with me it's a frozen game, okay. Someone's using sideline heaters. If a quarterback felt that ball, he would be generally aware that the ball had been warmed in this frozen game? There's no way to not be aware of that? You are a football player. You are aware of that?

A. I'm not a quarterback.

Q. Have you handled a football with the National Football League?

A. Yes.

Q. Okay. Do you think in a frozen game if someone put in a heated, you would notice, oh, this feels warmer than I thought it would?

A. With gloves on, I'm not sure.

Q. You are not sure about that? In any event, nothing was done to even investigate the quarterbacks in this matter, correct, by you?

A. Here, it says here in the article that he warned both teams.

Q. Right. But there was no investigation made of whether the quarterbacks knew about it or whether the quarterbacks asked the attendants to do anything? There was no investigation of that at all?

A. That's correct.

Q. And then finally, going back to NFL Exhibit 14, which are the notes you signed, and I want to look back on page 256. It states here, if you look at the -- this is the two different tests. And I'm looking at the one where it says, "Tests by Darrel" -- is it "Prioleau" ["pray-loo" phonetically]?

A. That's correct.

Q. It says here, "Belonging to JJ." Do you see that right at the top? Right next to the 11.8, it says, "Belonging to JJ."

A. Mm-hmm. Q. Now, you signed these notes, right?

A. Yes, sir.

Q. This page you signed, right?

A. Yes.

Q. Do you know what "belonging to JJ" refers to?

A. No, sir.

Q. Do you know if that refers to the fact that the gauge used by Mr. Prioleau was, in fact, a gauge that belonged to Mr. Jastremski?

A. Not to my knowledge.

Q. So you don't know what that refers to?

A. No, sir.

MR. KESSLER: I have no further questions.

MR. NASH: Just very briefly.

Recross-Examination by Mr. Nash

Q. Just the Vikings article, I want to follow up on the Commissioner's question. I'm not sure Mr. Kessler accurately described the article. I thought there was a suggestion that the article said that both teams actually warmed the football. What was your recollection of the incident?

A. That, my recollection of the game was that you had a game ball employee that was working that particular game, actually from the Carolina Panthers who actually took it upon himself to warm a football.

Q. And in terms of both teams, all this article refers to that both teams were warned?

A. That's correct.

Q. And it also says in the article that, "The sideline attendants involved in that likely meant well." Was that your understanding of that situation?

A. Yes.

Q. And again, did this or any other report that you received about the Vikings incident give you any indication that any player was in any way involved?

A. No player or anyone else was involved. No one else was involved.

MR. NASH: Thank you.

MR. KESSLER: Nothing further.

MR. LEVY: Thank you.

COMMISSIONER GOODELL: Thank you.

MR. KESSLER: You want to keep going or should we take a brief break? Mr. Wells, the witness, would like a brief break.

(Recess taken 3:54 p.m. to 4:03 p.m.)

MR. KESSLER: Our next witness will be Mr. Ted Wells. Please swear in the witness.

Testimony of Ted Wells

Direct Examination by Mr. Kessler

Q. Good morning, Mr. Wells. Would you state your full name for the record, please.

A. Theodore V. Wells, Jr.

Q. Okay. And what is your current occupation?

A. I am a partner at the law firm of Paul, Weiss.

Q. And Mr. Wells, were you hired to be the co-lead investigator in connection with the issues surrounding the AFC Championship Game of last year?

A. Yes, but I want to clarify your description with respect to "co-lead investigator." I was asked by Jeff Pash to become the independent investigator for the NFL with respect to what has become known as "Deflategate." That request was made on January 21st. A couple of days later, the NFL released a press release announcing that I had been hired and said -- and I don't have it in front of me; I apologize -- but it said in substance that I and Jeff Pash would be overseeing the investigation and I would be adding independence. I immediately telephoned Mr. Pash because I had not been told that we were going to be doing it jointly. And Mr. Pash explained to me that I would be the independent investigator, that he would be there to help facilitate on procedural-type issues and dealing with the Patriots, but that we were going to run it the same we had run the Dolphins investigation, which was I would be the independent investigator with my team. We would make -- "we" meaning Paul, Weiss, would make all of the decisions with respect to the investigation and that it would be my report and despite what had been said in that press release about his being my, quote, co- -- I don't even know if it uses those words, Jeff running with me, that we were going to run it like the Dolphins investigation.

Q. Okay. Let me ask you, you might as well get out a copy of your report.

A. Sure, I have a copy in front of me.

Q. Look at page 1 of your report, the Executive Summary.

A. Sure.

Q. And is it fair to say, Mr. Wells, that you stand by every word written in your report?

A. I hope so, yes, yeah.

Q. You try to have it written carefully and correctly, correct?

A. Yes, sir.

Q. So on the very first page 1 in the Executive Summary in the second paragraph, it says, "On January 23, 2015, the NFL publically announced that it had retained Theodore V. Wells, Jr. in the law firm Paul, Weiss, Rifkind, Wharton & Garrison ("Paul, Weiss") to conduct an investigation together with NFL Executive Vice President Jeff Pash into the footballs used by the Patriots used during the AFC Championship Game." And then it says, "The investigation was conducted pursuant." You see that?

A. Yes, sir.

Q. When you wrote this down, this was now when your report was issued, which was May 6, 2015, correct?

A. Yes.

Q. This is long after the NFL press release and after you had your conversation with Mr. Pash as to how the investigation was going to be conducted, correct?

A. Yes, sir.

Q. But you still thought it was appropriate, correct and accurate to, on the first page of your Executive Summary, describe the investigation as being one in which you were conducting an investigation together with Mr. Pash?

A. No. You totally misread the sentence. The sentence says that, "On January 23rd, the NFL announced." Now, that's the public statement. That's what that sentence is quoting. If you go down to the last sentence, "It was prepared entirely by the Paul, Weiss investigative team and presents the independent opinions of Mr. Wells and his colleagues." So there, I'm clarifying, despite what they announced in a piece of paper issued to the press on January 23rd, I'm saying to any reader of this report that this report was done by Paul, Weiss and it is the independent opinion of Mr. Wells and his colleagues. So I cut Mr. Pash out, though I have announced -- I'm sorry -- I've set forth in that first sentence what the NFL put out there.

Q. So when you prepared this report, did Mr. Pash see any drafts of this report before it was final?

A. I don't know whether that's privileged or what. You tell me.

MR. NASH: I would object to the extent that your answers would have to reveal any privileged communications. But otherwise, I think you can answer subject to that objection.

A. Okay. I don't want to waive anything, but the answer is yes.

Q. He did receive drafts of the report?

A. Yes, sir.

Q. Okay. Did he give you comments on the report before it was issued after seeing it either verbally or in writing?

MR. NASH: I think the best way -- I don't want to get into –

THE WITNESS: You guys tell me what to do.

MR. NASH: I think there's been a ruling about Mr. Wells's testimony. So to the extent that they are addressing Mr. Pash's role, I think the ruling had to do with whether Mr. Pash was substantially involved in the investigation or in the report itself. If they want to ask questions to that, they certainly can do so. But I would object on privileged grounds to questions about communications between Mr. Wells and Mr. Pash, the General Counsel of the NFL.

MR. KESSLER: Let me now state the following, if I can. Mr. Wells just testified he was independent and the NFL was not his client. Therefore, Mr.

Pash's communications with him could not be privileged under any possible application of the privilege, unless Mr. Wells wants to change his testimony and state that the NFL was his client in this matter, which would mean he is not independent.

MR. NASH: I object. You are mischaracterizing what he said.

MR. KESSLER: Okay.

Q. Was the NFL your client in this matter? Did you act as their lawyer when you did this investigation?

A. To my understanding, I was being hired by the NFL, and that's who pays my bills, to do what I have described as an independent investigation with respect to Deflategate. And what I mean by "an independent investigation," is that the opinions represented in this report and conclusions were those of myself and the Paul, Weiss team. Jeff Pash, and I don't think this waives any privilege, Jeff Pash did not attend any witness interviews. I did not deliberate or involve him on my deliberations with respect to my assessment of those interviews. Mr. Pash played no substantive role in the investigation itself. So I'm trying to give you facts without waiving.

Q. I will ask it this way.

A. Okay.

Q. Did you consider the NFL to be your client for purposes of the attorney-client privilege –

A. Yeah.

Q. -- with respect to the preparation of this investigative report?

A. Yes.

Q. Okay. That is fine. Now so, therefore, I will just ask you –

A. Okay.

Q. -- will you not, then, answer questions about what type of comments Mr. Pash made on your draft report before it was -- before it was issued?

A. I'm going to follow whatever -- it's not my privilege, sir. I just have to -- need to follow his advice.

MR. NASH: Yeah, I would object to the extent that I think Mr. Wells has already explained the role of Mr. Pash, the role of the Paul, Weiss firm and who the report was prepared by and who the conclusions -- who prepared the conclusions as well. To the extent that he wants to get further into communications, I think he's now trying to get into attorney-client privilege.

MR. LEVY: Without prejudice to the assertion of any privilege down the road, Mr. Wells can answer the question that was presented. The question was, did Mr. Pash give you any comments?

Q. Yes. Did he provide written or oral comments?

A. Yes.

Q. Okay. Were they written?

A. Not to my knowledge, but the truthful answer is he didn't provide any to me, okay.

Q. Did he provide it to another member of your team?

A. I believe so.

Q. Okay. And you don't know whether they were in writing or orally?

A. I do not.

Q. Do you know what the contents were of his comments?

A. I do not, except to say they couldn't have been that big a deal because I don't think I heard about them. But, you know, Mr. Pash is a very good Harvard-trained lawyer. If you give a Harvard-trained lawyer a report this thick, he's going to have some kind of comment. So I assume whatever it was, it was some kind of wordsmithing. I can tell you this without waiving any privilege. Mr. Pash -- Mr. Pash's comments did not affect, and from the time I gave him that -- whenever he got that draft of the report, did not impact in any substantive fashion the conclusions with respect to my findings with respect to violations by the Patriots or violations by Mr. Brady, nothing. You know, there was no substantive change.

Q. Mr. Wells, I assume that you are not the first drafter of this report, correct? One of your colleagues would have prepared the first draft and you would have reviewed it; is that fair?

A. I think that's privileged, but I will answer as long as it's not a waiver, yes.

Q. Okay. Would your principal colleague on this case be Mr. Lorin Reisner who is seated over there?

A. Correct.

Q. Now, Mr. Reisner, you observed, was representing the NFL and cross-examining Mr. Brady and Mr. Snyder in this proceeding; is that correct?

A. That is -- I saw it. You saw it.

Q. Okay. So, and Mr. Reisner was one of the principal lawyers working with you on this independent investigation, right?

A. If you read the report, it basically says that.

Q. So is it fair to say Mr. Reisner -- is Paul, Weiss also being compensated for representing the NFL in this hearing, conducting cross-examination? Have they been hired as NFL counsel for that purpose?

A. As I understand it, again, if I can answer without waiving any privilege, in terms of cross-examining both the experts and cross-examining Mr. Brady since we had already examined him and done the work, everybody thought it would be more efficient –

MR. NASH: I am going to stop you right there, Mr. Wells. I don't think this is an appropriate line of questioning and we are now getting into privilege. And I have to say it also isn't relevant to any issue in Mr. Brady's appeal.

MR. LEVY: Sustained.

MR. KESSLER: Okay. I would ask you to, just for the record, my observation that the statement that the Paul, Weiss firm is independent is clearly not correct. We now have testimony that they represented the NFL in this proceeding. They viewed the NFL as their client.

Q. I will just ask one more question about this.

A. Sure.

Q. Do you agree, Mr. Wells, as an attorney, that you, when you have a client or any client, the NFL, anyone else –

A. Sure.

Q. -- you have a duty under the ethical rules to zealously advocate and advance the interest of that client? Is that fair, under the ethical rules?

MR. NASH: Objection. We are now getting into arguments.

MR. LEVY: Sustained.

THE WITNESS: Okay.

Q. Let's move on to another subject. Now, going back to that same first page of your report, page 1, you say, "The investigation was conducted pursuant to the policy on integrity of the game and enforcement of competitive rules." Do you see that?

A. Yes.

Q. To your knowledge, that's the only policy that you were told about that you were conducting your investigation pursuant, correct?

A. That is correct.

Q. Okay. Now, at the time you did this report, did you have any knowledge or did you determine whether or not that policy was ever given out to players?

A. I have no knowledge one way or the other.

Q. Did you learn for the first time today at this hearing that it was not given out to players?

A. I think -- I think I heard something to that effect.

Q. Today?

A. In terms of whatever knowledge I have is what I heard today.

Q. Today? And it was prior to today and certainly at the time you issued this report you didn't know one way or another whether that policy was something given out to players?

A. That is correct.

Q. Now, with respect to your finding that Mr. Brady -- let's go to a specific finding. Let's look at, I am going to your Executive Summary. Let's go to your findings with respect to Mr. Brady.

A. Page 2?

Q. Page 2. So on page 2 of the report –

A. Second paragraph.

Q. -- it says the following. You say, "Based on the evidence, it also was our view that it was more probable than not that Tom Brady, the quarterback for the Patriots, was at least generally aware of the inappropriate activities of McNally and Jastremski involving the release of air from Patriots game balls." Is that a fair summary of what you concluded with respect to Mr. Brady that you put here?

A. Yes, just what I wrote.

Q. Okay. Now, am I correct that you don't make any finding in the report that Mr. Brady participated himself in engaging in any activities to deflate footballs, right? You don't make such a finding?

A. Well, what I say in the report is that, one, I believe Mr. Brady was generally aware of the activities of Jastremski and McNally. I also say in the report that, based on my personal observations of Jastremski and McNally, both of whom we interviewed, I do not believe that these two gentlemen would have engaged in their deflation activities without -- I may use the word knowledge and awareness of Mr. Brady. I'm not sure if those are the exact words, but that's the substance of what I say in the report.

Q. Okay. But you don't make any finding that, if you listen to my specific question –

A. Sure, okay.

Q. -- that it is more probable than not based on the evidence that Mr. Brady himself directed them to deflate the ball in that game, correct? You don't make such a finding here?

A. I'm hesitating about the word "direct," because what I do say in the report is I don't think they would have done it without his knowledge and awareness. Now, but I don't have a phrase, you are correct, where I say he directed them. What I say is I believe that they would not have done it unless they believed he wanted it done in substance.

Q. And that would apply even if he never told them to do it, even if he never authorized them to do it, even if he never said do it? What you were stating there is you believe that because he was Tom Brady, okay, that they would not have done something unless they thought it would be something he would like or want, right?

A. No.

Q. Isn't that fair to what you concluded?

A. No, no, no, that goes way too far in the sense that you are not looking at the evidence that I cite. For example, one of the core pieces of evidence that we cite against Mr. Brady is the text message where McNally says, "Fuck Tom." And Jastremski says in substance, "He asked about you yesterday. He said it must be a lot of stress getting the balls done." So that message we interpret in the report to mean that Tom Brady actually had a conversation with Jastremski and during that conversation, he actually asked about McNally and the statement was made by Brady that McNally must have a lot of stress getting them done, which we interpret to mean getting the balls deflated. So that's direct evidence of knowledge and involvement.

Q. That's the Jets game when those communications took place, right?

A. That's correct.

Q. Were the balls deflated in the Jets game or inflated?

A. In that particular situation, what they were -- what they were discussing was the inflation of the balls in the Jets game, but you have to step back in terms of how we viewed the evidence. Mr. McNally was a locker room attendant. Mr. McNally had no duties involving inflation or deflation of balls. Mr. McNally's job was to care for the referees. In fact, I'm not sure if we say it in the report, but the referees actually would get together and put together tips to give Mr. McNally at the end of the game. They only tipped two people, the bus driver and the locker room attendant. So Mr. McNally is somebody who Mr. Brady said he didn't even know, who should not have had anything to do with balls, yet Mr. Brady is saying that Mr. McNally must have a lot of stress getting them done, which as I said, we interpret to mean deflation, even though it was in the context, and you are correct, of the Jets game.

Q. Even though it was all about inflation, you interpret it to be about deflation?

A. That's correct, sir.

Q. And did you also look at the e-mail where –

A. E-mail or text?

Q. The e-mail. I will show you the e-mail. This is on page 86 of your report -- the text; I'm sorry –

A. I was just trying to make sure.

Q. -- where he said –

A. Hold on.

COMMISSIONER GOODELL: 86, did you say?

MR. KESSLER: Yes, 86. A. You just threw me off when you said "e-mail."

Q. Sorry. Okay, the text, when he's writing to his fiancé Panda and he says, "I just mentioned some of the balls. They are supposed to be 13. They were, like, 16." Do you see that?

A. Yes.

Q. Now, 13 would be within the legal limit, right?

A. Yes.

Q. So what he was saying here, he thought the balls were supposed to be 13, not lower than the legal limit? That's what he wrote, right?

A. That's what he wrote.

Q. Right. Do you have any reason to think why he would lie to his fiancé about this subject after the Jets game? What would be his motive?

A. I didn't say he lied to his fiancé.

Q. Okay. So then, you believe that Mr. Jastremski truthfully told his fiancé that he was trying to get the balls to 13 and they came out 16, right? That was a truthful statement, you believe?

A. Yes.

Q. Okay. And if he was trying to get them to 13, that was not a deflation below the limit, was it?

A. No.

Q. Okay, thank you. Now, Mr. Wells, how much was Paul, Weiss paid to do this report?

MR. NASH: Objection as to privilege and relevance. There is no question that they were paid. I don't see how –

MR. KESSLER: Definitely not privileged.

MR. NASH: I don't see how it bears on any issue relevant to Mr. Brady's appeal.

MR. LEVY: I am going to allow it.

Q. How much were you paid?

A. I don't know. The "paid" question is interesting.

Q. Billed, I will go with billed. How much was billed?

A. For the report, through May 6th, it's somewhere in the area -- and I'm not sure the bill was out, but it's going to be around somewhere in the range of 2.5 to 3 million.

Q. And you would be paid additional amounts for the work that Mr. Reisner is doing today or others assisting the NFL? That would be additional bills, right?

A. I hope so.

Q. Yes. By the way, are you billing for your testimony today as a witness?

A. I don't know. I haven't broached that.

Q. Okay. Now, let me ask you next when you were retaining Exponent in connection with this matter, did you have discussions with other experts before you retained Exponent?

A. Yes.

Q. Okay. And how many experts did you consider?

A. Well, what happened was as follows. Right after I was retained, there started to be a lot of publicity about the Ideal Gas Law. And I started getting parroted with articles about the Ideal Gas Law, so it was clear I needed to hire experts preferably physicists. We reached out to Columbia University. Columbia has a very respected Physics Department. It was close, in close proximity to Paul, Weiss. So our hope at that time was that we could find somebody at Columbia. Mr. Reisner sent an e-mail to the Physics Department at Columbia asking if they could help us, and I think he may have also talked to somebody. And he told them this is confidential. To our shock, after he contacted Columbia's Physics Department, there was an article, either the next day or the day after in the New York Times that Paul,

Weiss had reached out to the Columbia Physics Department. And we were, to say, the least outraged that we had reached out in what we thought was a confidential contact and then it was published in the New York Times. What happened, so that disqualified Columbia. Columbia was where we wanted to go. What happened next is that a professor from Columbia e-mailed Mr. Reisner maybe the next day, and the professor said that he understood we were looking for experts in physics and he recommended Exponent. And he said that Exponent was where many of Columbia's graduates who wanted not to go the academic route would go and work and he thought it was a first-class outfit and that that's who we should talk to. And he actually had in the e-mail, I think, Gabe's name, and we contacted him. So that's how -- so we get to Exponent through the recommendation of Columbia. Now, at the same time, because we don't know whether Exponent is going to work out, we contact the Princeton Physics Department. And they recommend that we should talk to Dr. Marlow. So at this juncture, we scheduled two interviews. We schedule an interview with Exponent and we schedule an interview with Dr. Marlow. And the fact that the people in the Physics Department at Columbia had leaked to The Times had us a little nervous about going the academic route. So we were somewhat more attracted maybe going to a traditional

consulting firm. We met, and I'm not sure what order, but it was within a day of each, we met with each of them separately. I thought Exponent had the resources, because we thought we would need testing, not only of the gauges, and we didn't know a lot. You know, this is in the early days. This is first few days. But we knew we had to test these gauges because the first question is, do the gauges work? Are they reliable? We didn't know if there was impact of -- on the footballs of just playing in the game, whether it's pounding, a 300-pound lineman falls on the ball or something. So we knew we needed people with resources to do testing. So we meet with Exponent and we liked -- and we liked them. And then we met the next day with Dr. Marlow and we liked him. But we were very concerned because of what happened with Columbia about doing any testing at Princeton because Dr. Marlow said if we wanted to do the tests in the Princeton lab, because of federal regulations or what have you, they have a lot of students and they couldn't guarantee confidentiality. So again, we were back into the academic world and concerned that we are going to have leaks. What we ultimately decided to do was to hire both. We hired Exponent to be the lead expert in terms of doing the tests that needed to be done and advising us on how to look at this data. And we hired Dr. Marlow as our consultant and his job was to watch Exponent. So we kind of had what I will call belt and suspenders. We have got a firm that we believed had the resources to do the testing, and we thought we would need physicists and engineers and statisticians, but also a lot of equipment that you might not have in an academic setting. And we wanted privacy, okay, we didn't want leaks. We were very conscious. We did not want leaks. So we get Dr. Marlow. Like I said, his job is to really watch. He's supposed to work with Exponent, but he's supposed to -- he's not doing testing. He is listening to their work plan. He's listening to, you know, their ideas. He's running numbers. They are going to run numbers, but he's my eyes and ears so I got to double-check. And one other thing I want to say is that I told them both in the interview before I even hired them, I said what this job involves is similar to being a court-appointed expert. I said you should view us like a judge or a court that's hiring an expert. I said we have no dog in this race. All we want to know is how to look at this data. That's the job. And we have no thesis. It's not like a normal, in the world we live in, Mr. Kessler, where you and I represent a client and we have got a particular position, be it the plaintiff or the defendant, and you got a thesis and you want an expert to know whether or not you can support that. We said we don't care about the outcome at all. We just want objective science, and understand that. So those, we told them those were the terms if they wanted to come on board. And they were both fine with that. So that's a long-winded way of how we got to Exponent.

Q. Is it fair to say, Mr. Wells, that Paul, Weiss is a law firm, not a law firm of statisticians or physicists or scientists? Is that fair to say on the whole?

A. That is true, but I will tell you we are blessed with such talent that we ended up finding that we had a Ph.D. physicist among our associates and we added that young man to the team. But I was shocked to find out that we had such a person.

Q. Let me ask the question differently.

A. Your answer is yes.

Q. Did you rely upon Exponent and Dr. Marlow to reach whatever testing, scientific, statistical conclusions were presented?

A. Yes.

Q. And so Paul, Weiss didn't independently make any scientific testing, statistical conclusions on its own, correct?

A. That is correct.

Q. Okay. And is it fair, then, that if for whatever reason it was concluded that Exponent's work was not a basis for reliable conclusions here, that then there would be no scientific conclusions that are reliable in your report? In other words, you don't have any other source of reliable evidence about the balls other than what you claim is done by Exponent as supervised by Dr. Marlow; is that correct?

A. I have no other source; that is correct.

Q. Right.

A. My only hesitancy about adopting your question in full is if it was established there was a mistake in some small area and it didn't impact the overall conclusion, that wouldn't necessarily invalidate the entire analysis. But I think we are on the same page.

Q. If it was something sufficient to render it unreliable, then there would be no reliable scientific findings here?

A. Yeah, I do not have any independent scientific analysis within my team or somewhere else. You are correct.

Q. Okay. Now, Dr. Marlow's specialty is theoretical physics; is that correct?

A. That's my understanding.

Q. He is not an expert statistician, right?

A. No, but as part of the -- well, I don't know that. I don't want to say that he's not an expert statistician because I do not know. I know Exponent, we have a professor of statistics with a Ph.D. who is a core part of our team who is here to testify today.

Q. You didn't look to Dr. Marlow to provide this statistical expertise?

A. No.

Q. That was not why he was hired by you?

A. No, no. That would be totally incorrect. The statistical work in the early days, Dr. Marlow from my personal observations, participated fully because - - because the way we did it, I just forget what page it was on (perusing). The way we approached it, Mr. Kessler, was as follows. You know, the first question we asked just looking at the raw numbers, was whether or not there was a difference. If you just looked at the numbers, it looks like the Patriots' balls drop more than the Colts. And then the question is, is that drop as a result of chance or something else? And so that was the question about statistical significance, just looking at the raw numbers. Because if they had told us it's just chance, maybe it's not there and you don't spend a lot more money. And so that was kind of the first look-see just looking at the raw numbers. And I remember right after we hired Dr. Marlow, he was on the phone with me giving me his views of the statistics. So that's why I say he was fairly active in those early discussions and throughout the entire representation. Dr. Marlow was, from my observation, very much into the statistics.

Q. Mr. Wells, you came to learn from Exponent and Dr. Marlow that there were many unknowns that could affect the application of the Ideal Gas Law to the footballs that were tested during the AFC Championship Game; is that fair?

A. I think the answer is yes. And let me explain why I'm hesitating, Mr. Kessler. The application of the Ideal Gas Law is, in and of itself is, it's kind of nuanced in the sense that the Ideal Gas Law is a theoretical concept that predicts the impact of temperature change on pressure. And it's a mathematical formula that you need a whole lot of things to be satisfied and in place for it to work. So that, the Ideal Gas Law was out there.

Q. Let me ask you differently.

A. Okay.

Q. Let me ask you this way. You came to learn that no one ever recorded the precise time that each of the balls were tested at halftime, correct?

A. I didn't need the experts for that.

Q. You learned that?

A. I learned that from the interviews.

Q. You came to learn that no one recorded the temperature inside the clubhouse at the time that the balls were tested at halftime, correct?

A. Correct.

Q. You came to learn that no one even specified whether or not the -- wrote down and specified whether the Colts' balls were tested after or before the Patriots' balls were reinflated? It was uncertain about that, correct?

A. Correct.

Q. Okay. You came to learn that no one indicated whether the balls were wet or dry when they were tested?

A. Correct. I don't have any data.

Q. Right.

A. And again, I have different witnesses who have different recollections. But I don't have any written documentation about what people saw at that moment in time, other than the raw data.

Q. And at all the points I'm covering, if you have different witnesses, they have different recollections because that's why you wrote it was uncertain?

A. That's correct.

Q. Because the recollections were different?

A. That's correct. When I had sufficient -- when I thought the evidence was sufficiently clear, we made a finding –

Q. Right.

A. -- or we stated this is the facts. When I thought there was uncertainty and I wasn't willing to make a finding, I stated with clarity that there was uncertainty.

Q. So there was, I think you wrote in your report that there was uncertainty about the time. There was uncertainty about the temperature. There was uncertainty about the order of the tests. There was uncertainty about the wetness or dryness. And you also came to learn all those factors could affect a determination as to whether the Patriots' measurements could have been due to natural forces or not? You came to learn that, correct?

A. Yeah. And, in fact, one of the things, we have had a lot of testimony about it today was the impact of timing within the locker room at halftime. And just what Dr. Dean Snyder was discussing, but -- but when we first get into the case, we haven't focused on that yet. All these articles I'm getting at the beginning of the case on the Ideal Gas Law are based on the assumption that they measured the balls in the warm locker room. They have taken them out to the field where it's, like, 48 or 50 degrees. And the story kind of ends. Nobody is really focused yet that when they came in at halftime and they brought the balls back into the room, that when they came from the cold back into the hot, the warmer room, the pressure started to increase as they heated up. And really, Exponent was the expert that really focused on that. And that's why I discussed in such detail in the report, because they are the ones that focused on that issue which really no one, you know, to my knowledge, had. And I wasn't even sensitive to it.

Q. And Mr. Wells, another point you came to as being uncertainty, you wrote was whether or not when the initial testing was done before the game, whether that was done by the logo gauge or the non-logo gauge, right? You concluded that was uncertain?

A. No, no. I made an express finding and so did the -- the experts made a finding and I -- and when I say "I," I mean collective "I," my team, we made an express finding that the non-logo gauge is the gauge that was used by Walt Anderson when he tested the balls. That is an express finding in the report.

Q. Now, Mr. Anderson was interviewed by you, correct?

A. Yes, sir.

Q. And he said his best recollection was that it was the logo gauge, correct?

A. That's absolutely correct.

Q. So you have decided to conclude something opposite to the best recollection of the only witness you have as to which gauge was used, right?

A. Well, no. When you say "the only witness, I have three witnesses as to whether the ball started. Because that's the issue. Let's talk about the -- let's forget people for a minute. The issue is where did the balls start in the locker room before they went outside? Because what we are trying to measure, we are trying to measure the beginning pressure from where they started in the locker room pre-game, and then the balls go outside. They deflate with the cold. Then they come back into the room at halftime and they start to slowly rise. And those measurements that Mr. Prioleau and Mr. Blakeman took, now you are trying to compare what was the starting psi and where was it at halftime? So that's the exercise, okay. So the question, the relevancy of non-logo, logo, is really to ask your question, where did the balls start? Now, the evidence we have is that the Patriots were emphatic with us that they set their balls at 12.5 or 12.6. That testimony came from Mr. Jastremski and it also came from Mr. Brady. Our balls are coming in at 12.5 or 12.6. So that's the Patriots. So I assume for the AFC Championship Game, the Patriots are set. They know where they are setting their balls. They have told me they are 12.5, 12.6. We then go interview the Colts. The Colts say their balls are at 13, maybe 12.95, maybe 13.1, but that's their number. But they are 13. And they are emphatic. You have two witnesses, the Colts at 13, Patriots at 12.5. And let's just forget Walt Anderson existed. If he disappeared from the face of the earth, I would have written a report that said these balls started at 12.5 and 13 because that's what the Patriots told me and that's what the Colts told me. Now, what happened next is Walt Anderson actually gauged the balls. And Walt Anderson said when he gauged the balls, they measured Patriots 12.5, may have been a couple, two exceptions, and Colts at 13. So Walt Anderson without talking to the Patriots, talking to the Colts, has said what he observed is just what the Patriots said and what the Colts said. Now, how do you get to what gauge he used? The only way Walt Anderson could get to 12.5 for the Patriots and 13 for the Colts is if he used the non-logo gauge.

And that is because the logo gauge always reads .3 to .4 higher. It is consistent. That gauge, it may read high, but we tested it hundreds of times. It always reads .3 to .4. It's like I tell people I have a scale in my house.

Q. Mr. Wells, can I break in to ask a question here. I know you would like to make a speech about your report, but I would like to ask a question.

MR. LEVY: Why don't we let him finish.

MR. KESSLER: It wasn't even the question.

MR. NASH: It was.

A. I have a scale in my house. I have two scales. One scale reads the same as the calibrated scale at the gym. I know that's the perfect scale. I have another scale that always reads three pounds lighter. I love that scale. But that scale is as calibrated as the good one. You know why? It's consistently three pounds under. That's how -- that's how the logo gauge is. It always is reading high. And the only way you could get those measurements where Walt says he saw just what the Patriots saw and what the Colts saw is with the non-logo gauge. And that's why we made that finding. Now, maybe lightning could strike and both the Colts and the Patriots also had a gauge that just happened to be out of whack like the logo gauge. I rejected that.

MR. LEVY: Why don't you ask another question.

Q. Okay, Mr. Wells, I know you have been in my shoes, okay.

A. Okay.

Q. Try to bear with me and answer my questions.

A. I just haven't been in this chair. This is kind of interesting.

MR. NASH: You asked for it.

Q. So my question is very specific. I am going to try to be very specific. You just testified that you never found the Patriots gauge, right? You now that?

A. That is correct.

Q. You never found the Colts gauge, correct?

A. That it correct.

Q. So as you are sitting here, you have no idea whether the Patriots and the Colts gauge would read exactly like the logo gauge or the non-logo gauge? You have no basis for knowing one way other the another?

A. In terms of the actual gauge, you are absolutely correct. I had to make a judgment.

Q. So bear with me.

A. Okay.

Q. If their gauges read like the logo gauges because they were older gauges that were given by Wilson and may have looked just like the logo gauge, then they might read like the logo gauge if that was true?

A. That's what I mean if lightning were to strike and what you would have to have happen in terms of my analysis, you would have to have had both teams for that Championship Game had gauges that were .3 to .4 off and then that all flowed into Walt Anderson using the logo gauge which was .3 to .4 off. And I don't think that happened and that's what I ruled. I think what I ruled is totally -- not only do I think it's correct, I think it's reasonable.

Q. Now let's talk about what else is here to make lightning strike. The Patriots didn't tell you -- you mentioned you had three sources. The Patriots didn't say anything about what gauge Mr. Anderson used, right? They didn't know what gauge he used?

A. Correct.

Q. The Colts didn't tell you anything about what gauge he used, correct?

A. Correct.

Q. The only person who told you anything about which gauge he used is Mr. Anderson?

A. Correct.

Q. Who said his best recollection was it was the logo gauge, direct?

A. Correct, but he also said it was possible he was mistaken.

Q. As you know as a lawyer, witnesses will say anything is possible?

A. Not Walt Anderson. You need to meet him. You should call him.

Q. He maintained with you he really thought it was the logo gauge?

A. But he also maintained that he could have been wrong.

Q. Now, let me direct your attention to NFL Exhibit 14.

A. I don't have it. I don't have it, sir.

Q. You don't have that?

A. Unless somebody gives it to me.

MR. NASH: I will get you one.

MR. KESSLER: I'm sorry; I apologize.

THE WITNESS: This is the whole book?

MR. NASH: That's the binder. It's 14.

A. I'm sorry; I didn't have it. Okay, go ahead.

Q. Take a look at page 260.

A. 260?

Q. Do you recognize these were the notes that were taken, this whole exhibit, at the various testing at the halftime and the post-game the day of the game? Do you recognize that that's what these notes are?

A. But just help me. Are these -- is this what is taken at the end of the game?

Q. Well, it's all of it. What's taken on page –

A. Page 260.

Q. -- page 260, as you can see, has four and four. So this would have been at the end of the game?

A. Okay, that's what I wanted clarification. I agree these are the notes taken at the end of the game.

Q. Okay. And I will show you the other pages, too.

A. Okay, okay.

Q. So at the top, it's written when it says, "Ending number 1," okay.

A. Right.

Q. It says, "JJ gauge, red Wilson sticker." Do you see that?

A. Yes.

Q. You know who JJ is?

A. Yeah, Jastremski.

Q. Okay. So somebody thought the gauge used by Indianapolis was the same as JJ's gauge, Mr. Jastremski's missing gauge, correct?

A. Yeah. Let me tell you what I recollect happening. These notes are made by Mr. Farley. Mr. Farley wrote things on these documents after they were signed. So the one I know -- I don't have an express recollection about 260. The same information, though, is -- he writes on 2 –

Q. 56?

A. -- 56.

Q. Yes. A. And this is in the report. I just don't think we addressed 260. But on 256, if you look at it, it says, I think it says, "Belonged to JJ." Do you see that?

Q. Yes.

A. He wrote that days later because Robyn Glaser, a lawyer for the New England Patriots, told him that that was JJ's gauge. And then he wrote it there. And when we questioned him, we said, Where did this come from and when? He said, This is what Ms. Glaser told me and we talked to her and she is confused, so that's how it got there. It was after the fact and it came from

Robyn Glaser. And I think we explained that in a footnote in the report, if my recollection is correct.

Q. Take a look at page -- take a look the Exponent report for a second, which is NFLPA Exhibit 8, if it's separate. Take a look at page Roman IX, the Executive Summary. It says in the second paragraph, "We have been told by Paul, Weiss that there remains some uncertainty as to which of the two gauges was used prior to the game." Do you see that?

A. Yes.

Q. Is that true?

A. You know that is true that I told them that, but ultimately, in the report itself, I make an express finding that the non-logo gauge was used. And, in fact, also in the Exponent report, they make the finding. But in terms of my role as the ultimate finder of fact, I made a ruling that I believe is absolutely correct based on the evidence that the non-logo gauge is the one that was used by Walt Anderson.

Q. Well, when did you tell them there was some uncertainty remaining?

A. At the beginning of the case because I didn't know, okay. We have uncertainty. They did one. They go out and buy hundreds of gauges and they do not only what they call exemplars, they take the logo gauge and the non-logo gauge. The right question to ask is whether both of these gauges, do they work, are they reliable and are they consistent? So they run the test on the non-logo gauge and they find that that gauge is almost perfectly calibrated. It works over hundreds of tests. It works close to what they call the master gauge. They have a master perfectly-calibrated gauge.

Q. So your testimony, I just want to understand, is that the Exponent report was issued the same day as your report, correct?

A. Yes, sir.

Q. And despite that fact, they wrote on that day that there was some uncertainty still about which gauge was used. You are saying they were wrong? There was no longer any uncertainty --

A. No, no, sir.

Q. -- the date their report was issued?

A. I said ultimately I made a finding in the report.

Q. Did that resolve the uncertainty?

A. Well, what I'm saying to the public, anybody that reads this report, you will see I say clearly, because I try to be transparent about what all the witnesses said. So I say Walt Anderson says it is his best recollection that he used the logo gauge. We then did tests that showed that there is consistent uptick on the logo gauge of .3 to .4. The scientists, the Exponent people say they believe based on their scientific tests that the non-logo gauge was used. I have a ruling that says there's uncertainty, but I am making a ruling as a finder of fact, because that's my job as the judge, that it's more probable than not that the non-logo gauge was used by Walt Anderson. That is set forth in those words or substance in both my report and in the Exponent report.

Q. Okay. So in your role as the judge, okay, you concluded that you were going to reject as a finder of fact Mr. Anderson's best recollection that he used the logo gauge, correct?

A. Not only did I reject it, I first said this is what he says and this is why I am rejecting it. And I set it out so everybody can see it. Look, this is no different than a case where somebody has a recollection of X happening and then you play a tape and the tape says Y happened. Now, the person could keep saying, well, darn it, I remember it was X. But the people are going to go with the tape. I went with the science and the logic that I had three data points. And that's what I based my decision on. It is a totally reasonable and, I think, correct decision.

Q. Okay. I'm not going to quarrel with you right now about what you did. I just want to confirm, so in addition to Mr. Anderson, there are a number of other testimony from people who you rejected in your conclusions in this case, correct?

A. You have to give me specifics.

Q. I am going to give you specifics.

A. Okay.

Q. You rejected the testimony of Mr. Brady that he knew nothing about the ball deflation in the AFC Championship Game, right? You rejected that?

A. I did reject it based on my assessment of his credibility and his refusal or decision not to give me what I requested in terms of responsive documents. And that decision, so we can all be clear and I will say it to Mr. Brady, in my almost 40 years of practice, I think that was one of the most ill-advised decisions I have ever seen because it hurt how I viewed his credibility.

Q. If he had given you that, you would have accepted his statement?

A. I do not know. I can't go back in a time machine, but I will say this. It hurt my assessment of his credibility for him to begin his interview by telling me he declined to give me the documents. And I want to say this. At that time, neither his lawyer nor Mr. Brady gave me any reason other than to say, "We respectfully." They were respectful. They said, "We respectfully decline." There wasn't anything about the Union or it wasn't anything, This was what my lawyer told me and I am going to follow my lawyer's advice. I was given no explanation other than, "We respectfully decline." And I did, I walked Mr. Brady through this request in front of his agents and lawyers. So I understood that he understood what I was asking for and they were declining.

Q. Did his agents or lawyer ask you what the authority was for you asking for those types of information?

A. No, that's not my recollection. They asked the authority for him to do the interview, I think.

Q. You don't recall them asking for the authority to demand e-mails or cell phones or anything like that?

A. My recollection, there's e-mail. The e-mail says what it says. But I thought the e-mails said authority to conduct the interview, but we ought to grab the e-mail.

Q. We will come back to that. Let me just go through where I wanted to go, other people you rejected. You rejected Mr. Brady as we just said. You rejected Mr. Anderson. You rejected Mr. Jastremski and Mr. McNally who denied any knowledge of any deflation on the AFC Championship Game, right? You rejected the two of them?

A. Yeah, because I did not think they were being candid.

Q. Okay. I just want to go through the various people who you rejected. In addition, do you recall, I think you already mentioned you rejected what Farley wrote down that it was Mr. Jastremski's gauge? You concluded that was not correct?

A. No. Mr. Farley told me that he wrote it down after the fact and Robyn Glaser confirmed that she told that to Farley and it was just a mixup. It wasn't a question of rejecting it. It was a question of when I looked this, the right question to ask was that statement put on there contemporaneously with the other stuff? Was it done on the night of January the 18th? Well, Mr. Farley said no, he wrote that days later and he wrote it because Ms. Glazer said it. So I actually accepted what Mr. Farley told me what happened.

Q. Do you recall that there was someone you interviewed who was named Rita Callendar?

A. I'm not sure. Somebody on the team may have.

Q. She worked for Team Ops, a security guest services company who worked for the Patriots.

A. Oh, she was the person that stood outside one of the locker rooms, right. Now I recall her. Go ahead.

Q. And Ms. Callendar told you that she estimated about 50 percent of the time, Mr. McNally took the balls out by himself to the field. Do you recall that?

A. Yes.

Q. And you got the same testimony from Mr. Paul Galanis who was stationed just outside the entrance to the Patriots locker room who said it was routine for McNally to walk to the field with the game balls unaccompanied, correct?

A. Correct.

Q. And you rejected their interviews with you, correct? You rejected that testimony as being inaccurate?

A. I don't think so. Could you show me where I do that?

Q. Well, didn't you conclude that it departed from some established protocol for McNally to take the balls by himself to the field and this was a fact that you relied upon?

A. My recollection is what we said is that based on our interviews of the referees, that Mr. McNally was either to take the balls out with the refs as they walked out of the locker room or if he was going by himself, he had to get permission first. That is what my recollection of the report is. And I don't think -- I don't think the report has any rejection of their testimony. And if it does, I will stand corrected if you show it to me.

Q. So you do accept the fact that Mr. McNally might routinely take the balls out by himself if he had permission?

A. I am just quarreling over the word "routinely." What we ruled and found in the report in terms of what was standard operating procedure based on the referees and those are the people we based it on, is that he had to get permission if he was going out by himself.

Q. But you are not saying you don't believe the people standing outside the door who said to them it was routine or half the time that he would go with the balls himself to the field?

A. I didn't feel I needed to reach a conclusion on that because there was no question that he had not gotten permission that day and that he had broken protocol. And I didn't need to drill down and decide when he walked down the hall 50 percent of the time by himself or was this person right or that person right. What I ruled was that he left without permission and that he broke protocol and didn't really turn on what those two individuals were saying. So I didn't have to make a judgment about them.

Q. Let me ask you this. You indicated in your report and at your press conference that you found that there was no bias by NFL or by the NFL in how it conducted the testing; is that correct?

A. That is correct.

Q. Okay. But you did not interview Commissioner Goodell in connection with that, correct?

A. To my knowledge, as I sit here, I don't think Commissioner Goodell had anything to do with the testing.

Q. Did you interview Jeff Pash in connection with that, your co-lead investigator, whatever his role was?

A. To my knowledge -- you are asking me to do with the testing?

Q. Yes.

A. To my knowledge, Mr. Pash had nothing to do with the testing.

Q. Did you interview Mr. Vincent?

A. Yes. I interviewed all the people who were there at the game.

Q. Did you ask them to give you e-mails and text messages, Mr. Vincent or the other NFL officials who were there? Were they asked to give you e-mails and text messages concerning the game-day activities on what happened with the Colts?

A. I do not think so.

Q. Okay. Did you ask anyone else except Mr. Brady, Mr. McNally and Mr. Jastremski and Mr. Schoenfeld to give you text messages or e-mails in connection with your investigation?

A. I asked people at the Patriots and I'm not -- I'm not sure in terms of anybody else. I'm just not sure as I sit here. But we can find out. I want you to have the answer.

Q. Did you ask anyone at the NFL for any of -- anyone who is employed by the NFL for e-mails or text messages to your knowledge in connection with this investigation?

A. I do not recall. But again, we can find out. I will get you an answer for the record.

Q. With respect to the request made to Mr. Brady –

A. Yes, sir.

Q. -- did you ever, yourself, determine whether you had the authority under any applicable policy to ask Mr. Brady to require him to turn over his e-mails or text messages? Did you ever look independently into that issue?

A. I can tell you when I did the Miami Dolphins investigation and I sat with either Ms. McPhee or Ned Ehrlich, I asked people for their phones, players, and they gave me the phones.

Q. When you did the Miami Dolphins investigation, was that under the policy that you cited here on competitive integrity?

A. No.

Q. Okay. And had you ever done an investigation previously under the privilege integrity policy?

A. No, sir.

Q. Okay. And would you agree with me that if that policy was not directed to players, that policy might not then impose any duties on players to cooperate or not? You haven't looked into that, right?

A. I haven't looked into it, but what I will say is Mr. Brady's agents at no time told me that was an issue, because if they had told me it was an issue, we would have had a discussion. Maybe I would have called Ms. McPhee. Maybe I would have called Mr. Ehrlich. I would have called somebody because I will tell you I did not -- I wanted -- I did not want Mr. Brady in a position where I would have to write that he didn't cooperate or when I interviewed him -- everybody said the guy was a great guy. Everybody said he was a great guy, great reputation. And I wanted to interview him without this cloud hanging over him, okay? And that's why I told Mr. Yee, I will take your word. You do the search and I will take your word.

Q. Now, let me ask you this. When were you retained in connection with this matter? Do you remember when?

A. Yeah, no, I know I was an hour away from surgery. January 21st, they called me. I was ready to get my knee operated on at 7:00 and they called me, like, at 5:00 or 5:30.

Q. Did you not contact Mr. Brady or his representatives to make any kind of requests for e-mails or phone records or text messages until February 28; is that correct?

A. That is correct. But I had given -- my recollection, we had given it earlier to Mr. Goldberg and then what Mr. Goldberg said -- Mr. Goldberg was --

Q. Who is he?

A. Mr. Goldberg is a lawyer for the Patriots who sat in on every interview, including Mr. Brady's. So I'm dealing with Mr. Goldberg. At some point, Mr. Goldberg tells me -- and I think I have given Mr. Goldberg at that time a written request for Mr. Brady's phone stuff. Mr. Goldberg says the agents are going to deal with it. You got to deal with his agents directly. He says, I'm out of it now. So then we write -- we take what we had already given Mr. Goldberg and we write it to Mr. Yee. So that's what happened.

Q. At no time did Mr. Goldberg ever tell you he represented Tom Brady, did he?

A. Mr. Goldberg, if you talked to him, said he represented everybody at the Patriots. That was how he held himself out. But then he made himself clear, with respect to Mr. Brady, I was going to have to deal with the agents. I mean, he made that clear.

Q. I just have some final questions for you, Mr. Wells. Would you agree that there were no established protocols that you found in the League to collect all the data that you would have liked to have to determine whether or not a drop in ball pressure was due to natural forces or some tampering? There was just no protocols to collect that, right?

A. I told you I agree. What I found in interviewing referees and just witnesses in general is that there was no appreciation for the Ideal Gas Law and the possible impact that that might have. And so people didn't appreciate that if you measured a ball in a hot locker room and then took it out to a cold field, you have automatic drop. Now, the Patriots had figured that out, okay. Mr. Jastremski had figured that out because he talks about it in one of his texts. But again, that didn't have anything to do in terms of procedures. You are correct, there were no procedures.

Q. Okay. And finally, there are many times when the Exponent report indicates that they've heard from Paul, Weiss that certain factors are unknown or uncertain, correct?

A. Sure, yes.

Q. And you would agree with me the fact that there were these unknowns is because there weren't these procedures to provide that information? Otherwise they would be certain, right?

A. That is -- that is absolutely correct. I mean, sometimes people break procedures, but you are right, I would have had data. Look, all of the things you said in terms of your opening statement that we had unknowns, we were aware of and we considered and we recognized that one of the options was maybe you had so many unknowns that you would have to say it's inconclusive. But we reached a different ruling and we reached it in great part because those gauges did work. See, look, the biggest thing when we started, we wanted to know did the gauges work? When I say did the gauges work, that so-called logo gauge that reads .3 to .4, it was tested hundreds of times. So you really know where it was. It wasn't an erratic gauge. If you had a gauge that some days read .7 over and other days it read .2 and other days it read below, then you couldn't base anything because that gauge was bouncing around. But because the logo gauge was consistently .3 to .4 over, and because the non-logo gauge was almost perfectly calibrated, we knew we had good gauges and that gave us the ability to do scientific analysis and make conclusions that we felt were reliable. And one of the things we say in the report is that the scientific analysis does not prove with, quote, "absolute certainty" whether there was tampering or not tampering. But the data ultimately was sufficiently reliable that we felt comfortable when we looked at the evidence in its totality. And the totality of the evidence involved not just the science. It involved Jim McNally calling himself the deflator and saying he had not gone to ESPN yet. And it involved the text message where Mr. Jastremski says he talked to Mr. Brady. And there's a reference to McNally must have a lot of stress getting them done. If those text messages did not exist, and all we had was a break in protocol and he goes into the bathroom and just the science, the result might very well be totally different. But when you combine the break in protocol, going into the bathroom, the text messages and the science, we felt comfortable reaching a judgment. It was a totality of all of the evidence analysis that gave us comfort in deciding it was more probable than not. We looked at all of the evidence together. And that's what juries do all the time. In most jury cases, each side will have an expert. One expert will say X happened to a reasonable degree of scientific certainty. The other side will say, well, my expert says Y happened to a reasonable degree of scientific certainty. The jurors sit there and they make a judgment about not just the science, but the whole case. And the judge gives them the discretion as long as it's not so unreliable that you can't make decisions. And that's what we did in this case. And that's why we reached the conclusions that we did and we think the conclusions are right and we think they are reasonable.

MR. LEVY: Mr. Kessler, do you have anymore questions?

MR. KESSLER: Just a couple more.

THE WITNESS: I'm sorry.

Q. Mr. Wells, did you make the decision not to use the data from the post-game measurements?

A. Well, we actually made -- we actually write in the report that, and there is a footnote. I just forget what page it is.

Q. 73?

A. Okay. That data we decided not to use. And the reason we decided not to use it is because we didn't know where the four Colts' balls came from. So they measured four Colts' balls at halftime. They then bring balls back in at the end of the game. They measure four bolts balls. They have no idea if the four Colts' balls they measured at the end of the game were the four Colts' balls they measured at halftime. So that was the Colts. With respect to the Patriots' balls, when they found out at halftime that the Patriots' balls were all under regulation, they pumped the air into them, but he didn't keep any record of how much air he put in. So we didn't have any records if the balls were 13.5 or what. So when the balls came back in, we didn't have any point to start at.

Q. Didn't your report say they pumped them to 13?

A. I'm not sure. My recollection is they -- it wasn't an exact number, but if that's what the report says, I will go with the report.

Q. I think your report says, if someone could check for me, I think the report says 13. So let's assume that's what it says. If they all were pumped to 13, if that's what the official said, couldn't you use the four Patriots' balls to test, then based on what had happened versus the 13, because they weren't going to be tampered with during that second half, right? They could have been used?

A. And you may have, that's correct, if that's what the report says. I will go with whatever the report says.

Q. Okay. And then secondarily, did you make the decision not to use the 12th ball that was tested three times by the same official with the same gauge?

A. No, it wasn't the same gauge. Al Riveron tested that ball and he tested it with two gauges. And it's not in the report because we didn't think -- at that point in time, the intercepted ball because nobody knew whether or not the Colts might have tampered with it or something, we didn't use that as part of the analysis. Later on after the fact, I don't know if it was the Patriots or somebody said, well, you could have used that ball as data that maybe the gauges were off, what have you. But the fact is that Riveron told us he tested it three times. I forget what the numbers are. And he used both of the gauges.

Q. That would be in the interview reports if you kept the interview reports?

A. That's my recollection.

Q. But you took notes of all that, either you or your staff, right?

A. Yeah.

Q. They exist, those interview notes?

A. Yes, sir.

Q. Okay. And they contain a lot of information that's not in this report, correct?

A. Oh, yeah, thousands of pages.

Q. Okay. Have you ever shared any of those interview reports with counsel for the NFL –

A. No, sir.

Q. -- in this matter –

A. No, sir.

Q. -- to prepare for this?

A. Not a bit.

Q. It wasn't just shared with counsel for the NFL today in front of me as I was looking across as they were preparing to do examinations? None of your interview notes have ever been shared with any counsel for the NFL?

A. No, sir.

Q. Anyway, those reports exist, correct?

A. I said that.

Q. And you know that it's been ruled that we can't get access to those reports in this case?

A. I understand that.

MR. KESSLER: I don't have any further questions at this point, especially since I am sure that I am bordering on the end of the time that you have given us.

MR. LEVY: We are going to continue to be flexible. Mr. Nash?

MR. NASH: Yes.

Cross-Examination by Mr. Nash

Q. Mr. Wells, you were asked about your role and your independence. And you gave some answers and I just want to ask you a few questions about that. First of all, what is your background in conducting investigations like the one that you were retained to conduct here?

A. Well, within the sports area, I've done four investigations. I have done investigations for the NFL with the Miami Dolphins. I did this investigation with Deflategate. I did the investigation for the NBA Players Association with respect to the practices of former Executive Director Billy Hunter. I did the investigation for the University of Syracuse Board of Trustees with respect to whether Assistant Basketball Coach Bernie Fine, their allegations of sexual misconduct. So those are the big four in terms of sports areas.

Q. And outside the sports area?

A. I have been involved in other investigations for private entities.

Q. And what is your view of your role when you are retained in these cases to be an independent investigator?

A. It is to do the best job that I can, to collect the relevant facts, examine the facts and then render a personal opinion as to how I see the facts. And I will say one thing because Mr. Kessler suggested somewhere is there a conflict between my duty to zealously advocate, represent the client. When I'm hired in the capacity of an independent investigator, my very job in terms of the representation I'm supposed to do zealously is to be independent and look at the facts and give a candid, objective opinion. That's what I'm supposed to do under the ethics rules.

Q. And is it fair to say that's what you did in this matter?

A. Yes, sir.

Q. Is it correct that you were not given any instructions as to reach any particular conclusion?

A. None at all.

Q. Would you have undertaken this role as the investigator if that were the case?

A. I would not. And if anybody tried to interfere with it, I would quit.

Q. Now, you were asked some questions, I think, it came when you were being asked about your finding about the logo versus the non-logo gauge.

A. Yes, sir.

Q. And I think you referred to yourself as the finder of fact and the judge. Can you explain what you meant by that when you say "judge" or you made a ruling.

A. Yeah. Look, my job was to investigate the facts and then render a personal opinion. That's what it is. It is an opinion. When a jury renders a verdict, it's their opinion. My job, and it's my team. This decision, the rulings in the report, though they call it the Wells report, were unanimous for myself and Mr. Reisner and Brad Karp, the partners on the team. This was our collective judgment and our personal opinion based on the standard of proof. And the standard of proof in an NFL investigation of this kind is the preponderance of the evidence. I mean, I have caught criticism because I used the words "more probable than not." And people act like, is that wishy-washy? It's not wishy-washy. That's the standard of proof that applies to most civil cases in the United States. And the NFL has made a decision to adopt that standard. In terms of the levels of proof, there are three levels. The highest is beyond a reasonable doubt. The middle one is clear and convincing, which applies in fraud cases. But the predominant standard in most civil jury trials in the United States is preponderance of the evidence, which means more probable than not. And when I wrote my conclusions in terms of "more probable than not," I did it very purposefully, because I did not want any readers to think that I had perhaps made a finding of liability beyond a reasonable doubt or by clear and convincing evidence. I wanted people to know this was the standard under the NFL rules and that's the standard I was making my ruling on. So I was doing it so people wouldn't get confused and think I had used some higher, higher standard.

Q. You were asked about your interview practices. You interviewed a lot of witnesses in this matter?

A. Yes.

Q. Other than what's in the report, did you interview any witnesses who told that you Mr. Brady was not aware or did not in any way know about the activities of Mr. Jastremski and Mr. McNally, that you didn't include in the report? A. No. I mean, just, I want to be clear. Look, Mr. Brady denied any involvement. Mr. Jastremski and Mr. McNally denied any involvement or that anything happened, including with respect to their knowledge of Mr. Brady. Coach Belichick said he had talked to Mr. Brady and that Mr. Brady had denied doing anything, and I think Coach Belichick said he believed him. I think those are the only witnesses who said something about Mr. Brady. And that's all in the report; I believe so.

Q. Now, getting back again to your role as the finder of fact, was it your role and your understanding to make any findings or conclusions about what discipline should be imposed on Mr. Brady or whether he engaged in conduct detrimental?

A. No, sir.

Q. You have been asked some questions about Exponent, and I want to -- you were here when Dean Snyder testified earlier, right?

A. Yes.

Q. If you could go to the Exponent report, IX, page IX, the Executive Summary.

A. Okay.

Q. And at the bottom of that page, there is a paragraph that, there is a "1" and a "2." Can you explain your understanding of what -- how Exponent approached this assignment?

A. Yes. The last paragraph on page Roman numeral IX reads, "As noted, Paul, Weiss retained Exponent to provide scientific and analytical support for its investigation and help determine based on the available data whether it is likely that there had or had not been tampering with the Patriots footballs. Specifically, Exponent conducted a science- and engineering-based investigation to, (1), analyze the data collected at halftime, particularly to determine whether the difference in the decrease in pressure exhibited by the footballs of the two teams was statistically significant, and (2), identify and evaluate any physical or environmental factors present on the day of the AFC Championship Game that might account for the difference in the magnitude of the reduction in air pressure between the footballs of the two teams measured at halftime." And what that paragraph says is that we proceeded in a sequential fashion. The first issue that was asked was whether or not there was a statistically significant difference between this delta that we recognized between the Patriots' balls and the Colts' balls, because if it was just by chance, then we didn't need to go out and do all of these experiments to figure out what might have caused a difference, because it was just chance. And as to what they looked at first was the question of statistical significance, they determined that it was. And then they moved to trying to figure out whether it could be explained by other factors. So we did all these experiments out in Arizona pounding the football, seeing if rubbing caused problems, seeing how you measure the ball sticking a needle in it a bunch of times, could that let the air out. And then they did what they called the timing -- what's the word?

Q. Transient?

A. The transient test. And what they did, they developed a model to try to figure out how timing impacts the measurements. So they built, you know, they actually developed a model and then after they developed that model, then they looked at game-day simulations. So, you know, this issue of timing that Professor Snyder talked about, I know he said it wasn't in the model. I don't know whether that's right or wrong. The experts can testify to that. But the way we approached it was first statistical significance and then we did the tertiary studies and we did the game-day stimulations, in addition to all these other studies, because the Patriots -- Patriots had all sorts of ideas what might cause this. Okay, Mr. Goldberg was writing me e-mails. You know, maybe it was the pounding. Maybe it was the wetness. Everything we got from Mr. Goldberg we sent out to Exponent and to Mr. Marlow, okay. If they raised something, we tried to go down that rabbit hole. We spent a ton of money, a ton of money trying to understand what might have caused it, other than tampering. And only the experts ruled that they couldn't get the numbers to match. And they didn't rule that the science absolutely shows there was tampering. They said here's the data. Now, we as the fact finder, Mr. Reisner and I, really, and Mr. Karp had to make a decision. Okay, but we looked at everything as a whole, which is how jurors make decisions every day.

Q. Did you consider -- you heard something about the AEI report. Are you familiar with that?

A. Yes. Q. And I think was it Dr. MacKinnon's report?

A. Look. To my knowledge when the report first came out, the New York Times and the guy that writes the 538 column was one of the most respected statisticians in the world. He wrote a column praising the science in this report. And he went out and interviewed other scientists and they praised the science done by Exponent and Dr. Marlow. Following that, the Patriots issued a rebuttal that contained a three-page letter from a Dr. MacKinnon who is a Nobel Peace Prize winner in chemistry. It's not a physicist or a statistician. And he took issue with some of the findings in the report. And then an entity called AEI issued a report in an op-ed in the New York Times and then Dr. Snyder had his PowerPoint that we got last week. But with respect to all three of those reports, I went to Dr. Marlow and I went to the people at Exponent and I told them I wanted them to review each of those reports criticizing their work. I wanted to know did those reports change their findings and conclusions in any way? Did it undermine their report? Did it make them feel that they got it wrong? And both Dr. Marlow and the people at Exponent told me they reviewed each of those reports, that each of those reports were flawed and failed to show an understanding of what they had done and that their conclusions had not changed in any way, shape or form. And that's what I did and that's what -- and they are going to testify here so Mr. Kessler can hear it and question them.

Q. I just want to ask you a few questions about the requests that you and your team made to Mr. Brady for texts and phone records.

A. Sure.

Q. And I think if I could get you to look at the binder, let me start with Exhibit -- it's NFL Exhibit 61.

A. Okay.

Q. Why don't you just tell us what this is. Is this the request that was made to Mr. Brady's counsel?

A. Yes, okay. In fact, it says, the first sentence says, to Steve, "In advance of our upcoming review of Tom Brady, we wanted to make sure you are aware of our prior requests communicated through the Patriots for Tom's relevant documents and communications." So that e-mail to the agent begins by saying, We had previously asked the Patriots for the materials. Now, as I said, my recollection is the Patriots later came back, once the Patriots -- once the agents were involved, and said to us, you got to go through the agents. But this confirms my recollection that we went, we started with the Patriots. And what we then did was basically redraft what we had sent to Mr. Goldberg. And so that letter sets forth and it's dated February 28, 2015, what we wanted. We wanted two buckets of information. We wanted him to take the phone, look at the text messages, e-mails, run the search terms that we set forth and give us any communications with anybody about deflation or inflation. So if Mr. Brady had talked to an assistant coach or talked to the second-team quarterback about these issues, we would get that material. We then asked him for all communications regardless of subject matter, I think, between Mr. Jastremski and McNally, regardless of -- and Schoenfeld, regardless of the search terms. So we wanted two buckets of information. And I know, I didn't get -- okay, I will stop.

Q. Yeah. So why don't you turn to the next Exhibit 70, because I think I can represent if you go to the third page of that exhibit, at the bottom, it's 001584. And there is an e-mail to you from Donald Yee who I believe is Mr. Brady's agent. And there is a reference to, I think, Exhibit 69, the request that was made on February 28th; is that correct?

A. This is page 1584?

Q. Yes, page 1584, you will see at the bottom there is an e-mail.

A. Yeah. Now, this e-mail is from Mr. Yee to me. It is dated March 2nd. It says, "Dear Mr. Wells, nice to meet you." Then he says, "On Saturday, February 28th, Mr. Burns at your office sent an e-mail to Mr. Dubin requesting that we, on behalf of our client, request a search of his text and e-mail communications dated from September 1, 2014 to present. We have considered this request. However, we respectfully decline." I want to say that's -- there is no statement as to why they are declining. They give us no information. They say, "We decline." Now, the next paragraph is important because it's something Mr. Kessler said. The next paragraph reads, "On another note, we understand that you would like to speak with our client in person about the past season's AFC Championship Game. Prior to confirming a time and date for such a discussion, we must ask with all due respect what is the precise basis for this proposed discussion? In our role as NFLPA certified contract advisors, we are obligated by the NFLPA agent regulations to be sensitive to collective bargaining issues, particularly if those issues may implicate player discipline matters." So that's what they asked me. They didn't ask me at any time about authority for the phone. They had already turned me down in the prior paragraph about the phone information. They were asking me did I even have any right to talk to Mr. Brady? And they wanted me to give -- to respond to that. And I sent them an e-mail telling them why I wanted to talk to him. But there was never any discussion directed to me or anybody on my team about not giving us the phone because of some concerns about the Union. In fact, to my recollection, you know, I know the Union was not permitted even to attend the interview, whereas they had Mr. Ned Ehrlich from the NFLPA was there at Foxborough that day. And we interviewed the kicker Gostkowski and Mr. Ehrlich did that interview, but Mr. Brady wouldn't let the Union even sit in on his interview.

Q. So I notice in Exhibit 70, the response you received about the request for Mr. Burns is one line. It says, "We have considered this request. However, we respectfully decline."

A. Right.

Q. Did Mr. Brady or his agents give you any other reason for that, for not giving you the texts?

A. No, at no time. Then what happens if you go, stay with the e-mail chain, so that's March 2nd. Then March 3rd, I write back, and I respond to the request why I think I want to -- why I want to interview him. And then I say, "Finally, we encourage you to reconsider your decision to decline our request for relevant e-mails, text messages and other material. Our request is narrowly tailored to the subject of our investigation and we would rely on you to perform the requested searches and produce only responsive material. We are hopeful that you will reconsider our request." So they have turned me down. I have now the next day I have written back and I said please reconsider. And then when they came to the interview on March 6th, I asked them had they reconsidered and they said, "We respectfully decline." And they did not give me any reason. And then I repeated the whole request in front of Mr. Brady, because I did not want Mr. Brady to be in a spot where later on he might say he didn't understand what we were asking for.

Q. When you said you repeated it, you are talking about the March 6th interview?

A. The request what I asked for, I made clear I didn't want to take access to your phone. Mr. Yee can do it. I did not, as Mr. Kessler said -- I want to be clear -- I did not tell Mr. Brady at any time that he would be subject to punishment for not giving -- not turning over the documents. I did not say anything like that.

Q. Did Mr. Brady or his representatives at any time tell you that they couldn't give you any of the texts because the phone had been destroyed?

A. No statements of that nature were made in any respect.

Q. If you would look at NFL Exhibit 96, this is a June 18, 2015 letter sent to Commissioner Goodell by Mr. Yee. I just want to draw your attention. In this letter, they talk about information that was now being provided regarding Mr. Brady's phone. And it says in the second paragraph, "Please note that in producing the cell phone and e-mail information, we have followed, in fact, we have gone further than the specific requests set forth in Wells's original electronic data request of February 28th made to us." Do you agree with that statement, Mr. Wells?

A. Well, I know, it is my understanding, I want to qualify, I haven't studied this, but it is my understanding that they didn't do any searches for the text messages for people other than Jastremski, Schoenfeld and McNally. So they didn't do that first big bucket I wanted that would have touched all people in terms of the search terms. And in terms of the text messages that they produced, to my understanding, and I didn't look through every page because the thing is real thick, like, 1,500 pages or something, there is no text message -- there's not one content. When I say a text message, I mean what did somebody say? They have phone bills that say on X date there was a text message, but there is no content. So that's like looking at a running log that said you sent an e-mail but you don't have the content. So I was looking for the content. Though, if Mr. Yee had come in and explained it to me -- look, I was trying to work with them. And so if he had explained, you know, we threw the phones away or whatever, you know, we would have talked about it. I did not want him in the position of not cooperating. I didn't want it for him. I didn't want it for me. Not only did it hurt him in terms of how we evaluated his credibility, but it put us in a hell of a spot because you have a person with this exemplary record and has done all these good things that people are saying, and yet they are conducting themselves in a fashion that suggests they are hiding something and may be guilty and not being forthcoming. So it was really hard to give them credit for the good stuff when he's basically looking you in the face and saying, I'm not going to give you my phone. But like I said, it not only hurt Mr. Brady, it hurt the investigation because it put us in a position we didn't want to be in because we wanted to be able to listen to him and evaluate his credibility without this cloud. That's why I kept saying, you know, reconsider. Give me -- I will take your word for it.

Q. The only other question I had is: You were asked about whether you had requested other, either e-mails or texts or other documents from anyone at the NFL; is it correct that you were provided with a number of documents from the NFL for your investigation?

A. Yeah, yeah, I was provided a huge number. And I just don't recollect as I sit here if we went through anybody's e-mails because the question Mr. Kessler asked me about was in terms of bias and with the testing. And what I found in terms of the testing, I didn't see any bias, so I didn't see any need to have to go back and look at e-mails for something I didn't see. If I had seen something in terms of bias being exhibited during the testing at halftime, I wouldn't have had any hesitation to go back and look for any e-mails, but I didn't see it. The problem with the testing that Mr. Kessler, you know, rightly pointed out, it doesn't have to do with bias. I had no records. People didn't record things at the front end. Mr. Anderson, he wasn't biased against anybody, but he didn't write things down. That was real. And, you know, there were issues in terms of record-keeping that I didn't have. But I didn't have record-keeping because of bias or somebody I felt was out to get the Patriots. The problem was, as he said, Mr. Kessler said, there weren't procedures.

MR. LEVY: Mr. Nash, do you have any questions?

MR. NASH: No, I don't.

MR. KESSLER: I have a few.

Redirect Examination by Mr. Kessler

Q. Mr. Wells, you had an interview with the press after your report came out, correct?

A. Yes, sir.

Q. And according to the transcript that's published, you said the following, Mr. Brady, the report set forth, he came to the interview. "He answered every question I put to him. He did not refuse to answer any questions in terms of the back and forth between Mr. Brady and my team. He was totally cooperative." Did you make those statements?

A. Absolutely, absolutely.

Q. And those are truthful statements, correct?

A. Yes, sir.

Q. Now, with respect to the issue of producing e-mails or texts, you asked Mr. Gostkowski to produce those things, correct?

A. We did.

Q. Again, did he produce them?

A. No, because we had decided that he wasn't that important a witness, and so we backed off. So what happened, I didn't resend. I didn't press because he just wasn't that important a witness.

Q. But his first response was that he declined?

A. Correct, he declined after Mr. Brady declined, but that is correct.

Q. He also declined?

A. Correct.

Q. To your knowledge, has Mr. Gostkowski been subject to any discipline for not cooperating with your request?

A. To my knowledge, as I said, I did not press the issue.

Q. Finally, you mentioned I think you had Exponent test all these things and it cost a ton of money or something like that?

A. It's true.

Q. How many millions was given to Exponent and to Dr. Marlow apart from what you were paid in this case, do you know, roughly?

A. Can I? Exponent was 600,000 and I'm not sure Marlow.

Q. An additional amount for Dr. Marlow?

A. Yes, sir.

MR. KESSLER: I don't have any further questions of you right now. Thank you.

MR. LEVY: Jeffrey, who is your next witness?

MR. KESSLER: Let me confer. So here is the issue in light of the timing and everything else, and I don't know what you want to do. You are going to call Exponent's people; is that correct?

MR. NASH: If you are done.

MR. KESSLER: Well, here's the issue. Okay. If you weren't going to call any Exponent people, then I would proceed to probably call Dr. Marlow first as I said I would because –

MR. NASH: You can do that.

MR. KESSLER: No, but I'm just saying, if you are going to call the Exponent people anyway, then in light of the time and the hour, I would be happy to proceed if this would be suitable to the Commissioner, because it may save some time to have them present, the Exponent people, cross-examine them and then maybe I will conclude I don't have to call Dr. Marlow. In other words, I would only be calling him if I'm uncertain as to whether anybody is going to testify for them.

MR. NASH: That's fine.

MR. LEVY: That's fine.

MR. KESSLER: So why don't we proceed next with your calling the Exponent people. We will do the cross-examination and then after that, I will let you know whether I feel it's still necessary to call Dr. Marlow or not at that point.

MR. LEVY: Agreed. Five-minute break.

MR. KESSLER: One other thing on the record –

MR. LEVY: Is there anybody else?

MR. KESSLER: No, but one other thing on the record, I would like the NFL to think about this: We have had this issue back and forth and we propose that there not be confidentiality in this matter and the NFL said they wanted confidentiality and we agreed to something and it was there. I would like to propose on behalf of the Union that we can release this transcript of this today. I would like the NFL to think about that. That's our proposal. Despite that, I'm not talking about any of the underlying things, but at least the transcript. I think there is a great public interest in this and in the interest of transparency, that would be something that we would like to see done. So I will submit my proposal for the NFL to consider as to whether that's possible or not.

MR. LEVY: Pending the agreement, the transcript is confidential.

MR. NASH: Yes.

MR. KESSLER: Well, we already have that agreement, which is why I have to make this proposal –

MR. NASH: Yes, we have that agreement.

MR. KESSLER: -- in order to see if the NFL would agree to that.

MR. LEVY: Five minutes.

(Recess taken 5:54 p.m. to 6:04 p.m.)

Testimony of Dr. Robert Caligiuri

Direct Examination by Mr. Reisner

Q. Can you please state your name for the record.

A. Robert D. Caligiuri, and I will spell it for you, C-A-L-I-G-I-U-R-I.

Q. Dr. Caligiuri, by whom are you employed?

A. I am employed by Exponent, Incorporated.

Q. What is your title there?

A. I am a group vice president and principal engineer. Group vice president is an administrative role. I am responsible for the company's core engineering practices.

Q. What kind of company is Exponent?

A. Exponent is a scientific and engineering consulting company that works for a wide variety of clients to solve their technical scientific problems, particularly, very significant ones.

Q. Where is your office located?

A. Our corporate headquarters are in Menlo Park, California.

Q. And what kind of work does Exponent do?

A. Engineering work, scientific work, both in the health arena, in the environmental arena, solving problems, do some litigation support, yes, all kinds of and types of engineering, problem solving.

Q. And do you have any particular expertise in terms of your own scientific and engineering focus?

A. My focus is on mechanical and materials engineering. And I bring those disciplines to basically find out what happened to things, to determine root cause analyses, looking at a wide variety of problems and particularly in consumer products and other areas trying to figure out what's going on here and use my material and mechanical expertise.

Q. Can you very briefly describe your educational background.

A. I have a Bachelor of Science degree in mechanical engineering. I have a Master's and Ph.D. of Material Science and Engineering from Stanford University.

Q. Were there other members of the Exponent team who assisted you on this matter?

A. There were a lot of people that worked on it.

Q. Can you just describe the principal members of the team and their area of expertise.

A. Sure. It became very apparent after we received the initial assignment from Paul, Weiss that statistics is a part of this investigation. So I went out and recruited Dr. Duane Steffey, who is a Ph.D. statistician, who also was a professor of statistics -- he's the director of our statistics department -- and engaged him on that aspect of the problem -- of the project. I also reached out to Dr. John Pye. He is a vice president of the firm and he's a Mechanical Engineer Ph.D. from Stanford University. He's very experimentally-oriented, does a lot of work for the United States Government. And I engaged him to take care of the experimental side of things. Dr. Gabe Ganot is a Ph.D. material scientist from Columbia University and I engaged him to do a lot of different aspects of the project. Those are the four key people on the project.

Q. What was Dr. Marlow's role in connection with Exponent 's work?

A. I think Mr. Wells said it pretty well here, he was working with us helping us doing some of the statistics analysis, reviewing our work, contributing to it, pointing out things, helping us plan the direction that we needed to go. He was very much involved in the project.

Q. At the outset of your work, what instructions, if any, were you given by Mr. Wells and the Paul, Weiss team about the role that Exponent should play with respect to its work?

A. I think Mr. Wells said it pretty well, too. He said we needed to consider ourselves court-appointed experts, which brings a level of independence. And I have actually served as that before. And at a very high level of independence and viewing things from very, very objective -- so objectivity and court-appointed independent expert, were very much important to this investigation for our role. It was also very clear that planning, the methodology and the approach, was left to us, and the scientific and technical aspect.

Q. Can you describe the assignment that you received from Paul, Weiss.

A. I think Mr. Wells did that pretty well, too. If we go to basically the paragraph he read, we were retained to provide scientific and analytic support in their investigation to help them determine whether or not, based on available data, there may have been tampering of the footballs by the Patriots, and based on that, to do two very large pieces of investigation. One was to analyze the halftime data and determine it's statistical significance; and two, to perform experiments and review and analyze the potential factors, usage, environmental, physical, that could influence any difference in the pressure drops that were measured.

Q. And can you describe in a little bit more detail the analysis and testing performed by Exponent.

A. The analysis, the statistical analysis?

Q. Start with the statistical analysis.

A. We took a look at, very carefully, at all the game-day halftime measurements that were made, analyzed them, put them through statistical models as has been discussed here already, and to determine is there anything there that supported it? Was it worth looking at more? We ran that through very, very careful examination of the halftime data. The second thing we did was to look at the gauges. The gauges that collected the data, was there something wrong with them? Were they messed up? Were they not reliable? That was a factor that would influence the observations that we made. The third thing we then did was do a whole series of experiments to evaluate the effects of ball usage, rapid insertion, repeated insertion of the needles into the balls, would they leak, all sorts of things that people had actually mentioned that could be contributing to the difference in the pressure drops.

Q. Can I just stop you there for a moment? And you have a copy of your report in front of you?

A. Yeah.

Q. Can you go to page XI, Roman XI of your report. And number 6 on that page describes the physical factors that were evaluated by Exponent?

A. Yes, it does.

Q. And can you describe those, please.

A. Sure. The first one I mentioned is the impact of gaming. Someone had mentioned, I believe, in prior testimony that the Patriots' balls were used more than the Colts' balls, unfortunately for the Colts, I guess, in the first half. So was there a factor being used more that caused the pressure inside to go down more relative to the Colts.

Q. And what did you do to test that?

A. Picture that made the rounds here of a football being squished in a mechanical testing machine. We took the football and we cycled it to 650 pounds to see if there was change or loss of pressure in the ball.

Q. The next thing was, "The impact of repeated insertions of an inflation needle into the football." What did you do to test that? A. Basically took a bunch of footballs and inserted a needle inside of it, and many, many times, to see is there leaking around the gland? Was there a change in the pressure over time with multiple, multiple, multiple insertions?

Q. And next, "The natural leak rate and permeability of properly-functioning footballs." What did you do to test that?

A. Basically we took footballs apart and measured the permeability to various materials inside the football to leakage of air.

Q. And the other listed factors are additional physical characters you tested, correct?

A. That's correct.

Q. What other testing did you perform as part of your work?

A. The -- beyond these physical factors, there were the environmental factors that we tested. And those tests fell into two kind of buckets. One bucket was the transient testing that's already been referred to here. And transient testing means monitoring. It is time-dependent, monitoring something over time. In this case, we took various footballs and put a gauge in the football and took them from various temperatures to various temperatures and monitored the time, monitored the change in pressure over time. That curve I believe that Mr. Snyder showed was one of them that he generated to see what is the effect of pressure on time, transient analysis. The second set of experiments that we did was to try to, based on the review of the videotape, was to try to simulate as best as we could with the information we had to actually recreate the game conditions on that game up to halftime. We put balls in 48 degrees Fahrenheit for a couple of hours, first in the locker room and then in the field, simulated field. We used different rooms at different temperatures to do that, brought them out and measured their pressures and that sort of stuff, tried to rub the footballs in the same way trying to stimulate the actual conditions as best we could.

Q. With respect to the transient experiments, I want to direct your attention to page 41 of your report.

A. Yeah.

Q. Can you describe what Figure 20 is.

A. Well, that's a set-up for the transient experiment. This is an actual game-day football. And you can see if you look at the top picture, Figure 19 is the instrument we inserted inside the football. And you can see the Tygon tubing that comes out to what is called a master gauge, which is a gauge that measured pressure calibrated to a Natural Institute of Standards standard of pressure to a thousandth of a psi. That is how we measured pressure.

Q. Can you describe again the purpose of the transient experiments?

A. It was to look at the effect of the temperature, external temperature, on the pressure inside a football as a function of time.

Q. Dr. Caligiuri, based on the testing that you described, did you reach conclusions?

A. Yes.

Q. Can you describe the key conclusions that you reached based on your work.

A. You said "testing." Are you including some of the statistical work, too?

Q. If you could just describe the key conclusions reached based on your work.

A. Sure. I think the conclusion section of the report says it pretty well, starting on page 64. The first thing we did as has been discussed here is we did a statistical analysis on the halftime data. And we looked at that data and we analyzed it and it's been discussed here. And we concluded from that based on the standard of five percent that the halftime data had some statistical significance and that it appears that the Patriots game balls exhibited a greater pressure drop than the Colts' balls, on average. So the difference in magnitude between pressure between the Patriots and the Colts as measured at halftime was determined to be statistically significant. So therefore, to us, that warranted further investigation into what could be causing it. So the next thing we did was to look at the gauges themselves and we tested the gauges, the logo gauge and the non-logo gauge. We tested hundreds of exemplar gauges we could get our hands on trying to see are these gauges capable of measuring these sorts of pressures.

Q. And what were your conclusions and where are they set forth on page 64?

A. Paragraph 3. It says, "The logo and non-logo gauges appear to have worked reliably and consistently on game day, and the difference in the pressure drops between the teams was not caused by a malfunction in either gauge." What we did notice in the testing was that the so-called logo gauge read consistently, reliably and repeatedly 0.3 to 0.4 psi higher. That's already been discussed here today. But it would do that every time. So it wasn't veering all over the map. It was consistently in that range.

Q. And directing your attention to paragraph 6 of your conclusions, what were your conclusions with respect to the potential contributions to the difference in the observed pressure drop with respect to the physical factors tested?

A. The difference that we are seeing basically usage really had no effect here. And as well as the ball preparations methods, we went and prepared balls the same way that the Patriots told us they did it and the same way the Colts told us they did it. So we prepared those balls and none of these factors, these ones that I listed, were having any effect on the difference of pressure inside the balls between the Colts and the Patriots. They were non-factors, so we excluded them from any sort of conclusions that we made.

Q. And directing your attention to the last sentence of paragraph 6, does that pretty much sum up your conclusions with respect to the impact of the physical factors? A. (Reading): "None of the above physical factors at the levels we understand were applicable on game day were found to contribute in any material way to changes in internal pressure of the footballs and do not, therefore, explain the relative difference in pressure drops measured by us."

Q. And directing your attention to paragraph 9, can you describe your conclusions with respect to the transient experiments that you were conducting?

A. We did a series of transient experiments that I told you about where we quantified the time-dependent behavior of footballs and to understand how such behavior might explain the difference in the magnitude of the pressure drops. So we looked at the -- very much looked at the effect of time here in our experiments, very, very much so. And we concluded that the timing does have an effect on the pressure, but the timing in and of itself did not account for the pressure drops that we saw. So timing is affecting the pressures, but that in and of itself is not contributing to the -- cannot account for the difference in the pressure drops.

Q. And does the last paragraph under Item 10 summarize your conclusions?

A. Yes.

Q. Can you read or summarize that into the record.

A. (Reading): "Within the range of game conditions and circumstances most likely to have occurred on game day based on information provided to us by Paul, Weiss, including the timing of various events understood to have occurred in the officials' locker room during halftime, we have identified no combination of the environmental factors listed above that could reconcile the Patriots halftime measurements with both results predicted by our transient experiments and the measurements of the Colts' balls taken at game-day." So environmental factors in and of itself cannot account for the difference.

Q. Very briefly, can you describe the conclusions reached based or your experimental game day simulations.

A. Experimental simulations, again, failed to account for the pressure drop difference between the Colts and the Patriots. Those were experiments that we tried to simulate the entire game day, and they could not account for it. And the game-day experiments also helped validate the transient experiments at the time because the data we collected from the game-day simulations overlay the data collected from our transient experiments, verifying that aspect of it.

Q. When you conducted the game-day simulations, you actually used Colts' balls and Patriots' balls that could be identified as having either been used in the AFC Championship Game or previously marked by Walt Anderson, correct?

A. That's correct.

Q. And you ran those balls through simulated events that basically replicated the conditions that were understood to be present on game day, right?

A. That's correct.

Q. Now, you were here during the testimony of Dean Snyder, correct?

A. Correct.

Q. And you heard Dean Snyder describe what he described as his three key findings or criticisms with respect to the Exponent report, correct?

A. Correct.

Q. I am referring to Exhibit 191 now. This is NFLPA 191. What he describes as his first key finding or criticism was, "Exponent's statistical analysis of the difference of the average pressure drops is wrong because it ignores timing." Do you have a reaction or response to that criticism?

A. Yes.

Q. What is your reaction or response?

A. It's totally unfounded criticism.

Q. Why? A. We did look at timing. We very much did so. The statistical analysis we did up front was really an intention to -- a gatekeeper to see if it made sense to follow up with everything else. And we concluded it was statistically significant. We did all sorts of experiments looking at time, time effects, time effects on pressure, all of those. We absolutely looked at timing. When we saw the effect of timing and when the balls were timed out and measured, we then went back to the statistical analysis as was discussed in Footnote 49 to our report. We went back and specifically put the effect of time back into our model. And to our -- I mean, it was interesting that the statistical analysis said it wasn't a significant effect, timing. Well, that seems kind of counterintuitive there. When experiments are saying timing is important, how could this analysis say it wasn't? Well, the reason is that the other factors, the physical factors that came into play, like ball wetness and dryness, differences in inflation pressure to start with, were masking the timing effect that you would have expected to see if it was all just due to increase in pressure at the time. So the reason you don't see a timing effect that we concluded in the statistical analysis is because it's being masked out by the variability in the data due to these other effects.

Q. And with respect to Dean Snyder's key finding or criticism 1, does that affect your views with respect to the appropriateness of the work done by Exponent or the conclusions reached by Exponent?

A. No.

Q. I want to direct your attention to key finding number 2 or key criticism number 2 identified by Dean Snyder, which is, "Exponent improperly draws conclusions based on the variability in halftime pressure measurements despite conceding that the variability is statistically insignificant." Do you have a reaction or response to that criticism?

A. I believe that one is unfounded as well.

Q. And why do you believe it's unfounded?

A. Because it's comparison of apples and oranges here. The statistical analysis we did up front is correct. We concluded the variability, which means the variation of the measurements as you look at the data set, the average of that compared to the average of variations, I will call it the average of the mean between the two could not be determined to be statistically significant. So you couldn't say that the Patriots' balls, based on that analysis, was more variable than the variability in the Colts' balls, based on that specific statistical analysis of that data. We came to the conclusion that part of the contributing factors, there were only four Colts' balls that were measured, as opposed to eleven Patriots. Maybe if we had more Colts' balls, we could have seen an effect. So that's correct, that's what happened. Then we went and did all that physical testing. We saw the effect of all those other parameters, the effect or no effect of those parameters. We looked at that and then we went back and looked at the variability of the data comparing, at the same time looking at the variation of the balls, individual balls. And could we account in the difference in pressures based on other physical factors. And the ranges and variability of factors were not predicted by the effect of, say, ball wetness and ball dryness that we saw. So we went back and said, you know, there is variability in here. The statistical analysis you can't conclude, but based on a review of the fluctuations in the data and looking at the physical experiments that we did, we concluded that there is a difference there and that difference is most likely the differences in starting pressure of the footballs, two different analyses. The statistical analysis did not preclude us from going back and looking at the physical realities that we measured. And that's what we did to come to that conclusion.

Q. And with respect to key finding or criticism number 2 of Dean Snyder, does that affect your views with respect to the appropriateness of the work done by Exponent or the conclusions reached by Exponent?

A. No.

Q. Directing your attention to key finding or criticism number 3 identified by Dean Snyder, which is, "If the logo gauge was used to measure the Patriots' balls before the game, then eight of the eleven were above Exponent's expected outcome." Do you have a reaction or a response to that criticism?

A. That's unfounded, too.

Q. Why is it unfounded?

A. Well, there's already been a lot of discussion here about logo versus non-logo gauge. If you were to take the logo gauge and assume that those measurements were made with the logo gauge, then, as was talked about today by Dean Snyder, the pressure the Patriots gave the balls to the referee pre-game were 12.2, below the League minimum.

Q. 12.17, right?

A. Yes. He calculated, I rounded it up, 12.17, correct, okay. And then if you look at the Colts' balls, if the same logo gauge was used, it's reading 12.6, 12.7. We were told that the Patriots and the Colts were insistent that they delivered balls at 12 and a half and 13, which means, geez, looks like the logo gauge wasn't used pre-game. But, anyway, if you take that number, 12.17, and you plug it into the Ideal Gas Law, which is a mathematical formula, you can get a lower pressure and you can change the results, that's correct. But that's like using numbers that don't make any sense. The other factor that he used to come up with this eight of eleven were above Exponent's expected outcome was, he assumed a temperature 71 degrees pre-game. That is a variable that we looked at. We looked at the range of temperature in the pre-game shower room. We actually measured it to be between 67 and 71, 72 degrees. That's why in all of our experiments, we looked at that as a potential range. If you use 71, yeah, you get the numbers that Dean Snyder calculated. But if you go use 67, which is the other end of the range, you find out six of the Patriots' balls were under the expected outcome. When I say "expected outcome," predicted by the Ideal Gas Law, okay. And if you look at the non-logo gauge pre-game, all of it, no matter how you look at it, all of it comes out that eight of the eleven balls fall below the expected outcome of the Ideal Gas Law. Number 1, the use of the logo gauge pre-game. Number 2 is the use of 71 degrees versus 67 degrees. And the third one is the same mistake that has been made by Professor MacKinnon, by AEI and now by Dean

Snyder. They assume in their calculations of the Ideal Gas Law what you have to do to use the Ideal Gas Law is the balls come off the field at 48 degrees Farenheit and stay at 48 degrees Farenheit throughout the measurement. That's the only way you can use the Ideal Gas Law. That we know didn't happen. The pressure is increasing with time. So this analysis by Dean Snyder doesn't make any sense, even just thinking about how the temperature was fixed throughout the measurement period, and we know that that's not correct. So those three factors, I can take no faith in that conclusion.

Q. And did criticism 3 or finding 3 of Dean Snyder affect your views with respect to the appropriateness of the work done by Exponent or the conclusions reached by Exponent?

A. No.

Q. Staying with the logo and non-logo gauge issue for a moment, to what extent did Exponent consider the possibility that the logo or non-logo gauge might have been used in connection with its transient experiments and its game-day simulations and account for that possibility?

A. Even though the evidence is pointing towards the use of the non-logo gauge, we said let's look at both conditions. What happens if the logo gauge is used or the non-logo gauge is used pre-game? We did that in the statistical analysis we did up front and we did it in every experiment we ran. You will see the experimental data shows for logo gauge and non-logo gauge. We also looked at the effect of ball wetness and ball dryness. Wet balls and dry balls, we did that consistently throughout all of our experiments. So even though the evidence pointed towards using the non-logo gauge, we considered it throughout our investigation.

Q. And those different scenarios are incorporated into the conclusions that you described, correct?

A. That's correct.

Q. One other thing with respect to Dean Snyder's analysis, if you go to the page with the Bates Stamp Number 3429, and this is his description in the difference in differences statistical approach used by Exponent. His bullet point 2, with respect to the difference in differences statistical approach used by Exponent says that, "The Colts' balls were used as control. Using Colts' balls as controls required whether the greater drop of psi in Patriots' balls was statistically significant." Were the Colts' balls used as controls in any way with respect to the statistical significance analysis performed by Exponent?

A. Absolutely not. I don't know where that idea came from. We did not consider the Colts' balls as controls in other statistical analysis. We looked at them both equally. And looked at the variation in the data for both the Patriots and the Colts. There was no assumptions about control or anything like that on the Colts' balls in our statistical analysis.

Q. You mentioned the AEI report. Did you review the AEI report that was published?

A. I sure did.

Q. And with respect to the AEI report, one of the criticisms or observations made by AEI was that, "There was no statistically significant difference between the pressure drop of the Colts' balls versus the Patriots' balls if you assume the logo gauge was used pre-game as opposed to the non-logo gauge." Do you have a reaction or response to that criticism?

A. Yes, I found that to be unfounded as well. What the AEI report did is look at four possible combinations pre-game. All the measurements were made with the logo gauge. All the measurements were made with the non-logo gauge. And then, for some reason, which there is no evidence of, Walt Anderson switched them out. He measured Patriots' balls with the logo and the Colts' balls with the non-logo and then the other way around. So he looked at four possibilities. Two of those possibilities just don't make sense because there's never been any indication that Walt Anderson switched the gauges in the middle of his pre-game measurements. We had no indications. We were actually told to assume that that did not happen because there was no evidence that that happened outside of AEI. We take those two scenarios off the table. The other two scenarios, there is one set of combinations within those within which you could get to the conclusion that the p-factor as we heard about today was 6.7 percent, but there's problems in that analysis as well. They had included in that analysis, AEI, a factor related order to order, which we had concluded was not a factor included in that. If you take that factor out, you cut that probability in half down to about two and a half percent.

Q. The AEI report also suggested that, "The evidence indicated that because the Patriots' balls were measured at the start of halftime, whereas the Colts' balls were measured at the end of halftime, after sufficient time had passed for the balls to warm up and return to their pre-game pressure, that was an explanation for the delta in pressure drop." Did you have a reaction or response to that observation?

A. Yes. That makes no sense, as I just talked about, because we specifically looked at that effect. It suggests to me AEI didn't even read our report. We looked at the effect of transient change, the change in pressure with time specifically as a possible contributing factor and concluded that it wasn't. So I don't know where they got that conclusion from, but it's not consistent with the data published in our report.

Q. And AEI in their report also suggested that, "There may have been a flaw in the statistical significance equation used by Exponent." Did you have a reaction or response to that criticism?

A. That one didn't make sense, either. The AEI report says that we used a multivariable regression analysis and they did something to try to repeat our numbers. They got most of them except they were unable to repeat our calculations. And they did something else. We didn't use a multivariable regression analysis. We used what's called a liner mixed mode analysis. They are statistical tools. So either they didn't understand what we did or just assumed we did something else. And that's why they couldn't reproduce our results. So yes, we used a linear mixed mode regression analysis, which is a standard statistically-accepted tool. So I don't understand where that criticism came from.

Q. And Professor, Dr. Caligiuri, after reviewing the AEI report, did it affect, in any way, your views with respect to the appropriateness of the work done by Exponent or the conclusions reached by Exponent?

A. No.

Q. You also referred to a report prepared by a Professor MacKinnon. Did you have any responses or reactions to the commentary that was set forth in that report?

A. I think I already mentioned one of them because his conclusion regarding the Ideal Gas Law calculations again made that same mistake assuming the temperature of the footballs at 48 degrees as it comes off the field remains at 48 degrees throughout the transient period and calculates Ideal Gas Law and compares it to the measurements. And that's just, you can't do that.

Q. And did Professor MacKinnon also make an error with respect to the conversion factor of the balls?

A. Yes.

Q. Can you describe that?

A. He failed to convert them all onto the same equivalent platform. We know there is a continuing error, if you like, in the logo gauge of about .4 psi, which is why you have to convert everything to a single master gauge calibration, which we did. We took a master gauge and made measurements and put the pressure on the logo gauge and said what the master gauge was doing and came up with a calibration curve. And we did the same thing for the logo curve. So we calculated and converted all the data to the same basis, the same equivalent playing field. Professor MacKinnon did not do that. He did not convert them all, so you are comparing apples and oranges.

Q. Directing your attention to the MacKinnon study, the MacKinnon report, did it affect your views in any way with respect to the appropriateness of the work done by Exponent or the conclusions reached by Exponent?

A. No.

MR. REISNER: Nothing further at this time.

Cross Examination by Mr. Kessler

Q. Ready to go? Good evening, I guess, now.

A. Sorry?

Q. Dr. Caligiuri, how do you pronounce your name? I want to get it correctly.

A. "Kala-jerry" [phonetically].

Q. "Caligiuri"? Do you like "doctor" or what do you prefer?

A. Whatever you like.

Q. I will call you Mr. Caligiuri, okay. Mr. Caligiuri, let's see if we can find some points of agreement. Do we agree that timing was a very important factor in determining whether or not natural causes could explain the results of the Patriots' and the Colts' balls?

A. You had to take that into account, yes.

Q. In fact, I think you wrote it was the most significant factor in your report; is that fair?

A. We certainly considered it a significant factor, yes.

Q. The most significant? That's what you wrote in your report.

A. Yes.

Q. You don't disagree with that?

A. No.

Q. Just trying to find points of agreement. Second, do you agree, you saw the criticism number 3 that Dr. Snyder presented, and he indicated that you should have recalibrated the starting pressures through the master gauge because you were comparing those starting pressures to the halftime pressures, which you did to the master gauge. Do you agree that you should have done that?

A. No.

Q. So you think it's appropriate to take one set of pressures, not do the master gauge and compare it to another set of pressures through the master gauge; that's your opinion?

A. No. The opinion is, in fact, the 12.5 we used is a master gauge reading. It is --

Q. You didn't do -- for the two balls you tested at halftime, logo or non-logo, you translated to the master gauge, right?

A. Correct.

Q. And for the starting time, you didn't do any translation to the master gauge, whether it was logo or non-logo, right? You didn't make any change?

A. You said "starting time."

Q. The pre-game measurement, you didn't do any translation to the master gauge there?

A. The master gauge is 12 and a half percent -- 12 and a half psi, and we used 13.0 psi for the Colts.

Q. Did you do any calculation for the pre-game testing to convert the measurements recorded to something in the master gauge?

A. The master gauge conversion, if you convert the 12.5 psi comes from use of the logo gauge pre-game. And that, as Dean Snyder says, is 12.17 percent -- 12.17 psi. You can put that in there and you can do Ideal Gas Law calculations, but they are not consistent with the physical facts.

Q. They are not consistent with what physical fact?

A. The fact that if that was happening, then the Patriots gave the referees 12.17 psi balls, below the League minimum.

Q. How do you know that the Colts -- and, I'm sorry. How do you know that the Patriots and the referee were both not using something equivalent to the logo gauge?

A. So you're asking me to assume that all three of these people, the Patriots pre-game, the Colts pre-game, and Mr. Anderson pre-game all used the same gauge that were exactly the same amount off? All the tests –

Q. No. A. I'm sorry; go ahead.

Q. I am asking the following. You have never seen or tested or looked at the Colts' gauge or the Patriots' gauge pre-game, right?

A. That's correct.

Q. Okay. So you have to make some assumptions about it, correct? A. Correct.

Q. Do you know if Wilson ever issued a version of its logo gauge to the NFL teams in the past, just like the one that was used for some of the measurements at halftime to NFL teams and that over the age of those gauges, they would all approximate what the logo gauge was? Did you ever consider that possibility?

A. So you're asking me to consider that Wilson gave the League gauges that were out of calibration?

Q. No, that over time they got out of calibration. A. All the gauges got out of calibration by the same amount?

Q. Over the same period of time.

A. I would say that's pretty highly unlike.

Q. You think that's unlikely? Did you do any test for that? A. How would we test that? We tested the logo gauge and found that it reads very repeatedly .3 to .45 above the master gauge. And we tested hundreds of gauges that we got, exemplar gauges. Yes, you are right, they are new. And they all read what the master gauge said they should be.

Q. Your testimony is the logo gauge, which the referee who was testing, he had two gauges, the logo gauge and the non-logo gauge, right?

A. He had those in his possession, yes.

Q. And sometimes you understood he would use the logo gauge, right? Sometimes in some games over his life, he would use the logo gauge, right?

A. I don't know if I know that for a fact.

Q. Okay. My question is: What you are testifying is, so every game he ever tested when he used the logo gauge, he could have been allowing illegal balls into play; is that what your testimony is?

A. If he was using the logo gauge and it was off by .3, by .45, and the team had set the ball at 12 and a half, it would have fallen below and he wouldn't have known.

Q. So there could have been numerous NFL games in which he used the logo gauge where the balls were underinflated, in your view, below the 12.5?

A. I haven't analyzed all the games in history and which gauge he used and didn't use.

Q. You just said all of the hundreds of exemplar gauges you used were new, correct?

A. We bought them, yes.

Q. Did you do any testing as to over time, if you have a gauge for one year, two years, three years, those gauges, what that does to the -- to how the gauges register in terms of their calibration?

A. Well, we have one data point, the non-logo gauge never got off by that much. We certainly didn't test these gauges for years on end. There wasn't any time for that. So we didn't watch one or multiples of our exemplar gauges over a three-years' period. No, we didn't do that.

Q. How do you know the non-logo gauge wasn't also a new gauge? Did you do any examination of that?

A. Didn't look very new.

Q. Do you know how old it was?

A. No.

Q. Do you know what its age was compared to the logo gauge?

A. No.

Q. You don't know any of that?

A. No.

Q. Okay. Now, you could have gone out to eBay or something and bought old gauges, right?

A. I think we looked pretty hard to find gauges.

Q. Did you look specifically for older gauges?

A. We looked for all the gauges we could find.

Q. So your testimony under oath is you specifically were looking for older gauges and you couldn't find them anywhere on the internet? That's your testimony –

A. I can't -- I can't –

Q. -- under oath? Is that your testimony, your sworn testimony?

MR. NASH: Objection.

MR. LEVY: You can answer.

A. We went out and collected all the gauges we could find. Were we specifically looking for older gauges that were, like, three years old? No, we didn't do that.

Q. With respect to timing, okay, is it correct as Dr. Snyder said that your difference of differences analysis as presented did not have any timing variable in the regression?

A. Initially, yes. We went back and put that back in after we saw the effect of time on pressure.

Q. So the initial test you did to determine whether there was anything to study did not have a timing variable?

A. Not specifically, no.

Q. Okay. And had you put in that timing variable, do you think Dr. Snyder put in the timing variable improperly?

A. I'm not sure. You mean the graphs that he showed?

Q. Yes. In other words, he states for his first criticism, he took your analysis and simply put in the timing variable in his first one, before he had three cases. The first case all he did was put in timing. Did you see that one?

A. Well, I think in all three cases, he put timing in some form.

Q. Yes. The first one was just timing, that exactly your thing, but putting in a timing, assuming that the Colts' balls were tested before the reinflation. The second one put in timing assuming the Colts' balls were tested after reinflation. And the third one added in the wetness factor. So those were the three ones. Do you remember that now?

A. Yes, I do.

Q. So in the very first one he did where he stated that he just put in a timing factor and made no other change and assumed that the Colts ball were tested before reinflation, do you think he did that improperly in some way? Do you have some criticism of his methodology for doing that?

A. I think I would leave that to the statisticians to discuss. But what I did notice, and I don't know exactly how he calculated the p-values he showed us, but if you look at what he did, he took the averages, took the averages of the Colts' balls and the average -- he looked at the average of the Colts' balls measured right after the Patriots' balls. And you can't do that. You can't compare averages because inside those four balls the Colts are doing, pressure is changing with time. You have to do a ball-by-ball movement and then do the analysis. To me, he just took a grab of averages and compared it to a grab of averages. The other thing he did was he used that curve he showed where he pulled data off; that's actually the wrong curve to use.

Q. Let me ask you this: Did you do any analysis of the fact that the Colts' balls could have been much dryer than the Patriots' balls because the Patriots' balls were used much more in the second quarter of the game?

A. Yes.

Q. Okay. And tell me what analysis you used which compared the Colts' balls being at a lower level of wetness versus the Patriots' balls being at a much higher level of saturation.

A. If you go to Figure 28 on page 55, that's sort of the summary of the transient experiments we ran, and then the overlay of the average data on the transients.

Q. Yes.

A. And you see wet and dry, wet and dry, wet for the Patriots, dry for the Patriots, dry for the Colts, dry for the Colts.

Q. You used the same wetness for the Patriots and the Colts' balls, right, when you did that analysis; you did the same spraying procedure?

A. They were sprayed the same way in the beginning of time –

Q. Right.

A. -- in the beginning of the measurement cycle. Let me finish my answer, okay. And then they dried. We didn't keep rewetting them throughout the transient period. So when we say "Patriots wet," they were wetted to that amount and they dried with time, because we didn't rewet them. The Colts' balls were wetted to the same degree to start and dried with time. Did we look at were the Colts' balls, on average, dryer when they went into the locker room? No, but there's no indication that that's actually the case.

Q. Ah, let's assume it was the case. You didn't test for that, right?

A. Did we look at wetness as a variability?

Q. Yes.

A. In the beginning, no, we didn't.

Q. Okay. Are you a football fan?

A. Yeah.

Q. You are familiar with the fact that when the defense is on field during a rainy game, the balls are in the bag?

A. The balls can be in the bag. We actually -- Paul, Weiss actually talked to the ball boys that were actually handling the balls on game-day. And that was part of our game-day simulation which we couldn't account for the pressure drop anyway. And some balls were in the bag; some weren't. They tried to keep them as dry as possible.

Q. Okay, try to keep them as dry as possible, right? It's easier to keep your ball dry if you are not in offense and the ball is not out in the field, right? You agree with that, right?

A. If all the balls are in the bag and you are not playing football and the balls are in the bag sealed up, balls will be not as dry -- not as wet as the ones you just picked up off the field.

Q. So you would have to agree with me it's a very plausible assumption that the Patriots' balls could have been much wetter than the Colts' balls because of the fact that the Patriots were on offense all the time with the balls? That's plausible, right? It's not not plausible?

A. It is a possibility, but there is no evidence that that occurred. The ball boys themselves said they tried to keep them as dry as possible.

Q. You don't know whether it occurred or not?

A. For all I know, what the ball boys said.

Q. Well, if you are on offense and you are playing with the ball, can you keep it dry when it's out there on the field?

A. No.

Q. Okay. So if the Patriots have those balls out there on the field, it's plausible those balls were wetter, sir, right? You are under oath.

A. Sure.

Q. Is it plausible?

A. Sure.

Q. Okay. And you didn't test for that plausible assumption, right? Did you test for it?

A. No, because –

Q. Thank you.

A. -- what would you test for?

Q. Let's move on to the next one.

MR. LEVY: Let him finish his answer.

MR. KESSLER: Okay.

Q. You didn't test for it, right?

A. What would you assume they were?

COMMISSIONER GOODELL: Let him finish his answer.

A. What would you assume they were? What are you going to pick? What are you going to pick? Well, the Colts' balls were five percent dryer than the Patriots and ten percent? There is no basis to pick anything. So we picked extremes of what we thought we could do and evaluated that.

Q. Right. The data was very limited, so it constrained what you could do, right?

A. Yeah. The ball boys weren't out there with the hydrometer measuring the wetness of the balls, no.

Q. No. The referees weren't indicating whether it was a dry ball or a wet ball when they did the test; is that true?

A. That's true.

Q. Okay. It's also true the referees weren't indicating if one ball was especially wet and one ball was a little wet; they didn't tell you that, right?

A. No.

Q. And you don't know if, on the number of balls tested, if there were more Patriots' balls that were wet as opposed to Colts' balls, just one way or the other, correct?

A. No, but you got to remember we tested the ranges of wet and dry, so all the balls would fit in these bands that are plotted in Figure 28, differences in wetness.

Q. Not the variability of wetness; you didn't test that? You just told me that, right?

A. We did.

Q. You didn't test if the Patriots' balls were much wetter than the Colts' balls? You just stated that.

A. At the beginning of the measurement period what you suggested, the balls were brought into the locker room and, on average, the Patriots' balls were wetter –

Q. Yes.

A. -- than the Colts' balls.

Q. You didn't test for that?

A. We did not test for that because there was no basis to test for it.

Q. Somebody else might disagree with that. Let's move on to another one, okay. You did an experiment to try to determine if natural causes could explain the drop in the Patriots' balls, right? You could explain the drop in pressure in the Patriots' balls? You did a series of experiments, right?

A. We looked at usage, physical and environmental factors.

Q. And on page 54 of your analysis, you say, "For the Patriots, it appears that so long as the average time at which the Patriots' balls were measured is no later than approximately two minutes after the balls were brought back into the official locker room, the game-day results can be explained by natural causes," right? That was your conclusion?

A. Yes.

Q. So the reverse is also true. It's your conclusion that if the Patriots' balls were measured earlier -- I'm sorry, if the Patriots' balls were measured later than approximately two minutes, then natural causes could explain it, right? The converse has to be true?

A. No.

Q. Well, I have to understand this, then. Read your sentence I'm reading. It says, "For the Patriots, it appears that so long as the average time at which the Patriots' balls was measured is no later than approximately two minutes after the ball was brought back into the official locker room, the game-day results can be explained by natural causes," right?

A. That's what it says.

Q. Okay. So what that means is, if the Patriots' balls are brought in and started to be tested in the first minute, then natural causes could explain them, right?

A. This is the average time. So that means that all eleven of the balls have to be measured within the first two minutes. Is that a possibility? Yes. I don't think that's very likely.

Q. When it says "average," "average" doesn't mean all within the first two minutes? It means, an average means when you take all the times, you average it together; isn't that what "average" means?

A. No. What it means is that if all the Patriots' balls were measured within zero and two minutes and the average falls within that, then the natural causes can explain it.

Q. That's not what it said. Is this a misstatement here? What I'm reading it says, "As long as the average time at which the Patriots' balls were measured is no later than approximately two minutes after the balls are brought back into the official locker room, the game-day results can be explained by natural causes." Doesn't that mean "average time" means "average time"? You add all the times and you come up with an average? You divide it by the number of observations? Isn't that what an average is?

A. Yes.

Q. Okay. So that would be some of the balls could have been later than two minutes, some could have been at 30 seconds, some could have been at one minute, some could have been at one and a half minutes, some could have been at two, some could have been at two and a half minutes and the average could still be within two, right?

A. Correct.

Q. And if that was done, then it is your conclusion that natural causes could explain what you measured for the Patriots' balls?

A. Yes, and I said that and -- but that means the balls got started measuring as soon as they got into the locker room, which I don't think is very realistic.

Q. Were you in the locker room?

A. No.

Q. Did anyone write down the time at which they started doing it?

A. No.

Q. Now, did you know that the officials felt rushed to try to get all the balls done? They didn't even finish all the Colts' balls, did they?

A. They did four.

Q. They only did four out of eleven or twelve, right?

A. Right.

Q. And so you don't think in that environment they would have started immediately? That's not a plausible assumption?

A. I think all the indications is that it would be very hard for them to get started with all the measurements and finish the average of it less than two minutes to get it done. I don't think that's a highly plausible explanation. Is it possible? Absolutely. That's why I put it in this report.

Q. Now, this statement here that you have is based on the assumption that the measurements were done by which gauge for the Patriots' balls?

A. I believe that's for the non-logo gauge.

Q. Okay. If it was done by the logo gauge –

A. No, I'm sorry. That's the logo gauge; I apologize.

Q. If it was done by the non-logo gauge, would they have a longer period of time? I believe if you look at your charts on page 55, that might help you.

A. Yes, that's correct.

Q. They would have a longer period of time if it was a non-logo gauge, correct?

A. Correct.

Q. And you wrote in your report it's uncertain as to which gauge was used? That's why you tested both?

A. Correct.

MR. KESSLER: So if we had the non-logo gauge, there's a longer window, Commissioner –

Q. -- if you would explain to him, that it is possible that your results would indicate natural causes could explain this, right?

A. And I have presented those possibilities in this report. You have to look at the totalities of the information availability and what's physically plausible leads us to the conclusion of what is more likely. But that's why we did all this testing, was to look at all the possibilities, and there were possibilities you could find. But you look at the totality of the information available and conclude what's most likely to have occurred.

Q. Do you agree that the relative temperature that should be measured, if you could, would be the internal temperature of the football and not the external room temperature?

A. The problem with measuring the internal, and we tried to do this, is that the air inside of a football is stagnant. It's not flowing. So that means you have very large gradients in temperature. So if you were to put a thermo -- and we tried to do this -- and you tried to measure the temperature in a football, you are going to get really wildly weird results, because the gradient is not uniform. So if you measure this spot, it's not representative of that spot over there or that spot over there. So that's why, yeah, I would agree with you, but there's no reliable way to do that unless you could monitor every cubic millimeter of air inside a football.

Q. Whether or not it's a reliable way to do it, you would agree that what actually the Natural Gas Law predictions you should look at is the internal temperature of a football if you could measure that, right?

A. If you are comparing external temperature to external temperature, then you can use the Ideal Gas Law. If you can measure the internal temperature in the locker room and measure the internal temperature on the field and then do the same thing, yeah, that's a good way to do it.

Q. Okay. Do you agree with me that the internal temperature of a football could be different from the external temperature?

A. That's why the pressure is increasing with time.

Q. Yes. So it can be different, correct?

A. It is different.

Q. And you have no measurements for the internal temperature of the footballs at any time, at halftime, post-time, before the game? You have no measurements for that at all, but you can't do them?

A. We tried to do it and I explained to you why that data is not reliable.

Q. Is that a long way of saying you don't have those measurements?

A. We have them. You can look at them.

Q. But you don't think they are reliable?

A. That's right.

Q. Okay, we will do it that way. Now, let me ask you this. Had you found originally through your differences from differences analysis that there was no statistically significant effect, is it correct, as was suggested, you would have closed up your books and not done any further analysis? Because that's what was suggested by counsel in the questioning. You may have been here for that.

A. I'm not sure that's the case.

Q. So you disagree with counsel about that?

A. I think we would want to pursue it a bit more because the statistical analysis was only one part of the overall program. MR. KESSLER: Could we do this, Commissioner? If I may, I know it's running late. I think if you give me a break, I can more consolidate my notes and possibly either significantly limit how many more questions I have or even possibly eliminate my questions. But I think it would be worth taking a break for five minutes rather than sitting here right now while I do that.

MR. LEVY: Yes.

(Recess taken 7:04 p.m. to 7:12 p.m.)

Q. Mr. Caligiuri, one of the things you tested for was the Patriots' gloving of the football, correct?

A. We looked at the effect of the Patriots' pre-game work on the balls to see if that could be causing the differences in pressure.

COMMISSIONER GOODELL: What do you mean the "gloving"?

Q. Just for the Commissioner's benefit, the gloving was that the Patriots indicated that as part of their preparation of the balls, they would have someone take receivers' gloves and vigorously rub the balls to prepare them; is that correct?

A. That's part of what they do, yes. I think that's what Mr. Brady talked about as part of the overall preparation program.

Q. And what you meant to do in your testing was to try to replicate what the Patriots did, correct?

A. As best we could, yes.

Q. Now in your gloving experiment, what you did is that you first took a measurement of the psi and then you did the gloving; is that correct?

A. The whole preparation treatment, the gloving was an important part, yes.

Q. But what the point here is in the gloving, when did you take your measurements? Did you take it before the gloving or after the gloving?

A. Before the gloving? Measurements of what? Figure 16 talks about it.

Q. I will try to be more specific. Let me find my specific reference to this. One second.

A. I think Figure 16 in the report is the answer to your question.

Q. So what does Figure 16 indicate? When did you take your measurement for the gloving?

COMMISSIONER GOODELL: What page is that?

THE WITNESS: I'm sorry, 34.

A. Sorry?

Q. Explain what that figure shows as to when you did the gloving and when you took your measurements.

A. It's very clear here we started out at 12.5 psi. We were measuring the pressure internally, continuously throughout the entire rubbing.

Q. So you first measured 12.5. Just tell me the order of what you did, if you can, please.

A. We took a football. We put a pressure gauge inside at times zero, 12 and a half psi and we are rubbing. And the pressure is going up as you can see in Figure 16. We are monitoring it continuously, so I guess I am not understanding your question.

COMMISSIONER GOODELL: I think that's the issue. You are doing it continuously?

THE WITNESS: Continuously.

COMMISSIONER GOODELL: Monitoring the pressure?

THE WITNESS: Yes.

Q. So you were monitoring the pressure from the beginning to the end of the gloving process; is that correct?

A. Yes.

Q. Okay. So based on your figures, if the Patriots were gloving the ball before setting their pressure to give it to the referees, let's assume that's correct, okay? You understand what I'm saying, that the Patriots' procedure was to glove their balls and this was done before they would go in to the referees for the measurement of the pressure at, let's say, 12.5, okay? You understand what I'm saying?

A. Yes.

Q. So in other words, there's a period on your Chart 16, there's a period before the 12.5 when the gloving is taking place? You understand my comment?

A. The rubbing was started about ten minutes after zero.

Q. Let's say it started at minus ten. In other words, the point is before the first measure at the referee, the gloving was done. Let's assume that for the moment, okay?

COMMISSIONER GOODELL: I'm not sure I'm clear.

A. No, I'm sorry. I really apologize for that. This is an experiment that we did where we started at 12 and a half and we did the rubbing experiment and the pressure came back down to the initial pressure within 30-some-odd minutes, 40 minutes.

Q. If, in your analysis, if after gloving the balls, the Patriots set the balls to a pressure of 2.5 or 2.6, let's say the Patriots gloved their balls and that's the pressure they are testing for and it's sitting before it goes to the referees, that's your understanding of what happened, correct?

A. I'm not exactly sure when the balls were prepared prior to giving them to the referees. I'm not quite sure of that timing, but the balls were given to the referees presumably at 12 and a half after the rubbing was done.

Q. After the rubbing was stopped, do you know that the rubbing was done a period of time before it was given to the referees? You know that?

A. I believe the preparation was done before the balls were given to the referees.

Q. It wasn't done the second before the referees, right? It was done some period of time before then?

A. Yes.

Q. Okay. So if they set their psi at 12.5, after rubbing, that was their procedure, under your analysis, how much below 12.5 would it drop as the rubbing effect wore off?

A. The rubbing effect is worn off within about 20 or 30 minutes of when you started.

COMMISSIONER GOODELL: Mr. Kessler, didn't Mr. Brady testify that he picked the ball up three to four hours before the game?

MR. KESSLER: Yes, he did.

COMMISSIONER GOODELL: So would that mean the rubbing was over at that point in time?

MR. KESSLER: The rubbing would have been done before he picked it up, correct, before he picked up the balls.

COMMISSIONER GOODELL: At least three to four hours by the time the referee checked the ball, right?

MR. BRADY: Can I talk?

MR. KESSLER: Why doesn't Mr. Brady explain.

MR. BRADY: On that particular day, like I said, we changed. They were rubbing in all the new balls, which was the first time we did it all season. So when I picked the balls, I still had them rub the balls as I left the equipment room to go for my game-day preparations. So I still had them, say, I like these, you know, however many, 17, 18, 19 balls. Just glove these five or six balls a little bit longer and then I left as they were still finishing those up.

COMMISSIONER GOODELL: Okay. But if they had rubbed them for two hours, that would have changed the balls significantly, I presume, for you –

MR. BRADY: Yeah.

COMMISSIONER GOODELL: -- once you left, right?

MR. BRADY: What do you mean?

COMMISSIONER GOODELL: This was three to four hours before the game, if I understood you correctly earlier?

MR. BRADY: Yeah.

COMMISSIONER GOODELL: You said you told them to continue to rub the ball a little bit. And I'm just, I'm making it up. If they rubbed it for two hours, there still would have been an hour to two hours before the referee saw it, I believe?

MR. BRADY: Yeah. I'm not sure what happened.

MR. KESSLER: You know what? The facts are too confused here. I'm just going to drop this subject. I don't think it's significant to the overall analysis. I have no further questions.

COMMISSIONER GOODELL: Okay. Did you finish? I'm sorry.

MR. BRADY: No, I did, yeah.

COMMISSIONER GOODELL: I understand your point.

MR. BRADY: Yeah. I said finish these five, glove them.

MR. REISNER: Very briefly.

Redirect Examination by Mr. Reisner

Q. Dr. Caligiuri, I want to direct your attention to page 55 of the Exponent report because I think there was a little confusion in the question with Mr. Kessler. And I want to direct your attention to the figures showing the non-logo gauge and logo gauge assumptions and comparing the transient results. Can you briefly describe the significance of the intersection, if any, of the transient curve in each figure with the halftime average indicated for each of the -- each of the Patriots' balls and the Colts' balls? And as a part of that, describe the significance of the triangle created as a result of any overlap and whether that makes it more likely that the non-logo gauge or the logo gauge yields results that could potentially be consistent with natural phenomena.

A. Yeah, I think there was confusion there when I think about it. If we look at the first figure in 28, the non-logo gauge, this is, the transient data for the Patriots is in red and the transient data for the Colts is in blue. Superimposed on that is the average values of the measurements for the Patriots and for the Colts. What the left-hand side of Figure 28 shows, comparing to the average, there is no intersection of the average –

THE WITNESS: Are you on there? Page 55.

COMMISSIONER GOODELL: Yeah, go ahead.

Q. And what does that absence of an intersection mean? A. There is no way on an average basis that the average data would have been consistent with the transient data for the non-logo gauge.

Q. And that's with respect to the non-logo gauge, right?

A. The non-logo gauge.

Q. So the extent that you said in responses to Mr. Kessler that the non-logo gauge presented data that suggested that there was a larger window of potential explanation of natural phenomena, that was inaccurate?

A. That's correct.

Q. Or an error that you made? Can you explain what the facts are based on those graphs.

A. The facts are, is that the average data does not overlap at all the transient curve for the Patriots' measurement. There's a slight, little, tiny triangle. If you look at two standard deviations, if you look at that overall air, there is a little tiny window there.

Q. What are you referring to when you referring to "the little tiny window," under the non-logo gauge?

A. Yeah. If you look at non-logo gauge, you look at the red line and there's kind of a reddish, lighter red band.

Q. And what's that band?

A. That is the standard deviation of the air to two standard deviations.

Q. Do you call that an error band?

A. An error band.

Q. So there is no intersection between the halftime average and the transient curve with respect to the non-logo gauge, correct?

A. That's correct.

Q. And now describe the circumstances with respect to the logo gauge.

A. If we look at the right-hand graph on Figure 28, it's the same overall plot, except this time it's the measurements, assuming it started with the logo gauge. And there is a window where the average line overlaps the transient curve. So there is a window in there where, on average, for if the average measurement time was less than two minutes, there is a window where it could be explained just by the environmental effect of the ball heating up with time.

Q. And Mr. Kessler asked you some questions about the average time it took to measure all eleven of the Patriots' balls. Do you have any understanding as to whether there were any findings by Mr. Wells and the Paul, Weiss team as to the likely time that it took to begin testing the Patriots' balls after the balls were taken into the officials' locker room at halftime?

A. I believe they concluded that it most likely was starting after two minutes.

Q. Does two to four minutes sound correct?

A. Yes.

Q. And Mr. Kessler asked you some questions with respect to your understanding of the wetness of the balls. By the way, did you, during your game-day simulations, did you actually watch the game on the television to try to simulate the events as you saw them occur on the television?

A. Yes.

Q. In the first half, just on TV, recognizing you weren't there, did it look like it was raining very much in the first half?

A. No, it wasn't, actually.

Q. And do you have an understanding with respect to the efforts by ball boys to keep the balls dry during the game?

A. Yes. My understanding is with discussions with the ball boys carried out by Paul, Weiss to try to keep them as dry as possible throughout the entire game time.

Q. And did you understand that meant ball boys sometimes put the balls underneath their slickers and between their slickers and their sweatshirts?

A. Yes.

Q. And do you have any understanding with respect to how frequently balls were swapped out in order to maintain their dryness?

A. Pretty frequently.

Q. Do you have any understanding as whether any of the game officials who were involved in testing the balls at halftime made any observations as to the wetness of the balls?

A. They said they were wetter is what I recall.

Q. Do you recall that Clete Blakeman said he thought they were damp at most and certainly not waterlogged?

A. Oh, yes, certainly. He said they were damp but not soaked with water or anything like that, yes.

MR. REISNER: Nothing further.

MR. KESSLER: I am afraid your questions have cause me to ask the following.

Recross Examination by Mr. Kessler

Q. I'm just reading what you wrote on page 5. With respect to the non-logo gauge, you wrote, "Had the non-logo gauge been used pre-game and using the information provided by Paul, Weiss, that the first Patriots' measurements most likely occurred no sooner than two minutes into the locker room period, there appears to be no realistic window in which the game-day results of both teams can be explained." Do you see that?

A. Yes. Q. So now I'm taking away the information given by Paul, Weiss that the first Patriots' measurements occurred no sooner than two minutes. Am I correct that if it occurred immediately, even for the non-logo gauge, that it was possible that natural causes would explain it, correct? That's what that sentence means?

A. That sentence says that, but it's accounting for that little, tiny triangle in the standard -- two-sigma standard deviation.

Q. That is your sentence in the report, not mine, right? A. That's right. Q. And I read it accurately, correct?

A. You did, and –

Q. And those were the results you recorded?

MR. REISNER: Please let him finish.

A. And I am explaining why that it says, "Most likely occurred no sooner than two minutes into the locker room period," that no realistic window in which the game-day results can be explained.

MR. REISNER: Read the next sentence.

THE WITNESS (reading): "The Colts' measurements are explainable, but the Patriots' measurements are not."

MR. REISNER: And the last sentence refers expressly to the only overlap being in the error band, doesn't it?

THE WITNESS: Yes, the only overlap between the Patriots' transient curve and the Patriots' game-day average is too early in the locker room to be realistic. And the overlap is only with the outer edge of the Patriots' error bands, which puts that possibility way down the probability chart.

Q. How early would it have to be? You said "too early." How early, how many minutes? What was it?

A. If you are looking at the error band now, is what we are talking about?

Q. The non-logo gauge. You just read a sentence at your counsel's request. It would be too early. What was too early? What was the time?

A. It was less than a minute.

Q. So was it 30 seconds, 45 seconds?

A. Well, based on this graph, it looks like about a minute, a little bit over a minute.

Q. More than a minute, not less than a minute, now looking at the graph, right? So if they came in and then a minute started, then it was possible, correct?

A. No, the average time had to be within that minute, minute and 15 seconds.

Q. Right. An average, again, we went through this before, means some could be more than a minute, some could start 30 seconds, some could be at 45 and you still could be within an average of a minute, right?

A. That would be pretty hard.

Q. Have you tried to do it to see if it's possible?

A. We actually tried to replicate the measurement process, and it takes about 30 seconds to measure the ball twice.

Q. Is that result reported anywhere in the reports?

A. I don't know if it's reported in here or not, but I know that's what we did.

Q. So did you put everything in the report you thought was significant that the world should know about?

A. You are asking me did we write down that we -- it took about 30 seconds. I don't recall if it's in the report or not.

MR. KESSLER: I don't have any further questions.

MR. REISNER: I don't have any further.

MR. LEVY: Call your next witness.

MR. REISNER: We call Duane Steffey.

Testimony of Duane Steffey

Direct Examination by Mr. Reisner

Q. Can you please state your name for the record.

A. Duane L. Steffey.

Q. And how are you employed?

A. I am a principal scientist and Director of the Statistical and Data Sciences Group at Exponent.

Q. How long have you been at Exponent?

A. Eleven years.

Q. And can you please describe, Dr. Steffey, your educational background.

A. I hold -- I took an undergraduate degree and then Master's and Ph.D. degrees in statistics all from Carnegie Mellon University.

Q. And can you describe any academic positions you've held.

A. For many years I was a Professor of Statistics at San Diego State University.

Q. During approximately what years?

A. From 1988 to, well, officially until 2006.

Q. And are you a member of any statistical associations?

A. Yes, I am. I'm actually an elected fellow of the American Statistical Association and I also hold membership in the Institute of Mathematical Statistics and the Society for Risk Analysis.

Q. And what was your role with respect to the statistical significance analysis performed by Exponent in this matter?

A. Well, that was the component of the investigation for which I had lead responsibility, given my background on the multidisciplinary team.

Q. Can you please describe as briefly as possible the statistical significance analysis performed by Exponent and the role of the statistical significance analysis as you understood.

A. I would be happy to. And I will be amplifying comments made previously by both Mr. Wells and my colleague, Dr. Caligiuri. For us, the statistical analysis was the point of departure for the investigation and not the final destination. We performed the initial analysis very early in our study to understand the halftime data, frankly, to find out whether the differences that were observed were in the noise level. And we looked at the halftime data as the they were recorded and we analyzed those data. We saw anomalies in the record of the halftime data that became even clearer after we did some experimentation. We identified four alternative scenarios, including switching of gauges.

Q. You tested all those scenarios, correct?

A. We tested all those scenarios and we accounted for the possibility that the balls were set pre-game with both the logo gauge and with the non-logo gauge. We accounted for that in our model with a gauge effect and said after accounting for the possibility that either gauge was used pre-game, the difference in average pressure drop that we see between the Colts' and the Patriots' balls were statistically significant.

Q. Now, Professor Steffey, Dr. Steffey, you were here during Dean Snyder's testimony, correct?

A. Yes.

Q. And you heard him describe three key findings or criticisms of the Exponent work, correct?

A. Yes.

Q. Key finding 1 or criticism identified by Dean Snyder was that, "Exponent's statistical analysis of the difference in average pressure drops is wrong because it ignores timing." Do you have a reaction or response to that criticism?

A. Yes. I think that criticism is without foundation.

Q. And why?

A. Well, for several respects. First of all, it mischaracterizes the purpose of the statistical analysis. You need to remember that this analysis originally was done very early in the investigation before we had done extensive experimentation to understand how important timing was. We were just looking at the data saying, does this average pressure drop differ for whatever reason? Is there some factor that the difference we are seeing, is it meaningful and is it worth exploring further, just from a purely empirical look at the data? So that's point number 1. Point number 2 is that as it became clearer through the experimentation that the timing was, we saw a pronounced timing effect in the experiments, we went back to the halftime data and said, well, you know, and frankly, I had looked at the data and I didn't see an obvious time trend in the record of measurements. But I said let's be sure. And we don't know the exact clock time of when the measurements were taken, but we do know the order in which they were taken. Everybody has testified, look, they were measured in the order in which they were recorded, eleven Patriots' balls measured by two officials with two gauges and then at some point later, either immediately after or after a delay, the four Colts' balls were measured. So we had the order of measurement, which is essentially a proxy for time. Because there is, as Dr. Caligiuri indicated, it takes some time to go through the process of measuring each ball. And so obviously, you know, balls later in the order, 14 or 15 were measured at times later than balls measured at two or three. So it's a proxy for clock time without having to impose an assumption about what clock time was.

Q. Does it affect your view with respect to the appropriateness of the work done by Exponent or the conclusions reached by Exponent when you take into consideration the criticism identified by Dean Snyder?

A. Not at all, not at all.

Q. And why is that?

A. Well, one point that -- I think the implied claim is that there's an adjustment that's being advanced by Dean Snyder and his team and that if you make that adjustment, that timing explains the difference in average pressure drop, okay. There are a couple of important points to keep in mind. The average pressure drop is just one part of the investigation to look at. Variability is another. And as we looked at -- re-looked at the halftime data later, after the experimentation is done, just asking whether the sequence of measurements makes sense, there is a claim that what Dean Snyder and his team have done is to adjust for timing. Now, understand that my comments are going to be based on what I would regard as a preliminary analysis of PowerPoint slides that I got a few days ago. So I don't have a lot of extensive documentation, and a lot of the technical details weren't really drawn out in the testimony today. But I was able to replicate nearly exactly the p-values that are reported by Dean Snyder in his slides, taking our significance finding of .004 and then imposing adjustments under three cases. Case 1, as best as I can tell involves looking at the transient curves and saying, well, if I think about the average time at which the Colts' balls were measured, and I shift them to correspond to the average time at which the Patriots' balls were measured, what is the psi effect? And in his Case 1, it looks like it's about .31 psi. So I believe what he did is to add .31 to the measured pressure drop for the Colts' balls to each of the Colts' balls, same numerical value to each of the Colts' balls and saying if they had been measured earlier, they would have seen a larger pressure drop. Now, I have got a couple of problems with that. The main problem is that this is claimed to be an adjustment for timing. But remember that eleven Patriots' balls were measured. And if it takes roughly 30 seconds between the measurements of balls, there's at least four or five minutes that elapse between the measurement of the first Patriots' ball and the measurement of the last Patriots' ball. Dean Snyder's adjustment for timing doesn't make any adjustment to the Patriots' data. So to claim that there is an adjustment for timing I think is inaccurate. Now, following that logic, though, I looked at how the p-value is calculated. And, again, the technical details of this aren't really transparent. But because I was able to use two different approaches and get values very close to the reported p-values, I believe what was done is to take, again, and analyze the difference of differences. The two ways I did it were to basically redo the -- what we described -- what has been described, accurately described as the linear mixed effects model. That's our main model in the appendix. And then I also did a simpler analysis just looking at the logo gauge separately and the non-logo gauge data separately, and doing what is called a two-sample t-test to compare the differences in the average drops for the Patriots and the average drops for the Colts. Now, what wasn't acknowledged or discussed here is that in order to replicate -- nearly replicate the p-values that are reported here, there is another implicit assumption, which is that the variability in the Patriots data and the Colts data are the same, and that the t-test, for example, was carried out with what's called a pooled variance. So you are assuming that the Colts' data is as variable as the Patriots' data and you use that. Now, if you do that, then you get a p-value a little bit above five percent. It's about six and a half percent. Interestingly, you can do that test without imposing that assumption. You can do the comparison and use the variability in the Patriots data to estimate the variability and the uncertainty in the Patriots average drop. You can use the Colts' data to estimate variability in the Colts average drop. And if you do that, the p-value that you calculate under this Case 1 adjustment is actually below two percent. So it remains statistically significant at the five percent level. And that's, frankly, consistent with what we were saying. Timing helps to explain the results we see at halftime, but it's not the whole story. And similarly, if you take Case 2 which is making a larger adjustment, the reported p-value's in the neighborhood of .2, a little bit above .2. Again, if you do the analysis without imposing an equal variances assumption, you get a p-value that's below ten percent. So it's statistically significant at the ten percent level, not at the five percent level. The other important point in thinking about statistical significance is that it's not a black or white line at .05. And there's no direct way that you can connect .05 certainly to a legal standard for preponderance of evidence. So it's not that if you are .04, it's more likely than not, and if you are .06, it's less likely than not. We have to be clear about that. So for all of those reasons, I think that first finding is without foundation.

Q. I think this is the last question. Is it fair to say that what Dean Snyder purported to do is not really a statistical significance analysis to look at the likelihood of chance explanation the variation, but introduce into his analysis one of the potential explanations for the deviation?

A. What we didn't do is we didn't go back. As I said, we went back to the halftime data and looked for a time effect there. We didn't see it. We didn't alter the halftime data and reanalyze the data based on assumptions that we weren't in a position to validate. And I think that, you know, the conclusion that we came to in part is that, you know, the arithmetic doesn't add up. If you look at the first Patriots' measurement, whether it's made by the logo gauge or the non-logo gauge, the very first one, it's higher than the last four Patriots' footballs, which are being measured at least three minutes, probably later. And so the actual, if you look at the sequence of Patriots' measurements, and this is the point we make in the report, it's going exactly in the wrong direction compared to what we know to be the timing effect. And so the timing effect goes in the wrong direction. The ball conditions that we tested experimentally we know can affect the measured pressure by no more than about .3 psi. And yet, you are seeing differences in pressure that go well beyond -- they go opposite the timing effect and they go well beyond what's attributable to differences in wet versus dry balls.

Q. And did you also review a commentary or criticisms by either AEI and Professor MacKinnon with respect to the Exponent work?

A. Yes.

Q. And do you have any responses or reactions to the observations or commentary made by each of those reports? A. They are similarly without foundation.

Q. And why?

A. Can we take them in turn?

Q. Yes, please.

A. The AEI report which has already been discussed, I mean, I would really try to amplify what's already been said about the AEI report.

Q. Please.

A. The notion that we made a mistake and we made an error, what's been characterized in the media as a freshman statistics mistake, is just wrong. The mistakes that AEI attributes to us, in fact, are theirs. They weren't able to replicate our results. The first part of their report says we can't reproduce our results. They misidentified the statistical model we were using. We weren't using a multiple regression model. We were using what's called a linear mixed effects model. They were ultimately able to replicate most, but not all of our estimates. I spent a little time with that report and I finally figured out what their mistake was. They couldn't match our estimates of gauge effects. And the reason was that when they were thinking about gauge effects, they were taking the average -- the simple answer is that they were using a weighted average to estimate gauge effects, and they should have been using an unweighted average. What do I mean by that? Their estimates of gauge effects were looking at the average of all the fifteen measurements that were taken by each gauge. Now, eleven of those were Patriots' measurements and four of them were Colts' measurements. But we had to consider the possibility of team effects in the data. And statistical theory tells us that if you have got a model that has both team effect and gauge effect, to properly account for the team effects, the way you estimate the gauge effects is not to average all of the data because you got more Patriots data than Colts data, because that's how the halftime measurements were done. What you have to do is calculate an average for each gauge for the Patriots. And, for example, for the logo gauge, you have to calculate the logo gauge average for the Patriots and you have to calculate the logo gauge for the Colts, get those two averages and then take the averages of averages. And had AEI done that, they could have replicated our results. Other statisticians understood what we were doing and effectively were able to replicate our results. So that point was wrong. We talked earlier about the fact that they then go on to present findings purporting to show that if the logo gauge was used pre-game, that you can again get a p-value above .05. Well, first of all, that's a limited victory in that doesn't really speak to the "more likely than not" legal standard. But if you look at their model, as Dr. Caligiuri pointed out, the way they got there is to include an order effect, which is essentially the same order effect that we went back and put into the model and said it's not statistically significant. Not only is it not statistically significant, but the coefficient for that term doesn't make physical sense. The order coefficient that they have in the model is positive and they are looking at pressure drop and how does pressure drop change. And so their model, the order effect that they put in, which has the -- the order effect that they put in basically is saying that pressure drop should increase with time. And again, that doesn't make physical sense because the balls are getting back to equilibrium and the pressure drop from where you started pre-game should be getting closer.

What happens if you remove that order term? Well, as Dr. Caligiuri mentioned, and I think it's worth emphasizing, if you take out that nonsignificant order effect, guess what happens to the p-value? It drops below .05 again, and it basically renders void the claim that you can get -- you can get nonsignificant results depending on which logo gauge is used. And so I think those are the main points that I think I wanted to make in response to the AEI report. I think Dr. Caligiuri tackled the other part of the AEI report on the misinterpretation of the Ideal Gas Law. And with regard to Dr. MacKinnon, I think the only comment that's probably worth emphasizing is that he was citing evidence that there was a lot of measurement error. In fact, I think Dean Snyder referred to measurement error. As Dr. Caligiuri pointed out, when we studied the gauges, the gauges don't always read the same thing; we know that from the halftime data. One gauge may read higher or lower than another. And we studied 50 gauges made by the same -- essentially they were the same in manufacturer to the non-logo gauge. They don't all read the same from one another. We didn't read any that read as high as the logo gauge did. Most of them were pretty well-calibrated to the master gauge. But if you were using that gauge repeatedly, you got consistent measurements at those nominal pressure levels. And so if you are looking at differences and you are using the same gauge to make measurements of difference, you are getting a good measure of difference. So if you are looking at, if you are using one gauge pre-game and you are using that same gauge at halftime, you are getting a pretty accurate measure of what the pressure drop was. So the notion that differences in pressure drop could reflect gauge measurement error is simply not supported by the extensive experimentation that we did and reported in our report.

Q. Was there anything in the AEI report or the MacKinnon commentary that made you question the tests undertaken by Exponent or the conclusions reached by Exponent? A. No. MR. REISNER: No further questions.

MR. KESSLER: I will try to keep this short and simple.

Cross-Examination by Mr. Kessler

Q. Despite how complex I think this testimony was, Mr. Steffey, you agree, do you not, that you found that timing was an important factor? I think you said "very important factor" in your direct testimony?

A. In -- well, I think I would stand by what we said in the report. In terms of explaining, if we ask the question what factors can we vary that have the greatest impact on the ball pressure that we measure, if the ball is in a dynamic state in that the ball is either warming or cooling, that the timing of measurement is very important.

Q. Okay. So that was a way of saying "yes," correct? I'm trying to move this along. You agree timing was a very important factor, right?

A. Well, I would just like to put it in the appropriate context.

Q. I know, but we are here very late, so if you can answer "yes," "yes" would be good. Let me go to the next thing. Take a look at your Appendix

A. This is your statistical model that you presented to the world, correct?

A. Yeah. Well, this is the model that explains how we conceived of analyzing the halftime data.

Q. There is no other statistical model presented in Appendix A? There's only one, correct?

A. In terms of the general structure of the model, yes, that's right. Q. So there is not an Appendix B, C? This is the model you presented, this one-structured model, right?

A. Correct. We've presented that as the structure with which we used to analyze the halftime data under multiple scenarios about the data themselves.

Q. Okay. This one-structured model that you chose to present as your only structured model in this appendix and in the entire report, okay, has no timing variable in it, correct? That was testified by Mr. Caligiuri, right?

There's no timing variable in this one-structured model that you chose to present, correct?

A. We didn't put it in the final form of the model because we put in a term to account for timing. And found it wasn't significant for the halftime data as recorded.

Q. Okay. So you didn't put it in? That's another way of saying "yes," right? It's not in there, right? I will get to why you didn't put it in. Would you just give me it's not in the model?

A. There's no term in there that says time effect or order effect.

Q. And when you say, "There is no term," there is no statistical variability in your regression analysis that would have time as a factor affecting the dependent variable, correct? A. That's correct. And just for —

Q. "That's correct" will be good. A. I am referring to the equation that's about a third of the way down on Page A3.

Q. And that's the only equation you present for your structured model, right? There's no other equation I'm missing in Appendix A that does have a timing variable, right?

A. Well, there's another version of that equation that's got a lot of Greek letters in it later on, and that's for the more technical readers. But there's no other equation either in prose or in symbols that have a timing effect in it. That's addressed in the footnote.

Q. Even if I could understand the more technical one, I won't find any timing variable in that in Appendix A, right?

A. That's correct.

Q. Okay, thank you. Now, you then said the reason you didn't put in a timing variable is because you found it was statistically insignificant, and that's what your Footnote 49 says, right?

A. That's correct.

Q. Now, it's completely the opposite of everything else you found, that timing was the most significant variable to conclude that it also is a statistically insignificant variable; is that correct or not?

A. I'm not sure I followed the last part of that.

Q. Okay, let me try again.

A. Try again.

Q. You did all this work that said timing was the most significant variable affecting ball pressure in your analysis?

A. Yeah, mm-hmm.

Q. And then you are saying the reason you didn't put timing into the analysis is because when you tested ball order, you found it was an insignificant variable, correct? That's what you testified? That's what Footnote 49 says, right?

A. Yes. I think what Footnote 49 is pointing to is an inconsistency between the results that we demonstrated experimentally, which were consistent with physical theory and the observed pattern in the halftime data. They don't match.

Q. Right. So your halftime data analysis does not match with all the other studies you did that said that timing was significant? The results are inconsistent, right? A. That's right. And one thing to keep in mind is that the experimental results that we generated used balls that were at the same starting pressure.

Q. Now, let me ask you this. You mentioned that you tried to replicate Dr. Snyder's work, correct? You believed you were able to do that?

A. I believe I was able to do that.

Q. And you pointed out that by doing some variability analysis for the second measure, you could achieve a statistical significance that's above ten percent statistical level, not a five percent, right?

A. The p-values I calculated were between five and ten percent.

Q. It would not be significant at the five-percent level, right?

A. That's correct. And again, the statement applies only to the difference in mean pressure drops and isn't addressing the anomalous fluctuations that are in the Patriots halftime data.

Q. It is true, is it not, that Exponent chose in this analysis to make five percent the relevant statistical significance level? That's Exponent's choice, correct?

A. Well, yes. I think as others have testified earlier, that is a standard level to use as a threshold for statistical analysis.

Q. And you would agree with that, correct?

A. Well, yes, that's the threshold that I instinctively applied.

Q. Professor Marlow agreed with that, who was supervising you?

A. I think we were in general agreement with that.

Q. No one disagreed and said let's use ten percent? Everyone said let's use five percent?

A. It's a common threshold and to use it in evaluating halftime data was reasonable.

Q. And, in fact, five percent is the measure that Exponent uses in almost all the statistical studies as a matter of practice; isn't that correct?

A. As a matter of practice. I would just qualify that by saying remember, in a real problem where you have to make a decision, there is not necessarily a huge difference between .045 and .055. That's something that you have to think about as a practical, real-world decision-maker.

Q. You mentioned civil cases in which you have testified, right?

A. Yes.

Q. And you talk about the preponderance of evidence there, correct?

A. Correct.

Q. Okay. Are you familiar with the fact from -- how many cases have you testified in?

A. At trial or in depositions?

Q. In any way, trial?

A. Trial, a handful of times; maybe 30 depositions.

Q. Are you familiar with the fact that even in the civil case with a preponderance of evidence like here, if the Court finds that you haven't met a relevant level of statistical significance, what happens to the study; does it get admitted into evidence or is it excluded from evidence, in your experience?

A. I don't think I can answer that as a general proposition. And you have to think about the context in which we were doing this analysis. We did this analysis very early in the study. We were looking at whether the mean pressure drop was statistically significant. We also looked at whether the variability between the Patriots' measurement and the Colts' measurement were statistically significant. And the other thing that is known in general statistical practice is that if you have a finding of non-significance and that finding is based on a relatively limited amount of data, you have to be somewhat cautious about taking that as evidence of no difference, because when statisticians encounter that situation, what they think about is what they call the power. They are saying, well, do I have enough data so that if the difference actually existed and it was appreciable in magnitude that I would have enough data, that I would have a high probability of detecting that? And so, findings of non-significance have to be treated, especially in situations with small sample sizes, with a little bit of circumspection as opposed to findings of significance. If you get a finding of significance with a small amount of data, that's generally an indication that you have a pretty strong effect and it's strong enough to manifest itself even with a relatively limited amount of data.

Q. Small data sets are less reliable than big data sets, correct?

A. I don't think I said that.

Q. Is that true?

A. You have to put that statement in context.

Q. Is it true, yes or no? How about answering that? Before giving me the explanation for why, is it true that, in general, small data sets are less reliable than bigger data sets?

MR. NASH: Objection.

COMMISSIONER GOODELL: He asked you a question. Answer the question.

A. You have to explain what you mean by "reliable." If you are making a decision based on whether or not an effect is significant and you do an analysis with a small data set and that effect is still significant, then your data set was small, but it was large enough for you to discover that effect and make a decision on it. And having more data wouldn't affect the decision you make. Now, if you are trying to estimate something to a certain margin of error, is it true that you get a smaller margin of error if you have more data? Well, yeah, it is. Is that important or not? I think it depends on the context.

Q. Is this one of the smallest data sets you have ever worked in on any of your statistical analyses in all the cases you have testified in? Is this one of the smallest ones?

A. No, I wouldn't say it stands out as being exceptionally small. It is small. Obviously, four observations for the Colts isn't that many, but it's certainly, you know, there is information there.

Q. I will ask you this: Have you ever done a case you can recall where you had four observations was your entire data set and that's all, or less? And if you can't identify, "no."

A. I have reviewed evidence that has been put forth where people have taken one or two measurements and tried to reason on that basis.

Q. And you think that's a proper thing for a statistician to do with one or two observations?

A. Typically, it is not. Typically it is not because there is uncertainty. But if you had a situation where there was no variability, you had a population that had no variability in it and you wanted to learn about that population, one measurement would be enough because there is no variability.

MR. KESSLER: I don't have any further questions. You can keep going if you want, but I'm done.

MR. REISNER: Professor Steffey, one question.

Redirect Examination by Mr. Reisner

Q. Is there any statistical principle that requires the inclusion or introduction of the type of timing variable described by Dean Snyder in order for a statistical significance analysis to be valid?

A. Well, no, especially not in this context. I guess I would respond in two ways. We were doing that analysis before we did a lot of transient experiments where we understand exactly what the magnitude of the timing effect was. And the second thing is, I think there are flaws with the approach to adjustment for timing that Dean Snyder and his team did. They basically, as near as I can tell, just altered the Colts' data by shifting all the numbers down and didn't really address the time that elapsed in the Patriots' measurements, and frankly, the anomalies in the Patriots' data when you look at it sequentially. And when we first looked at variability and we said, gee, when we look at the variability in the Colts halftime measurements and the Patriots halftime measurements, although the Patriots' data is more variable than the Colts, it's not statistical significant, that might be because of small sample sizes for the Colts. But then we did the experiments and we understood the importance of timing and we looked at that data again, looking at the sequential nature of the Patriots' observations and said, look, we can't explain this, either by timing or ball conditions.

MR. REISNER: Nothing further.

MR. KESSLER: Nothing further from me.

MR. REISNER: We call Professor Dan Marlow.

THE WITNESS: Thank you.

MR. REISNER: Last witness.

COMMISSIONER GOODELL: Welcome.

Testimony of Daniel Marlow

Direct Examination by Mr. Reisner

Q. Can you please state your name for the record.

A. Daniel R. Marlow.

Q. And how are you employed, sir?

A. I am a Professor of Physics at Princeton University.

Q. What is your current title at Princeton?

A. I am the Evans Crawford 1911 Professor of Physics.

Q. How long have you been at Princeton?

A. 31 years.

Q. And other than your current position, have you held any other positions at Princeton University?

A. I was department chair.

Q. During what period of time were you department chair?

A. 2001 to 2008.

Q. When you refer to "department chair," which department are you referring to?

A. The physics department.

Q. Professor Marlow, do you have any areas of particular emphasis of academic research and expertise?

A. Yes. I'm an experimental particle physicists.

Q. What does that mean?

A. Well, particle physics studies -- it's also called subatomic physics. It studies the constituents of matters, the interactions between them. This is research we do at the Large -- right now, the experiment I'm working on is at the Large Hadron Collider at CERN.

Q. And to what extent is the discipline of statistics relevant to your work?

A. It's quite relevant. We don't study statistics, per se, but we depend on statistical analyses a lot in our work.

Q. And what was your role with respect to the analyses, experiments and other work done by Exponent in this case?

A. Well, one way to describe it is, I guess I was the designated skeptic. I looked over what Exponent was doing. I thought about the problem a lot myself, just probed when they did an analysis, I would do it myself. When they made measurements, I would look at the data, say, does this make sense? Does this agree with what I would expect from theory? And then I also spent a lot of time thinking about things that weren't included, trying to think about that.

Q. How frequently did you interact with Exponent?

A. It was roughly once a week, maybe sometimes a little bit more, sometimes a little bit less during the, you know, main, most intensive part of the investigation.

Q. And can you just describe the form in which those interactions took.

A. Well, there were mostly phone calls where Exponent would come and report what they had observed. Usually there would be a document that preceded the phone call. I would spend some time studying it. Again, I would do my own calculations to see does this make sense, you know, does this look like solid work?

Q. And what role, if any, did you play in the development by Exponent of the statistical significance model they used?

A. Well, I took a much simpler approach, which gave it essentially equivalent results. Again, and there is a lot of confusion on this point, it was never an intention to do anything other than to say are we wasting our time here by even looking at this? If we had found initially that there was no difference between the Patriots' and the Colts' balls, speaking for myself, I would say forget about it. There's just no point in studying this further. But we found a large statistical significance.

Q. And what role, if any, did you play in the development of the transient experiments and game-day simulations used by Exponent?

A. Well, that was more along the lines of looking at what they did. Before -- before any measurements were made, I had actually realized that this transient effect would be potentially important. What I didn't know basically was how quickly the footballs would warm. But I thought that was something we definitely had to look into, and it turns out it was an important effect.

Q. Did Exponent share data with you in the course of their experimentation?

A. Absolutely.

Q. And did you discuss that data, its significance, and follow-up that should take place?

A. Yes.

Q. Do you have a view with respect to the appropriateness of the statistical significance model and analysis used by Exponent?

A. For the purpose that it was put to, it was fully appropriate.

Q. And do you have a view as to the appropriateness of the transient experiments and the game-day simulations used by Exponent?

A. Yes.

Q. What is your view?

A. Perfectly good. I was, especially with the simulation experiments, I was, frankly -- "amazed" may be overstating it, but I was highly impressed with the level of detail, thought, planning and execution. It was really a first-class piece of work.

Q. Did you review the report prepared by Exponent?

A. I did.

Q. And did you review carefully both the substance of the report and the conclusions set forth in the report?

A. Yes, I went through it. There were a couple of drafts. I went through all of them and looked at it for, obviously, for any mistakes, and then also I was looking is this presented in the clearest possible way?

Q. And do you have a view as to the conclusions reached by Exponent as set forth in its report?

A. Yes.

Q. What is your view about their conclusions?

A. I believe the conclusions are correct. And there are uncertainties, but those are very clearly laid out in the report. And we talked earlier about these transient curves, the Figure 28. And I think, I know it could be difficult for people to ponder graphs and try to understand what they mean. But if one takes the trouble, then it's quite clear. I think that captures not only the central result, but also the uncertainties.

Q. Were you here during the testimony of Dean Snyder?

A. Yes.

Q. Did you hear his description of his three key findings or criticisms?

A. Yes.

Q. Directing your attention to his first key finding or criticism, "Exponent's statistical analysis of the difference in average pressure drops is wrong because it ignores timing." Do you have a reaction or response to that criticism?

A. Well, there were never any claims that timing was in it. There was a lot of confusion on this point. But it's -- how do I put this? I think it's quite clear what Exponent did, what the philosophy of the analysis is. And I don't understand how people have so much trouble understanding that.

Q. And directing your attention to key finding or criticism number 2, "Exponent improperly draws conclusions based on variability and halftime pressure measurements despite conceding that the variability is statistically insignificant." Do you have a response or reaction to that criticism?

A. Yeah. It's a kind of very pedantic, technical point. And it also, again, misses the basic point. The reason that first result is not statistically significant, I point out it is actually -- it's very suggestive. There is a pretty clear effect there. It just doesn't quite rise to this or synch to this .05 level, but that doesn't prove it's not there. And you can look at other data and that's essentially what Exponent did, is they looked at their simulation data. And what struck me was in all the data sets I looked at, they all consistently had a much lower variability than what we saw in the Patriots' balls.

Q. And directing your attention to key finding or criticism 3, "If the logo gauge was used to measure the Patriots' balls before the game, then eight out of eleven were above Exponent's expected outcome." Do you have a reaction or observation, reaction or response to that criticism?

A. Well, I think, as has been pointed out, there was a lot of discussion of the logo versus non-logo gauge. I think there's ample evidence that the non-logo gauge is what was used. This business of whether or not it was corrected is such a tiny detail. I mean, obviously, if you say the logo gauge was used, then it's not a small correction, but it's a tiny correction if you say the non-logo gauge is used. And furthermore, that analysis ignores something that everyone agrees on, and that is that as the balls warm up, their pressure goes up. So it's just a little bit off topic.

Q. In other words, it freezes the balls at the outdoor measurement?

A. Freezes the balls, yes.

Q. And based on the criticisms or findings described by Dean Snyder, did it affect your views with respect to the appropriateness of the work done by Exponent or the conclusions reached by Exponent?

A. No.

Q. And have you had an opportunity to review each of the AEI reports and the MacKinnon report that were described earlier?

A. Yes.

Q. And after reviewing the commentary on those reports, did that affect your views with respect to the appropriateness of the work done by Exponent or the conclusions reached by Exponent?

A. No.

MR. REISNER: Nothing further.

Cross-Examination by Mr. Kessler

Q. I will try my best -- so far I have been failing -- to try to ask questions. If you can just answer very simply without explanations, I hope you will try to work with me.

A. As long as you don't editorialize.

Q. You are an expert in experimental particle physics?

A. That's correct.

Q. Will you agree with me that the Exponent report is not -- doesn't have anything to do with experimental particle physics? Will you give me that?

A. There are common techniques.

Q. Does it have anything to do with experimental particle physics as a science?

A. No.

Q. Thank you. Second point, you stated with respect to the first criticism that there was never any claim made that timing was included in the statistical model in Appendix A. That's what you just stated, right?

A. Well, let me speak for myself. I never saw that particular test as having anything to do with timing. I think there is confusion on this point.

MR. LEVY: You may continue.

THE WITNESS: Okay.

A. There is confusion on this point and that is because there's this large variability in the Patriots' balls, you don't see a timing effect. You expect to see them rise, but they don't rise. And if they didn't have this variability, you would see it. Now, that's Part 1. Part 2 is there's another effect which is you can't really get from the halftime measurements by themselves. And that is the time at which the Patriots' balls are measured and the times at which the Colts' balls were measured. And that is discussed in the report, but that comes from reconstructing what went on during that period in halftime when they were measuring. So no statistical model is going to tell you what that is.

Q. I will try again. Is it correct, as you stated, that there was never any claim made that there was any timing variable in the statistical model that is set forth in Appendix A?

MR. REISNER: Objection.

A. Well, I will try again. I will try again. There is some inclusion of a statistical -- a time effect in the statistical model, but it's only there to look for a rise in the balls during the Patriots' measurements. It's not there to look for the difference between the Patriots' and the Colts' balls. Do you understand this now?

Q. Yes, I do.

A. Good.

Q. There is no timing effect to account -- to try to account for whether that was a factor in the differences between the Patriots and the Colts' balls, correct?

A. That's correct.

Q. Okay, good. Now, the next one, you said that -- you concede that there was no statistically significant effect for the variability analysis, correct, at the five-percent level?

A. If you only look at the halftime data, yes.

Q. Okay. You didn't look at the post-game data, right?

A. I did.

Q. You did look at the post-game data?

A. I did.

Q. Did you do a study of that?

A. Yes.

Q. Did you report it in your report anywhere?

A. No, because we didn't want to use the halftime data or the post-game data to speak to the mean. However, since you asked, I did do the analysis. It's not in the report. The reason it's not in the report is because of potential uncertainties with it. However, any uncertainty I can think of, and I will ask you to think of an uncertainty, or you (indicating), so think of an uncertainty that would lead to a smaller variance in the data, and there are none. So if you include that, then suddenly this variability becomes statistically significant.

Q. Who made the decision to leave out the post-game data? Did you participate in that decision?

A. Yes. I expressed my opinion and I was overruled.

Q. So others decided not to include it, but you wanted to include it?

A. That's correct.

Q. In any event, it's not there, correct?

A. It's not there.

Q. Looking just at the halftime data which you did include, there is no statistically significant effect, correct?

A. That's correct.

Q. Now, you then said even though it's not statistically significant, you used the word, it's "suggestive." Do you remember using that word?

A. Yes.

Q. Okay. Is "suggestive" a scientific term recognized by any statistician? Is that a scientific term, "suggestive"?

A. Well, it's a term in plain English. And I can tell you how we use it in science. If you see something where an effect is suggested, you pursue it, all right. So you say, look, we have this data set. There is some suggestion here that something is going on. And we do this all the time at CERN. And you can bet your bottom dollar -- you can bet your bottom dollar that if you see a suggestion of an effect in data, you are going to look very hard for other data to see whether or not you are right. Sometimes the other data shows that you are wrong; other times it doesn't. But the notion that because this is insignificant, well, forget about it, is just silly.

Q. It's just silly?

A. Yes. If you say because this is not significant, we will never look anyplace else, that's just silly.

Q. Didn't you just testify on direct examination that you set up the exercise on the difference between the differences and that if it was not statistically significant, your decision would be there would be no point to doing anything further? Did you testify to that, yes or no?

A. Yes.

Q. Was that silly?

A. No, and there is a reason, if you will let me explain.

MR. KESSLER: I have no further questions.

COMMISSIONER GOODELL: Let him finish, please.

Q. Explain, explain.

COMMISSIONER GOODELL: There is no reason to be disrespectful to any witness.

Q. I'm sorry. I apologize for that.

A. I can explain. If you hadn't seen a mean shift, then there would be no point in going on, all right. However, we did see a mean shift, so we said look, we have to understand why this happens. Then we look at this variability. The variability data in the rest of the experiments' measurements that Exponent made comes for free. So if you get free data, of course, you look at it.

COMMISSIONER GOODELL: Okay. Were you done, Mr. Kessler?

MR. KESSLER: I don't have any other questions for this witness.

MR. REISNER: Very, very briefly.

Redirect Examination by Mr. Reisner

Q. Dr. Marlow, the variability analysis that took into account the post-game data that you wanted to include in the report but didn't get included in the report, your view that wasn't included in the report would have been more prejudicial to the Patriots, correct?

A. Yes, yes, and that was part of how I interpreted why I was overruled is we didn't want to be too aggressive in it. We were trying to be fair.

Q. In your view, based on the variability and analysis, taking into account the post-game data would have made it more likely that the Patriots' balls did not start at the same psi level when they were introduced on the field and after Walt Anderson had gauged them, correct?

A. Yes. The very -- the most natural explanation for the variability is that they started at different pressures, yes.

Q. And is it fair to say that this was not included in the report because there was a consensus between you and Exponent that it was better to take a conservative approach and not use the post-game data because it might open you up to some criticism, much of which we have heard today?

A. Yes, that's fair. That's why I went along, but I couldn't contain myself here; I'm sorry.

MR. REISNER: Nothing further.

MR. KESSLER: I'm going to resist any temptation to ask any further questions at this point.

MR. LEVY: All right.

MR. KESSLER: Thank you.

MR. LEVY: Thank you. We are done for the day. I understand that the parties are going to consult and agree on a proposed due date for post-hearing briefs. The Commissioner will agree to any schedule that's reasonable. In your briefs, the Commissioner would like you to address the question of whether he should hear from Mr. McNally and/or Mr. Jastremski before resolving the issue, before deciding the matter.

MR. KESSLER: Other than that question, you have indicated that we should address the legal issues. Can we limit our briefs to that rather than, you know, arguing what happened in the factual record today and all that, or would it be helpful for you to have that as well? Post-hearing briefs are -- I want to find out what would be useful to the Commissioner for his decision.

MR. LEVY: Recognizing there are 25 people who are here that would like to leave, why don't I ask the two of you to consult, see if you can come up with an agreement on that. And I am happy to participate.

MR. NASH: That makes sense.

MR. KESSLER: Okay.

MR. LEVY: Thank you all for your patience.

COMMISSIONER GOODELL: Thank you.

(Hearing adjourned at 8:27 p.m.)

Printed in Great Britain
by Amazon